RECOVERY FROM AUTISM

RECOVERY FROM AUTISM

A RESOURCE HANDBOOK DRAWN FROM
BIOGRAPHICAL NARRATIVE ACCOUNTS &
CURRENT RESEARCH

JENNIFER POOLE PhD

Matador
9 Priory Business Park,
Wistow Road, Kibworth Beauchamp,
Leicestershire. LE8 0RX
Tel: 0116 279 2299
Email: books@troubador.co.uk
Web: www.troubador.co.uk/matador
Twitter: @matadorbooks

ISBN 978 1789015 911

British Library Cataloguing in Publication Data.
A catalogue record for this book is available from the British Library.

Typeset in 11pt Minion Pro by Troubador Publishing Ltd, Leicester, UK

Matador is an imprint of Troubador Publishing Ltd

To Sydney Weaver

CONTENTS

List of Figures and Tables ix

Acknowledgements xi

Introduction xiii

Chapter 1 1
An Ecological Theory of Autism

Chapter 2 21
Researching Recovery in Autism/ASD

Chapter 3 50
Parents as Researchers

Chapter 4 64
Personal Narratives of Recovery

Chapter 5 175
Programmes Adopted in the Narratives

Chapter 6 249
The Structure of Recovery

Chapter 7 271
The Mother/Infant Dyad in Recovery

Chapter 8 298
The Recovering Personality

End Note 326

References   329

Appendices
Appendix I: The ATEC Questionnaire   347
Appendix II: Bibliography of Personal Narratives   348
Appendix III: IRP Blank Form   349

LIST OF FIGURES AND TABLES

Figure 1	Main areas of the brain	1
Figure 2	Entrained mother and child	2
Figure 3	Accumulating an allostatic load	5
Figure 4	Physical effects of an allostatic load	6
Figure 5	Un-entrained mother and child	7
Figure 6	State of motivational conflict	8
Figure 7	Triad of impairments	9
Figure 8	Elements of genetic identity	10
Figure 9	Four concepts of an ecological theory of autism	15
Figure 10	Multiple outcomes from the same environmental factors	19
Figure 11	Disorders of an unregulated fight/flight mechanism	27
Figure 12	PPCE therapy: during, after and later	32-33
Figure 13	Florica Stone's perception of autism	69
Figure 14	Difference in sensory activity with Irlen glasses	200
Figure 15	Interrelated elements of communication and language development in DIR	210
Figure 16	Traumatic impact of hypoxia	250
Figure 17	The three domains of recovery	250
Figure 18	As AL/MC resolves development re-establishes	254
Figure 19	Programmes within the three recovery domains	255
Figure 20	Sample individual recovery plan	257
Figure 21	The three Rs of recovery	263
Figure 22	Mother/infant dyad as developmental foundation	273
Figure 23	Social interaction programmes and typical development	291
Figure 24	Personality Variation in health and illness	306
Table 1	Interacting variables in autism/ASD	18
Table 2	Reliability of the ATEC	39
Table 3	DIR/Floortime intervention outcomes	42

Table 4	Parent ratings of the behavioural effects of biomedical interventions	44
Table 5	ATEC scores for Alexander	71
Table 6	ATEC scores for James	92
Table 7	ATEC scores for Campbell	98
Table 8	ATEC scores for Temple	114
Table 9	ATEC scores for Max	132
Table 10	ATEC scores for William	140
Table 11	ATEC scores for Mark	154
Table 12	ATEC scores for Donna	173
Table 13	Sample ABA curriculum	207
Table 14	Four temperament dimensions and their extreme personality variants	302

ACKNOWLEDGEMENTS

My thanks go to all the courageous people affected by autism, determined to pursue a better life for themselves or their children. To Antonio Giuseppe Farruggia-Bochnak for valuable feedback on an early draft; to Alex Liddle for her proof-reading and constant friendship, and to Mike Franklin for all his love and support.

Jennifer Poole

INTRODUCTION

Recovery from autism is the sequel to *An Ecological Theory of Autism/ASD*. That book resulted from an eight-year research study into the nature of autism. It presented a clearly argued rejection of the long-held assumption that autism/ASD is 'genetic' and therefore fixed. Rather, it proposed that autism/ASD is about 95% *epigenetic* and results from an individual's physiological interactions with single or accumulated environmental exposure, at a critical time of their development. This position left the way clear for an examination of the potential for 'recovery'; the subject explored in this book. The concept of 'recovery' has traditionally been considered both impossible and damaging by established experts in the field, despite evidence that individuals have recovered from autism in the past. In fact, a decade ago funding for this research was refused on that basis: hence this project has been a 'labour of love' and straightened financial dependency: as is frequently the case for those who are first to take seriously non-orthodox concepts. Very recently, however, US psychologists, such as Andrew Zimmerman of the Massachusetts Hospital for Children, Deborah Fein at the University of Connecticut, and Lisa Shulman at the Albert Einstein College of Medicine have begun to note that some children may indeed 'grow out' of autism. This is a most welcome departure because the logical conclusion of the historic 'flawed gene' explanation is the hopeless 'life-long' prognosis inevitably given. In fact, as will be seen, when freed from a perception of genes as fixed and deterministic, a range of potential improvements in health and social development are seen to be possible. This book examines how these have come about for a number of individuals who have (or whose parents have) written of their work towards 'recovery': including the meanings attributed by them to this term. In so doing it deconstructs the recovery process and suggests there may be an optimum approach: one from which each individual can find what they may, themselves, need.

PERSONAL NARRATIVES

In this volume I bring together a range of programmes and methods drawn from personal biographical narratives and accounts of what has proved helpful to individuals with ASD. Where available these are augmented with academic research, although at present this is somewhat sparse. Some programmes have been established by professionals who are themselves parents of children with autism. Most are drawn from parental efforts to assist their children where little or nothing was offered by professional service providers: particularly in the area of physical health improvement. Personal narrative data is essential in showing what may be possible for, as a result of decades of such dedication, many parents are now better informed than 'experts' on how to help the ASD child/ individual. Their stories are recommended to anyone concerned with the welfare of those with autism/ ASD. Appendix II provides a bibliography of accounts I read prior to commencing this research. Others are cited throughout. The internet has since made many more available.

PRACTICAL SOLUTIONS

For too long autism/ASD has been dominated by rigidity in what assistance is possible and who is best to provide it. The narratives make this limitation very clear. I therefore make no apology in exploring the many 'non-established' and neglected health solutions that have formed such a vital role in the recovery process, and in parent-led methods. Many have been side-lined for years out of misplaced concepts of what constitutes 'evidence' in psychology or medicine. But what matters most to parents is their children's wellbeing. For this reason, this book is about helping those affected become happier; more healthy; able to sleep; eat normal food without pain; start to talk/or regain speech where it has been lost (if possible); to express the love they feel for those around them, and to share in the joys of life, instead of withdrawing from sensory overload by 'zoning out' or screaming from frustrated efforts to keep everything in a frightening world the same, and under control. It is aimed at relieving the often immense pressure and strain experienced by those with autism/ASD and their families, who bear the burden and worry of finding practical lifelong solutions for them. *Recovery from Autism* is written for those who care more for the child's health and wellbeing than preserving established theories. It also offers an incentive to those wishing or needing to adopt a less trammelled viewpoint in the area of autism/ASD generally. As the narratives show, many recovered individuals emerge as emotionally fulfilled, sensitive people with personalities and talents previously unimagined. There is much to be discovered of practical benefit, which needs only to be made more accessible to alter current misperceptions and limitations. This book is a step in that direction.

THE LAYOUT OF THE BOOK

Chapter 1 provides a summary of the ecological theory of autism from which the potential for recovery logically follows. Chapter 2 looks at researching recovery, including establishing the meaning/s of 'recovery'. Chapter 3 examines the vital role of parents as researchers. Chapter 4 presents eight personal narratives, chosen to demonstrate a range of recovery experiences; while Chapter 5 outlines all of the programmes and methods cited in the narratives, their research base and how to access them. Chapter 6 breaks down the structure and process of recovery, explaining the variety of outcomes found, and developing a generic *individual recovery plan*. Chapter 7 illustrates how recovery depends upon emulating aspects of the mother/ infant dyad. Chapter 8 shows how the recovering personality 'emerges' and also addresses current notions of an 'autistic personality'.

Jennifer Poole
October, 2018

CHAPTER 1

AN ECOLOGICAL THEORY OF AUTISM/ASD

In this chapter I describe the four basic concepts of *An Ecological Theory of Autism* (Poole, 2017) which together offer a theoretical framework in which recovery – and/or 'growing out of autism' – can be understood. Each of the concepts is outlined below. These are followed by some frequently asked questions about autism/ASD from this new perspective.

1 THE CONCEPT OF *ENTRAINMENT*

Entrainment is a biological term for the state in which two separate open systems, in close proximity, become one system through synchronicity or resonance. In child development, entrainment refers to the nature of the mother and child when attuned to each other as a *dyad* (Newton, 2008). At birth, the infant is 'centred' in the emotional limbic system of the brain, which also houses the survival areas. Until such time as the child's higher cortex and conscious thinking have developed, s/he requires the mother and (later) other adults, to regulate her emotional experiences, including fear. The main areas of the brain are illustrated in Figure 1, below:

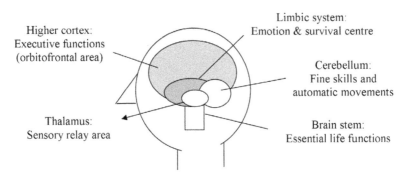

Figure 1 Main Areas of the Brain

Entrainment allows the mother to adopt the role of 'executive' and to direct, modulate and synchronise her feelings and communications with those emerging in her infant (Newton, 2008, p38). She emotionally and socially 'interprets' the world, regulating the inner and outer environments and providing a secure base from which the infant develops more widely. Mother/child entrainment is illustrated in Figure 2, below:

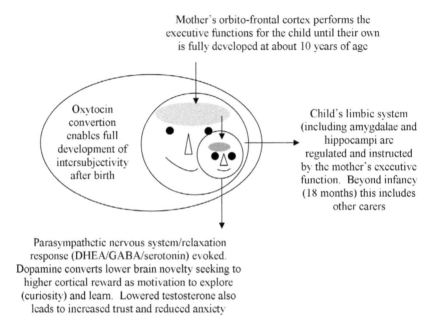

Figure 2 Entrained Mother and Child

As shown, when entrainment occurs, a particular neurochemical pattern is created which supports the child's desire to explore and learn in the wider world. Foetal oxytocin becomes converted to mature oxytocin – known as the 'social hormone' – enabling the pair-bonding necessary for social relations and development through *intersubjectivity*.

INTERSUBJECTIVITY

This is the ability to 'give and take'; to know when to speak or respond, and when to stop speaking and allow the other person to say something in their turn. Trevarthen and colleagues described how:

"...infants freely and sensitively seek to communicate from birth, and they need sympathetic company to develop their minds...."
(Trevarthen et al., 1998, p7)

And:

"...the efficiency of sympathetic engagement between an infant and the adult signals the ability of each to 'model' or 'mirror' the motivations and purposes of the partner, immediately."
(Trevarthen, et al., 1998, p59)

The intersubjective relationship with the mother underlies all of the social interaction of the developing infant and toddler, including the establishment of 'joint attention'. This is where a child will look at an object pointed out to them or engage the attention of another person to share with them what they have seen. Intersubjectivity also enables the newly born child to develop a sense of 'self' including within a social context. It forms the foundation of all relationships and social interactions between individuals. It is these social aspects that are the main difficulty for those with autism/ASD. Lack of intersubjectivity is generally considered to be the 'core deficit' or missing developmental step in autism/ASD.

THE MOTHER/CHILD DYAD

In typical development the mother acts as the vital bridge between the child and the wider world. Consequently, I have adopted the term 'mother' to refer here to the biological mother and to embrace the fact that the mother/child has evolved as a dyad, in the interest of maximum survival. The child will refer to the mother to see how s/he should react to any new situation or possible threat (Sorce et al., 1981) and/or to relax. Rothschild (2000) cites the work of Schore (1994) and Perry et al. (1995) in understanding the crucial role of the mother in helping the child regulate stress, concluding:

"A healthy attachment between infant and caretaker enables the infant to eventually develop the capacity to self-regulate both positive and negative stimuli."
(Rothschild, 2000, pp22-3)

In understanding autism/ASD, it is particularly important to recognise that mother and child are in a relationship *prior* to birth. For example, from extensive research in this area it has been found that the newborn child is already familiar with their mother, and also of other individuals consistently around her. The newborn will express a 'preference' for their mother's voice (DeCasper & Fifer, 1980) and breast milk (Nishitani et al., 2009). Likewise, the mother can identify her own infant at birth, and vice versa, from the chemical pheromones present in the womb for the past seven months (InfoRefuge, 2013). So, while it is common to hear that a mother is 'expecting a child', from the earliest time of auditory development (eight weeks in utero) the child is also 'expecting a mother' and only has to put a face to her after birth. Human infants are innately drawn to faces and will look at even a picture of a face from the first day of life, although boys are more easily distracted towards other similar shapes than girls (Baron-Cohen, 2013). Interestingly, a study by Geraldine Dawson compared 34 autistic children with 21 typically developing children, and 17 'mentally retarded' but non- autistic children, in a face recognition task using pictures of their mothers. She found that both the typically and mentally retarded children showed different brain activity (as young as six months of age) when seeing their mother's face compared to a stranger or object (Smith et al., 2000). This difference did not occur in the autistic children (Dawson, 2001). Face recognition depends upon experience (use of) a specific area of the brain (the fusiform) and on eye contact (Schultz, 2005). Consequently, this is likely to reflect lack of face to face stimulation rather than a 'brain defect'.

2   THE CONCEPT OF *ALLOSTATIC LOAD*

Allostatis is an alternative word for the limbic function of the brain (see Figure 1). An *allostatic load* (AL) is McEwan's term for the accumulation of 'wear and tear' from single or sequential environmental factors (EFs) on the limbic system (McEwan & Lasley, 2001). Similar concepts have been proposed by Lemur (1996) in 'Total Load' theory and the 'Toxic Tipping Point' by Jepson & Johnson (2007). An AL may either accumulate in the individual's lifetime, or build upon effects carried over from previous generations. Evidence for this can be found from the presence of epigenetic 'tags' and 'markers' in human DNA. These 'tags' show how environmental factors (EFs) have altered the expression of genes, without altering the genes themselves. A study at Johns Hopkins University identified such tags in the DNA of fathers of children diagnosed with autism/ASD (J. Hopkins, 2015). Interestingly, Happe (1996) found about 50% of the fathers and 30% of mothers of boys diagnosed as autistic possessed 'proto-autistic' traits. These are characteristics associated with autism/ASD but which are too mild to give a diagnosis in the parent. This phenomenon is known as the *broader autism expression* (BAE). Figure 3 illustrates the concept of an accumulating allostatic load. It shows sequential environmental factors, in this case, over more than one generation, including the parental BAE/DNA 'tags':

Figure 3 Accumulating an Allostatic Load

TRAUMA

The limbic system attempts to adjust to each environmental factor/event as it accumulates, and to the combined load. Ultimately, however, the load can become too great for the limbic system and it cannot cope further without detrimental effects on the individual. When this stage is reached the limbic system experiences the allostatic load as a *trauma* Crucially, the limbic system – which is the survival-based area of the brain – does not recognise the difference between a physical or emotional trauma and will react with the same global fight, flight or freeze (F/F/F) response for either causation (Evans et al., 2000). At this point, there will be a cascade of stress chemicals into the brain and the immune system will also be triggered, stimulating further 'alarm' cytokine messages, to alert a greater response (as for example in fever and inflammation). The main physical effects of an allostatic load are shown in Figure, 4, below. As a result of this, many of the body's functions, including the digestive, immune and nervous, systems become chaotic and disordered. This also alters the biochemistry required for optimum cognitive development and functioning because, as Lathe states, 'body and mind are intertwined' (2006, p152). Thus there is a combined body/mind traumatic response.

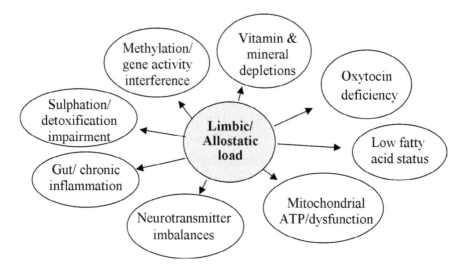

Figure 4 Physical Effects of an Allostatic Load

BREAKING THE DYAD

Understanding autism/ASD requires recognition of the mother/child as a dyad, rather than as two separate individuals, and that this relationship extends from *in utero*. In autism/ASD the allostatic load/trauma breaks this relationship disrupting and/or preventing entrainment. Critically this is *before* the child has developed the higher cortical executive functions typically performed by the mother within the dyad. Following the break the now un-entrained infant has no choice but to attempt to regulate the resulting, sub-cortical (limbic) fight/flight response without her executive role. This state is illustrated below in Figure 5.

A distressing aspect of the break in entrainment is that, despite her desire and effort, the mother becomes unable to perform the developmental function of regulating her child's fears, and so ending the 'closed loop' of MC. This is because the child has now taken on this role for him/herself, unaware of any alternative. Taking on this function for themselves is an act of survival for the child who has now become 'responsible' for their own safety and security, unaware that this is the mother's role. This point is important, as it renders the mother unable to 'reach' her child, who is now psychologically isolated from her as the dyad has become two separate systems. The child will feel threatened by anything which places additional stress on their ability to cope and maintain a state of biochemical equilibrium, which is one in which the child's survival system is constantly 'looking out' for any threats to security.

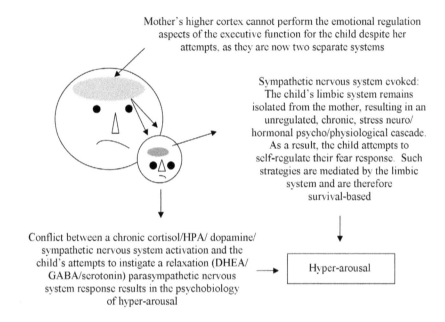

Mother's higher cortex cannot perform the emotional regulation aspects of the executive function for the child despite her attempts, as they are now two separate systems

Sympathetic nervous system evoked: The child's limbic system remains isolated from the mother, resulting in an unregulated, chronic, stress neuro/hormonal psycho/physiological cascade. As a result, the child attempts to self-regulate their fear response. Such strategies are mediated by the limbic system and are therefore survival-based

Conflict between a chronic cortisol/HPA/ dopamine/ sympathetic nervous system activation and the child's attempts to instigate a relaxation (DHEA/ GABA/serotonin) parasympathetic nervous system response results in the psychobiology of hyper-arousal

Hyper-arousal

Figure 5 Un-Entrained Mother and Child

3   CONCEPT OF *MOTIVATIONAL CONFLICT*

As shown in Figure 5, the un-entrained child enters a state of hyper-arousal/ hyper-vigilance. This state has been termed *motivational conflict* (MC) by Niko Tinbergen (1989/ 1993). The child's development is constrained by survival-based physio/psychological functioning. Hence there is a *conflict of motivation* between the need to be safe and secure (limbic system constraint) and the innate curiosity and desire to expand outward into the world (developing higher cortex) of the typically developing child. Figure 6, below, illustrates this concept:

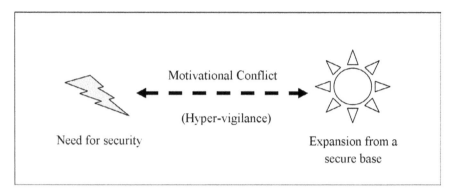

Figure 6 State of Motivational Conflict

The state of motivational conflict (MC) means that development may only take place in 'safe' areas: For example, as a 'special talent' or limited interest, rather than through the social-based learning of the typically developing child. The child will engage in activities that bring a reduction in the hyper-vigilant state and in a sense of reward within this social isolation. Curiosity and desire to explore do exist but are constrained by the underlying trauma, as any changes or additional pressures in the environment will represent threats to the coping state. The overall result is a derailment/suspension of the child's typical development and the subsequent behaviours and characteristics of autism/ASD.

'TRIAD OF IMPAIRMENTS'

As described, continued hyper-arousal will engender a degree of anxiety and increased need for control (for sameness) over the environment. In addition, higher-to-sub-cortical development cannot take place fully when the child in MC is constrained to a dominant survival-based (limbic/mid-brain and brain stem) function. The resulting developmental suspension/derailment of the child's social experience, and other typical higher-cognitive aspects, has historically been highlighted in *the triad of impairments* (DSM-V, 2013) shown in Figure 7, below:

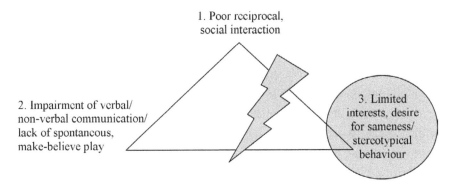

1. Poor reciprocal,
social interaction

2. Impairment of verbal/
non-verbal communication/
lack of spontaneous,
make-believe play

3. Limited
interests, desire
for sameness/
stereotypical
behaviour

Figure 7 'Triad of Impairments' (DSM-V, 2013)

The term *impairment* (designated by Wing & Gould, 1979) has now been generally discarded in favour of the concept of 'difference' or *neuro-diversity* (discussed in Chapter 8). However, it is still utilised as part of diagnostic terminology. These and other characteristic behaviours act as guidance in establishing a diagnosis of autism/ASD. Those in corners 1) and 2) of the triangle are the direct result of delayed or derailed development stemming from the break in entrainment and the intersubjective relationship. The cognitive aspects of autism (theory of mind and executive deficiencies) are due to poor higher cortical and mid-to-higher cortical development, while weak central coherence (seeing parts not wholes) results from lack of the brain hemisphere and sensory integration which would occur in a typically developing child. Limited interests and desire for sameness (corner 3 of the triangle) represent the individual's attempt to self-regulate their hyper-arousal and cope without the role of the mother. Examples are the calming activities of rocking or 'stims' and fixation with endorphin-stimulation (such as with lights). As Donna Williams (an 'autie' author whose narrative is in Chapter 4) explains:

"Everything I did, from holding two fingers together to scrunching up my toes had a meaning, usually to do with reassuring myself that I was in control and no-one could reach me, wherever the hell I was."

(Williams, 1992, p 26)

(*An Ecological Theory of Autism*/ASD provides a detailed exploration of the biochemistry of motivational conflict and how this leads to the characteristic behaviours found in Autism/ASD).

4   CONCEPT OF *GENETIC IDENTITY* (GI)

The allostatic load and resulting motivational conflict will be expressed in tune with the inherited, individual differences or *genetic identity* of the person. The concept of *genetic identity* (GI) replaces the notion of 'flawed genes' and/or 'faulty brain' which for decades has tended to stigmatise those with a diagnosis of autism/ASD. This change is also necessary because, contrary to what is generally stated, extensive research has found no 'genes for autism/ASD'. Rather than 'genetic flaw' the concept of GI suggests there may be developmental outcomes resulting from interactions between susceptible, healthy natures and particular environmental factors (EFs). The elements of GI are shown in Figure 8, below:

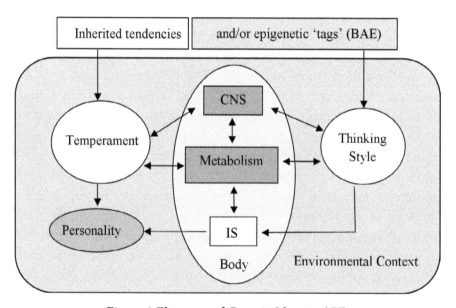

Figure 8 Elements of Genetic Identity (GI)

As can be seen, GI comprises inherited tendencies towards body type, including central nervous system (CNS) metabolism and immune system (IS); and also traits for temperament and thinking style. The whole is embedded within our environmental context (both physical and psychological) and continually interacts with those influences and exposures. Because of the natural diversity of GIs susceptibility to specific environmental factors will vary between individuals and is also likely to run in families.

TWO STREAMS OF ASDS

Given all of the above, two streams of autism/ASD are probable: an individual stream (IS) and a broader autistic expression + individual stream (BAE+I).

1   Individual Stream (IS)

In the individual stream (IS) autism/ASD results from an interaction between a particular susceptibility and single or cumulative environmental factor/s, which create/s an allostatic load/trauma sufficient to break entrainment. In this stream there are no obvious, wider BAE 'pro-autistic' traits apparent in the familial background.

2   Broader Autism Expression + Individual Stream (BAE+IS)

In the wider BAE+IS stream, the individual is diagnosed in the presence of additional familial 'proto-autistic' traits or characteristics. Here, a particular environmental exposure is sufficient to 'prime' the potential parent. This 'priming' effect is passed forward to the next generation, becoming 'full blown' in an individual with a similarly susceptible GI when they experience their own allostatic load/trauma and leading to a diagnosis of autism/ASD.

MULTIPLE PATHWAYS TO AUTISM/ASD

It can now be seen why there is no single 'cause' of autism/ASD. Rather, each individual shows a personalised 'pathway' within one or other of these two streams (IS or BAE+IS). The 'cause' in either stream lies with the *interaction* between the individual's natural susceptibility/GI to one or more environmental factors (EFs) with the most recent acting as the 'trigger'. In autism/ASD, these susceptibilities /vulnerabilities are likely to run in families with similar GIs; hence the presence of the broader autism expression (BAE). For this reason there are many possible variations and triggers, depending upon different GIs and EFs, and the susceptibilities and interactions between the two. As a result of these individual differences autism/ASD will present as a syndrome – with similar but varying expression according to the GIs of those affected. The example 'pathways' below are drawn from the personal biographical narratives. They are illustrative of the variety that may occur within this basic, yet flexible, theoretical framework.

a)   Temple's Pathway

This example is based on information provided in Temple Grandin's account (Grandin, 2014) which is described on page 267-8 of this book. Following a physical trauma of unknown origin at aged 1-2 years, her brain 'rewired itself' naturally to compensate, in keeping with her innate, preferred thinking style (TS). Her father also demonstrated some 'proto-autistic' traits (BAE). It is important to note that, contrary to established 'wisdom' in the past, it is now well known that the brain is highly 'plastic' in its ability to form new connections in response to environmental stimulation and exposures. Programmes (usually with mice or rats) aimed at sensory enrichment have clearly demonstrated a difference in brain development compared with more stimulant-lacking contexts (Diamond & Hopson, 1999). This must be so, or else no new learning, new skills or personal growth could possibly occur, nor could any form of brain rehabilitation. In infants and children 'plasticity' is particularly marked, so that early interventions and life experiences (including emotional states) will literally 'shape' the developing brain (Gerhardt, 2004). In Temple's case, the neurological 'recovery' made from the earlier trauma provided her with a 'special talent' in the area of perception. Based on her account the following pathway is suggested for Temple:

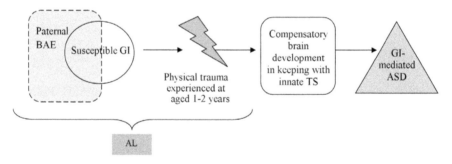

b)   Male Gender Pathway

An example in the narratives of a pathway where gender is relevant is that of James (Narrative 2, Chapter 4). In his case a number of 'risk' factors accumulated to form an allostatic load: the presence of an increased allergy rate (and therefore immune dysfunction) in the family background; his lungs were under-developed in the womb; he was cyanosed ('blue') at birth and he was vaccinated: which his mother (a doctor) suspects negatively affected him. He was also the only male child of triplets (his sisters being unaffected). We know from comparative studies that boys are more vulnerable to vaccination than girls (see Poole, 2017, Chapter 8) and also to other early disruptive trauma (Baron-Cohen, 2003). A potential male gender-based pathway for James might therefore be as follows:

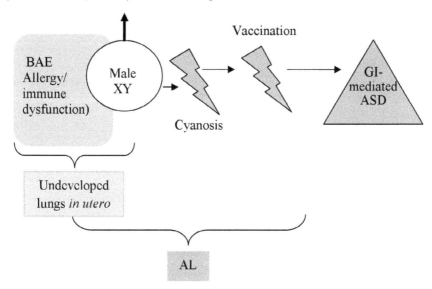

c)   Maternal Stress Pathway

There is some evidence that trauma experienced during pregnancy can transmit to the unborn child. An inherited traumatic 'memory' effect has been found in the children of women who had developed post traumatic stress disorder while pregnant at the time of the 2001, US World Trade Building terrorist attack (Yehuda et al, 2005). This effect was particularly connected with the first and third trimesters of pregnancy. Research by Beversdorf et al (2005) found a higher incidence of prenatal stressor events in autistic children at 21-32 weeks gestation, with a peak at 25-28 weeks, while Walder and colleagues (2014) noted an association between the 1998 Quebec hurricane and subsequent autism diagnoses 6.5 years later. Similarly, a 2016 study by Kinney and colleagues showed a highly significant association between autism prevalence and prenatal exposure to hurricanes and tropical storms in Louisiana (Kinney et al, 2016). And research with mice found epigenetic markers indicative of trauma could pass through two generations (Morgan et al., 2011). Susceptibility to stress may depend upon the GI of the mother. For example, a study by Hecht et al. (2016) identified individual differences in the transportation of serotonin (which affects stress toleration) in the body: a vulnerability which might equally apply to an unborn child of the same GI. A maternal stress pathway might be therefore be expressed as below:

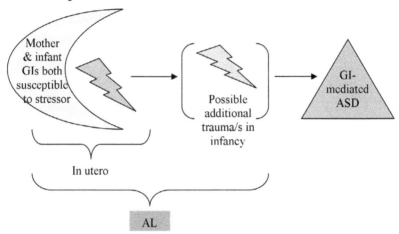

The infant may directly experience the mother's stress as sufficient to trigger their own limbic response, or it may act as a priming factor in an accumulating series (shown in brackets) leading to a full blown AL. In either case, the AL/ASD will be expressed (mediated) through the infants own GI.

d)   Birth Hypoxia Pathway

In this pathway the infant experiences a lack of oxygen during the birth process, or shortly afterwards. Such a situation is described in *For the Love of Ann* (Copeland & Hodges, 1973) who was left in the cold for some time after her birth and became cyanosed ('blue'). Ann was eventually recovered by her parents (see Appendix II). A possible pathway for birth hypoxia is shown below:

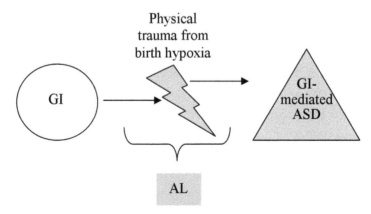

All infants are likely to be 'susceptible' to hypoxia at birth and where this contributes to an accumulating load it may provide an AL tipping point. For example, James required steroids to develop his lungs *in utero* and then experienced mild cyanosis after birth, adding to the allostatic load already carried from his under-developed lungs.

SUMMARY OF CONCEPTS

The ecological (AL/MC) theory of autism described in this chapter is underpinned by the four major concepts of *Entrainment, Allostatic Load, Motivational Conflict* and *Genetic Identity* illustrated in Figure 9, below:

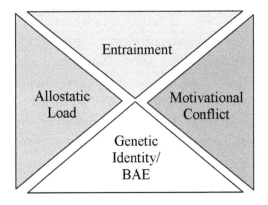

Figure 9 Four Concepts of an Ecological Theory of Autism/ASD

The emphasis in AL/MC theory is on the *interaction* between an accumulated allostatic load (AL) and an individual's genetic identity (GI) which leads to a traumatic break in entrainment and the intersubjective relationship with the mother. This results in a state of hyper-vigilance/arousal and motivational conflict (MC), leading to the typical signs and characteristics of delayed/derailed development, including those of the *triad* historically used in a diagnosis of autism/ASD.

SOME QUESTIONS AND ANSWERS ABOUT AUTISM/ASD

Given all of the above, answers to some commonly asked questions from the perspective of an ecological theory of autism/ASD can be offered:

WHAT IS AUTISM?

Autism/ASD is the result of a traumatic *allostatic load* (AL) which breaks mother/child entrainment and the intersubjective relationship, before the child has developed the capacity to act as their own 'executive' higher cortex. This physio/psychological trauma places the infant in a state of chronic hyper-arousal/hyper-vigilance or *motivational conflict* (MC). The child is not physically but *psychologically* 'detached' from the socio-psychological supportive dyad and wider network which would typically ensure their emotional regulation, sense of safety and social integration. The impact of this traumatic break provides the context within which the typical behaviours and characteristics of autism/ ASD occur, as the infant must now perform the mother's executive role and regulate their own emotional state whilst centred in and constrained by limbic (survival-based) sub-cortical functioning.

IS THE MOTHER TO BLAME?

Absolutely not. The break in entrainment is not deliberately caused by mother or child and, as described earlier, the mother frequently sufferers greatly as a result. In the past, Freudian psychiatrists assumed 'refrigerator' mothering was to blame for the child's apparent withdrawal (for example, as was Pat in Mark's Narrative in Chapter 4). However, this idea was de-bunked in the 1960s by Bernard Rimland's work on the biological foundations of autism/ASD (Rimland, 1964). Similarly, AL/MC theory stresses the biochemical foundation of motivational conflict within a combined body/mind model.

WHY DOES AUTISM AFFECT INFANTS AND YOUNG CHILDREN?

This is due to the timing of the traumatic break which occurs before the infant has developed the 'executive', regulating faculties of the higher cortex. Even when they subsequently do so, the survival brain retains a *constraining influence* through motivational conflict. The child with autism/ASD may physically grow up, but still lack the internalised regulatory skills that would typically have developed with an entrained mother and child. The child has missed vital intersubjective developmental experiences and so does not have the inner structure necessary to comprehend or tolerate social relations as a typically developing child would do. It is through the entrained mother/ child dyad that we learn to regulate emotions for ourselves. A trauma initially occurring at an older age would not constrain the development of the lower-to-higher cortex in the same way, so that higher faculties would be available to the individual with which to consciously address their own traumatised state (such as through therapy). In autism/ASD the child is not 'aware' consciously but, rather, is placed in a 'developmental limbo' by the need to cope with the hyper-arousal and hypertensive effects of the trauma and to regulate their own environment to this end. All the while entrainment is lacking, however much the mother (or other adults) might wish (and try) to 'reach' them, the child remains unaware of any need, or any regulatory resource they might offer.

WHAT IS THE DIFFERENCE BETWEEN 'BRAIN FLAW' AND BRAIN DAMAGE?

In the AL/MC theory of autism the historical concepts of 'genetic flaw' or 'faulty brain' have been rejected as both stigmatising and inaccurate. 'Genetic flaw' offers a hopeless and potentially self-loathing suggestion of blame, as does the idea that the individual has a 'faulty brain'. In contrast to fixed and determinist genetic notions of autism, we now know that the brain is capable of great compensation (especially in children under eight years of age) due to its plastic nature. Consequently, the idea that autism/ASD as a fixed state is out-dated. This can be seen from the narratives (Chapter 4) and from recent research that some children can 'grow out of autism' (Lawrence, 2013). There will clearly be limits to this recovery, depending upon the degree of damage caused by the trauma itself, but the potential remains nevertheless.

WHY IS AUTISM A 'SYNDROME'?

Autism is a 'syndrome' because there are a variety of genetic identities (GIs) and potential environmental factors which may interact to bring about the trauma leading to autism/ASD, as shown in Table 1, below:

Time of Trauma:	*In utero*	Birth	Early Childhood	
Trauma Type:	Toxic	Non-toxic		
Gender:	Male	Female		
Stream:	BAE	IS		
GI Thinking Style:	Verbal	Visual	Kinaesthetic	
Temperament:	H/A	RD	NS	P
Somato-type:	Ectomorph	Exomorph	Mesomorph	

Table 1 Interacting Variables in Autism/ASD

These include the time of the trauma (three variables), type of trauma (toxic or non-toxic), gender, whether there is a familial BAE, and the elements of the GI; including thinking style, temperament and body (somato) type with their associated physiological corollaries (metabolisms). The combinations of these variables lead to the different 'types' and expressions of autism/ASD. If we understand autism/ASD as a trauma state expressed through the BAE and/or GI of each individual, we can better see how one person might become 'autistic' while another 'hyperactive'. McCandless, (2009) for example writes:

> "...I consider attention deficit disorder (ADD) and attention deficit hyperactive disorder (ADHD) to be milder versions of the same problem."
>
> (McCandless, 2009, p3)

It might also be relatively easy to 'mis-diagnose' ADHD for autism/ASD. For example, it was found in a recent assessment that 1:42 boys are being 'wrongly diagnosed' with ADHD when in fact they might be autistic (JADD, 2016). The assessment authors state:

> "The misdiagnosis is to some extent understandable because around 30% of children with autism also present with ADHD."
> (JADD, 2016)

Figure 10, below, illustrates how multiple outcomes are possible from the *same* environmental factors, depending upon individual susceptibilities and environmental exposures:

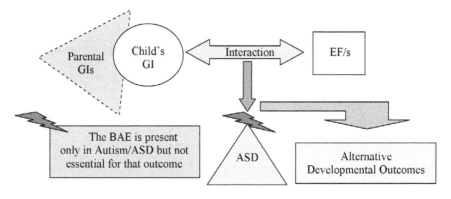

Figure 10 Multiple Outcomes from the Same EFs

An ecological theory of autism/ASD allows and accounts for the situation above; where one child might develop ASD, another ADHD, another obsessive compulsive disorder (OCD), or another specific allergies or cancer. We can also now see how it might be possible for an autistic child who 'grows out' of their diagnosis to present with a different but related condition. For example, Griswold (2017) describes research by Mukaddes and colleagues (2016) in which some children undergoing (mostly behavioural) programmes, whilst developing social and communication skills which no longer rendered them 'autistic', nevertheless exhibited OCD and/or anxiety. Within the current ecological theory of autism/ASD this can be explained as a shift in the surface expression of the AL/trauma, without the deeper change that would ultimately resolve it. That is: the chosen programme has addressed the higher cortex, but not the limbic system sufficiently.

WHAT ARE THE IMPLICATIONS OF AN ECOLOGICAL THEORY OF AUTISM/ASD?

An ecological theory of autism/ASD has serious implications. One of these is in relation to child development as a whole in that the mother/child dyad profile is enhanced in both developmental importance and relevance (see Chapter 7). Another is the suggestion that, despite the current 'mushrooming' of neurological and health conditions in children, these may stem from the same, relatively few environmental factors being expressed according to the individual's GI. A third relates to the suggestion that autism is a 'fixed' and 'permanent' state with no 'cure' or means of 'recovery'. In contrast, by adopting an ecological perspective, autism can be seen as a derailment or suspension of the child's development, rather than a brain or genetic 'flaw'. Given this; 'recovery' as a concept gains more potential. The foundation for researching recovery and the meaning I attribute to this term are established in the next chapter.

CHAPTER 2

RESEARCHING RECOVERY IN AUTISM/ASD

In contrast with the ecological theory of autism summarised in the previous chapter, genetically-driven theories of autism are unable to account for recovery, or to meaningfully explain how any child diagnosed with autism/ASD may 'grow out' of it (James, 2012). Indeed, since its original classification by Kaner in 1942, 'experts' and other medical personal have described autism as 'a life long condition'. Any recoveries made have historically been denied (for example: Frith, 1989/2003). And this is still the case, usually by doubting the original diagnosis or baldly re-stating, as does Dr Georgina Gomez-de-la-Cuesta, of the National Autistic Society:

> "…a child with autism will grow up to be an adult with autism."

Or Matson:

> "When you're autistic, you're autistic. It's a very stable condition."
> (In: James, 2012)

This is despite work by the developmental psychologists Greenspan and Wieder in 2006 which clearly indicated that their programme (DIR/Floortime, described in Chapter 5) led to children no longer diagnosable as autistic on a standardized diagnostic measure. Then, in 2012, Andrew Zimmerman of the Massachusetts Hospital for Children, US, surveyed 92,000 parents of children aged 17 and younger. Of the 1,366 with a child previously diagnosed with an ASD, 453 said their child no longer had the diagnosis: about one third (In: James, 2012). But it wasn't until a US study by Deborah Fein the following year that researchers began to seriously examine the subject of recovery from autism (Fein et al., 2013). Further research by Catherine Lord's team (Anderson, et al., 2014) followed and it is now generally assumed that a small percentage of children with autism (7-9%) can 'lose their diagnosis' and/or achieve an 'optimum' or 'very positive' outcome (Griswold, 2016). These findings are explored in more detail later in this Chapter.

THE MEANINGS OF *RECOVERY*

A number of terms have been adopted to indicate positive outcomes from interventions for autism/ASD. Consequently, it is important to be clear about the meaning/s attributed to these and/or in the 'recovery' literature. Mark Blaxill is co-founder of *SafeMinds,* an organisation which investigates the effect of mercury on children's brain development. He is also the father of an autistic daughter. He gives the following definition of recovery:

> "The goal of treatment is recovery: defined as a more rapid developmental trajectory, restoration of specific functions and, in the best case, a normal life. Recovery is not the same as a cure."
>
> (Autism Research Institute, *Website*, 2010)

However, Blaxill does not specify in what way recovery differs from cure. *The Autism Research Institute* (ARI) in San Diego, USA, was established in 1967 by Bernard Rimland a US psychologist and parent of a son with autism. Rimland was responsible for rejecting the original, Freudian suggestion that 'refrigerator mothers' were to blame for their child's autism and replacing this with a neurological/biological theory (Rimland, 1964). Edelson, an ARI Director, explains Rimland's perception of recovery:

> "Dr. Rimland did not want to use the word 'cured' to describe these children. Instead, he preferred the more appropriate term 'recovered'. He liked the analogy offered by Stan Kurtz, director of the *Children's Corner Schools* in Van Nuys, California…to illustrate what recovery means:
>
>> "Assume that a person is hit by a car. His legs are broken, and he suffers brain damage. At this point, he is considered disabled. Now let's say after intense rehabilitation he is able to walk again

with a slight limp and has some remaining neurological issues but can live a normal life – or maybe he heals so well that you couldn't tell he was in an accident at all. That's recovery."

He continues:

"...many children once diagnosed as autistic may exhibit only nuances of their former behaviours; for instance, some still have mild 'stims', or an exaggerated focus on favourite topics. Despite lingering issues, recovered children will, in many cases, be able to live independently and happily, have productive careers, and enjoy rewarding relationships with others. They may not be 'cured', but they are certainly recovered from the devastating symptoms that once blocked their path to a normal future."

(Autism Research Institute, *Website*, 2015)

Greenspan and Wieder's research with their own *developmental, individual-difference, relationship-based* programme (DIR/Floortime: described in Chapter 5) showed a majority (58%) of children treated had recovered beyond being diagnosable using the *Childhood Autism Rating Scale* (CARS). However, these authors do not refer to 'recovery' as such. Rather, they adopt a range of terms to describe their positive outcomes. For example:

"There are others...who make unusual progress, advancing significantly beyond the 'high functioning' level."

(Greenspan & Wieder, 2006, p7)

The terms 'unusual progress' and 'advancing significantly' appear to stand in for 'recovered' and 'recovering' in this appraisal. Similarly, Annabel Stehli, whose daughter recovered completely using *auditory integration training* (AIT: described in Chapter 5) adopts the term 'exceptional progress' in her anthology of recovery narratives (Stehli, 2004). Others include 'grow out of autism', 'optimum outcome', 'lost the diagnosis', 'resolution of autistic symptoms', 'left the autistic spectrum' or 'shed their autism'. The choice of words may be aimed at avoiding 'false hopes' of full recovery; not appearing to reject those individuals who do not make as much progress as others and/or at avoiding aggravating/alienating the psychological/ medical establishment. For this reason, perhaps, it is probably no coincidence that DIR is a more accepted programme (among professionals) than Son-Rise, for example, despite some clear parallels, whose approach is more open:

> "Oftentimes parents are given prognoses that are frightening and negative. They are told what their children will never do and can never have. We do not believe that anyone has the right to tell a parent what their child cannot achieve. We help parents focus on their attitude and reclaim their optimism and hopefulness. We help them to see the potential in their children and then 'go for the gold'. From this perspective, we have seen, all things are possible. Additionally, caring professionals are not often given the resources, guidance or support that they need to help the children that they are working with. We understand the pressures that many professionals deal with and offer a unique attitudinal perspective that allows you to feel both re-energized and armed with excellent tools to help your students."
>
> (Son-Rise, *Website*, 2010)

Like DIR, Son-Rise carefully avoids using the words 'recovery' or 'cure', preferring 'progress'. Indeed, they state explicitly:

> "You don't have to 'cure' your special child in order for his or her specialness to have meaning and value. The value lies not in 'results' but in how you treat your situation and your child."
>
> (Kaufman & Kaufman, 1995, *Foreword*)

The Kaufmans emphasised the complete recovery made by their son, Raul, openly referring to this as a 'miracle'. And given that Raul, now in his 30s, is no longer autistic, has a genius IQ and that his parents were advised by the professionals they consulted that he was 'an incurable retard' who should be institutionalized, the word 'miracle' appears entirely justified in his case. So, whilst it may not be the expressed goal of any of these professionals to bring about recovery, they offer hope that the child can progress as much as is possible despite their diagnosis. Recovery is perceived, not so much as an outcome, but as part of an ongoing (possibly lifelong) process, much less limiting than the prognosis typically offered to parents and individuals by established service providers, and far more positive in most cases.

REDUCING DISCOMFORT

For many offering help to individuals with autism/ASD recovery means reducing the discomfort of either the core autistic (triad) state, or the co-morbid illnesses experienced. For example, *Treating Autism* (TA) is a charity run entirely by parents. Its aim is: to 'provide support and information to persons affected by ASD, their family members and professionals'. They state:

> "Our charity works to relieve the suffering of people with autism and their families through the provision of information and support services, free of charge, in particular concerning the treatments for autism"
>
> (TA, 2017)

As with ARI, this parent-driven organisation began when no other help was forthcoming. The purpose is not 'recovery' but reducing the discomfort of the affected individual. That recovery is sometimes the 'accidental' outcome is noted, but in a way that will not deter others from doing as much as they can:

> "Although these are not a series of miraculous cures and complete recoveries from autism, all of these children have made notable, sometimes remarkable progress. These are the stories of hope."
>
> (TA, 2017)

When it does occur, however, 'recovery' indicates no longer any signs of autism. There are one or two stories of this type among the many narratives to be found on the TA website. One of these is that of Ryan, diagnosed aged 4, whose mother recovered him as a child.

RYAN'S DEFINITION

Now aged 26, Ryan is now an aerospace engineer with a love of surfing. He states that he has 'recovered' from autism:

"Some people think we should just accept autism. And that if a child is treated, it changes who that kid is. I am still the same person I was only now I'm happy and can enjoy life."

(TA, 2017)

IS 'LOSING THE DIAGNOSIS' RECOVERY?

One question which emerges from this research refers to 'losing the diagnosis' and whether this equates to 'recovery' from autism/ASD? Chapter 1 cited work by Mukaddes and colleagues who found that some children (about 9%) might lose their diagnosis of autism but retain signs of a different, related condition such as anxiety and obsessive compulsive disorder. Previous research indicated a similar result, but with such problems at a lower rate, possibly reflecting cultural differences (Griswold, 2016). A study by Lisa Shulman and colleagues reviewed 569 children who had been diagnosed with ASD from 2003-13. A variety of therapeutic interventions had been used with the children, who were also from racially and socio-economically diverse backgrounds. Of the 569 children, 38 showed no autistic symptoms when re-evaluated four years later. However, most of the children continued to exhibit other learning and behavioural symptoms. Shulman states:

"Autism generally has been considered a lifelong condition, but 7 percent of the children in this study who received an early diagnosis experienced a resolution of autistic symptoms over time....The majority of the children at original diagnosis displayed intellectual disability but at the point of resolution of autistic symptomatology displayed normal cognition."

(Shulman, et al., 2015)

Despite this improvement in cognitive functioning (measured as intelligence quotient: IQ) the researchers found 92% of the children showed 'residue learning and/or emotional/behavioural impairments'. Similarly, Eigsti (a co-author of Fein et al, 2013) notes that children who became no longer diagnosable showed 'unusually active language regions' in the brain, relative to children with mild autism or those originally without the condition. Although expecting that those who had 'shed their autism' would show brain activity more similar to the typical group, the team found 'a unique signature of brain activity reflecting a tendency to compensate for difficulty with language'. The children utilised the right hemisphere of the brain in addition to the left-hemisphere language processing areas (i.e. they adopted whole-brain processing). The intervention appeared to have: 'sparked compensatory brain changes rather than promote neurotypical brain development' (In: Griswold, 2016). Of this, Fein suggests 'the brain functioning is not normalized. It looks like they might be compensating' (in: Carpenter, 2015). And in research by Mukaddes and colleagues, of the 26 children (21 boys) who lost their diagnosis of autism/ASD, 24 had received help for a psychiatric condition other than autism. More than half met the criteria for attention-deficit hyperactivity and nearly half had a specific phobia and/or severe anxiety about an object or situation, such as spiders or heights. Roughly one in five had obsessive compulsive disorder (In: Griswold, 2017). As shown in Figure 11, below, these are all results of a limbic system in fight/flight:

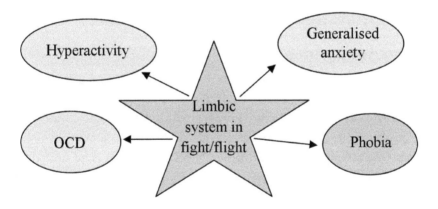

Figure 11 Disorders of an Unregulated Fight/Flight Mechanism

This observation is supported by research from Albert Einstein College of Medicine, US, which proposed that the symptoms of autism may be 'reversible' as 'the brains of autistic individuals are structurally normal but dys-regulated' (Mehler and Purpura, 2009). These authors discovered the *locus coeruleus*-noradrenergic (LC-NA) system of the brain to be involved in autism. The LC-NA system secretes the stress hormone adrenaline: a key neuro-transmitter of the flight/flight response and of attentional capability. They write:

"What is unique about the *locus coeruleus* is that it activates almost all of the higher- brain order centers that are involved in complex cognitive tasks."

(Mehler & Purpura, 2009)

In addition, Mehler and Purpura point to the interesting phenomenon of fever which can sometimes appear to restore normal functioning in autism/ASD, as it too stimulates the LC-NA system of the brain. This could not happen if autism was caused by a lesion or structural abnormality, nor a 'faulty gene'. It can be seen from the studies cited above that the residue psychological states (phobias, generalised anxiety, hyperactivity and obsessive compulsive disorder) in children who had 'lost' or 'shed' their autism diagnosis all result from of an unregulated limbic system. So, how are we to understand these outcomes? Does 'losing a diagnosis' equate to recovery? To understand this, it is necessary to return to our new understanding of autism/ASD from an ecological perspective.

DEPTH OF RECOVERY

Fein states: 'so far at least, which children move off the autism spectrum and why remains a mystery overall.' However, within an ecological framework the 'mystery' becomes more comprehensible. The ecological theory of autism (AL/MC: described in Chapter 1) proposes there is an underlying limbic-mediated physio/psychological trauma at the root of autism which breaks the mother/child dyad and entrainment. This leads to delayed or derailed development of the higher cortical /cognitive aspects of autism/ASD. There are therefore 'layers' to autism: 1) sub-cortical/limbic and, 2) higher cortical aspects, which means that different 'depths' of recovery may be occur. Studies that measure purely cognitive outcomes, such as by using intelligence quotient (IQ) will therefore be measuring only the surface (higher cortex) aspect of autism and not the underlying trauma state. As the diagnostic *triad* is largely formed of observations and behaviours rather than their underlying causations, it is highly possible that the child will no longer be 'diagnosable' on a cognitive measure, whilst retaining aspects of related (and deeper) limbic system dys-regulation in the range illustrated in Figure 11 above. Vestiges of both the damage (from the trauma) and the derailed developmental results may remain.

FACTORS AFFECTING OUTCOMES

In addition, the nature of the intervention utilised in these studies will play an important role in outcomes. For example, 40% of the OO children in Fein's study had received a behavioural intervention (ABA: described in Chapter 5) some commencing this as young as 18-24 months (Ornstein et al., 2014). ABA is a language-based (cognitive) programme. A 'verbal layer' over an initial trauma could have two effects: 1) it might provide language and rudimentary social interaction to the child enabling them to articulate their fears, emotions and insecurities to adults who could then help regulate these. And, 2) the disciplined framework of behavioural programmes provides security and structure in itself, which could have the effect of 'turning off' a degree of anxiety and insecurity (and therefore the fight/flight/LC-NA system) resulting from the original trauma. However, this may be insufficient to fully address the underlying allostatic/ trauma effects, which must be reduced or resolved for a deeper 'recovery' to occur, and/or for developmental steps such as intersubjectivity (social reciprocity) to re-instate. And, clearly, the degree of damage and derailment originally suffered will be key in any outcome. When assessing outcomes, it is important to bear in mind that autism/ASD is not a 'cognitive/social problem' alone but the result of physical/ psychological trauma, and recovery is therefore a form of rehabilitation. There will consequently be degrees of recovery depending upon degree of harm. Outcomes will also depend upon other factors, such as the genetic identity (GI) of the child. For example, some ASD children, particularly Aspergers, may be of a language-based thinking style, so that an ABA programme may particularly suit them. However, others may be more visually (Melillo & Leisman, 2009) and/or right-hemisphere dominant (Escalante-Meade, et al., 2003), so may need to form compensatory brain connections to accommodate a left-hemisphere/ language-based programme to their natural GI. In fact, it is considered that the majority of those with autism are of right/whole brain dominance and processing preference (thinking style). This may explain the compensatory brain activity found by Eigsti.

REMAINING DIFFERENCES

Returning to Fein's study (2013), the 'optimum outcome' (OO) children had been similar to those who retained an autism diagnosis when younger, although they had exhibited milder social difficulties than the rest of the non-OO autism group. Subsequently, the researchers found almost no difference between the OO and typically developing children, as Fein writes:

> "We looked at so many variables, we were beating the bushes to find anything different [between them] and there was so little."
>
> (Fein, et al., 2013)

One difference they did observe was that, although the repetitive behaviours and rituals characteristic of autism were greatly reduced in the OO children, they continued to exhibit more rituals and routines around mealtimes and bedtimes than the typically developing group. However, these behaviours did not interfere with their lives in the way they had done previously. This finding suggests the underlying trauma of autism/ASD had diminished to a great extent – hence the rituals were much reduced. The OO group were also more likely to use unusual phrases or scripted language when narrating a story, but this appeared to reflect a 'quirky sense of humour rather than communication deficits'. In summary:

> "…individuals who shed their diagnosis improved across all the symptom domains of autism….it is not just that they no longer meet the diagnosis criteria because they have learned social skills, for example."
>
> (In: Deweerdt, 20104)

Taking all of these factors into account 'loss of the diagnosis' by itself may not equate to recovery as perceived within an ecological theory of autism, but it can give valuable insights into the possibilities of different interventions and the varying level of need of different individuals.

THE DEFINITION OF RECOVERY USED IN THIS BOOK

It would appear from all of the forgoing research that a partial 'recovery' from autism/ASD can occur and the individual will no longer be diagnosable as such. However, some trauma effects may remain. So, within an ecological theory of autism, and for the purposes of this enquiry, I have taken 'recovery' to comprise two things together:

1. A significant degree of physical recovery from the physio/ psychological *trauma* which initiated autism/ASD and:
2. Sufficient re-instatement following the resulting *developmental derailment* that the individual is now able to enter into intersubjective relationships

Under this definition, recovery may occur along a continuum with no fixed time scale. Some sensory or physiological elements of 'delayed' or 'disrupted' development' may remain as remnants of the original derailment, and the individual may then benefit from additional programmes/interventions. The process of recovery from this point of view is examined further in Chapter 6.

THE 'INCONVENIENT FACT' OF RECOVERY

Whilst there is still some scepticism in conventional circles regarding the results cited earlier, this is mild compared with the historic tendency to ignore any evidence not emanating from an orthodox source. And it is very recent indeed that psychologists have begun to 'notice' that some children diagnosed with autism can lose their diagnosis and/or achieve an 'optimum outcome'. As Geraldine Dawson, a psychologist and researcher at Duke University, US, states:

> "Those of us who work closely with children with autism have known clinically that there is this subgroup of kids who start out having autism and then, through the course of development, fully lose those symptoms…and yet people always questioned it."
>
> (In: Padawer, 2014)

Given the traditionally hostile environment surrounding any such suggestion, it is not surprising that an established researcher like Dawson has never presented this clinical observation before Fein's study was published. The determined stance that autism/ASD is a life-long state has led in the past to rejection of the body of qualitative (experiential) evidence of recovery. But to fully understand recovery from autism (as with autism itself) it is essential to 'hear' the voices of recovered and recovering individuals themselves. This requires a willingness to accept, without selective bias, what the sociologist Max Weber called 'inconvenient facts' (Weber, 1918). These are facts (evidence) which may fly in the face of established opinion and theory. Sadly, the scientific impartiality required for this has not always been achieved by those working in ASD research (or elsewhere). For example, in a major text on autism, Roth (2010) presents a photograph (shown in Figure 12 a, below) of *Prolonged Parent-Child Embrace* (PPCE), a form of holding therapy:

Figure 12 a) 'During PPCE': From: Tinbergen and Tinbergen (1983/93)

This illustration is one of a sequence in Tinbergen & Tinbergen (1983.89) but is the only one shown by Roth. It is given, perhaps, to illustrate an autistic child in distress during a therapy unpopular with many autism 'experts'. It certainly shows a somewhat unhappy child. However, Roth fails to remark that, for the first time, she is making good eye contact with her mother; something most individuals with autism/ASD find difficult to do and consequently avoid. In addition, Roth completely omits the plates giving the subsequently positive outcome of the session, both of which show a now happy child interacting with her mother and therapist in turn, illustrated in Figures 12 b) and c) below:

 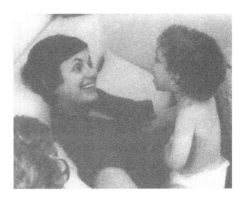

b) "Later: Exploring her   c) "Afterwards: Interacting
   mother's face"   with Dr Welsh"

Figure 12 b) & c) 'After PPCE'. From: Tinbergen and Tinbergen (1983/93)

Following the therapy session, the child is happy and unharmed physically or psychologically. Now able to make good eye contact, she appears willing and able to interact with her mother and others around her. As described in Chapter 1, lack of this ability (intersubjectivity) is considered to be the 'core deficit' in autism. Given this, one can justifiably imagine the developmental gains that may now follow for this child. It is undoubtedly the case that since PPCE was devised, more desirable and less coercive measures have been developed that are likely to achieve the same results. PPCE in its original form appears therefore both unnecessary and less than optimum as an intervention (see Chapter 5 for a description and detailed discussion). However, regardless of one's own opinion, if we are to understand what is possible or not in autism/ASD, it is surely most important to acknowledge the 'inconvenient fact' of this child's apparent recovery using this method?

SIMON'S EXPERIENCE

Whether it is acceptable for the child to be made unhappy appears to depend on who is doing the making. For example, a contemporaneous narrative describes how Simon Lovell attended a *National Autistic Society* School, at that time run by Sylvia Elgar. His mother has written a personal account of his and her experiences and describes Simon's response to the school routine:

> "The changes that took place in him [Simon] during that new term were visible. The first was a new and plainly marked reluctance to go to school. He could not tell me about it, but he demonstrated it very efficiently by stages in a go-slow at breakfast time. Until then, I had never experienced the slightest difficulty with him over meals-he seemed to like all foods indiscriminately, and was always hungry....Now breakfast began to assume a distinctly nightmarish quality. He would not eat, except at a pace a snail would have found slow, he would not look at us, and he often cried silently. In the end, thoroughly worried, I phoned Mrs Elgar about it. I remember hearing the smile in her voice. 'He's having to work for the first time in his life', she told me 'and he's none too enthralled about it. Give him time and don't worry.'"
>
> (Lovell, 1978)

As instructed, his mother ignored his distress, sending Simon to school without breakfast if he had not eaten it by the time to leave. After a while all this behaviour stopped. (Simon's experience is described further in the next chapter).

FOR THE LOVE OF ANN: AN OBJECT LESSON

An object lesson in establishment selectivity is found in *For the Love of Ann* (Copeland & Hodges, 1973). *For the Love of Ann* describes what is now accepted to be a basically behavioural approach to reclaiming a child, invented *ad hoc* by her parents for want of any other help. Immediately after birth, Ann had been left unattended and uncovered by hospital staff, resulting in her becoming 'blue' (cyanosed) – apparently from cold. She was later found to be autistic. Her parents followed their own instincts, largely driven by her father Jack, and recovered Ann. The methods they used appeared quite harsh (it included the occasional smack) but, nevertheless, by the end of the narrative Ann appears to be a happy, independent young woman with her life ahead of her. At the annual National Autistic Society

(NAS) conference of 1985 (over 30 years ago), while many books were available to buy, Ann's story and the Tinbergens' *New Hope for a Cure* were absent. At the same conference a talk given by an autistic child's mother, accepting the hopelessness of her child's prognosis and not in any way looking for help to recover him, was greeted with sympathetic admiration. If I had not already read Ann's story at school, and previously corresponded with Niko Tinbergen, I would not have been aware that some children can 'recover'. Examples of professional censorship continue. Applied behaviour analysis (ABA: described in Chapter 5) was found to have been given early in the lives of 40% of those children who gained an 'optimal outcome' in Fein's study: which was published exactly 40 years after Ann's recovery narrative. ABA is, arguably, a more humane version of the original behavioural techniques upon which it is based, and features prominently in many published recovery narratives (see Chapter 4). Yet many psychologists still consider there is 'no evidence' for ABA, despite the real life experiences of children and parents (Keenan, 2004). While ABA may not be ideal for all children at all times, if the personal experiences of Ann's family had been acknowledged, including that Ann had recovered to a degree inconceivable to some (then and now), many professionals would perhaps not still be in the position of only just beginning to discover that a well-managed ABA programme can help some children regain lost development.

ACCEPTING 'INCONVENIENT FACTS'

So, despite the belief that autism is/was considered to be life-long, some children 'no longer have the condition' and/or may begin 'functioning in the normal range'. This 'inconvenient fact' raises important questions about our understanding of autism/ASD and child development generally, such as: how can recovery be possible if the standard theory of autism is correct, and why don't all children with autism recover, or show related difficulties? In addition, more attention must be paid to what parents/ recovered individuals have already found helpful, and to the degree and type of autism theirs was. We must also find a way to accept the recovery of some, whilst protecting those who may not recover from feeling less 'successful' or 'lesser' people. These points are addressed throughout this book.

TYPES OF RECOVERY RESEARCH DATA

In the study that formed this book, three types of research data were found. The first (A) comprises research studies undertaken with children who had received a diagnosis of autism/ASD using a standardised measure, and who were later re-assessed: three such studies are discussed below. The second (B) presents parental feedback on programmes found helpful with their children. The largest source for this type of information is provided by the *Autism Research Institute* (ARI), which has collected parental data from 1,124 children, largely from biomedical treatments (including diet). The chief aim of ARI research is to help parents identify which programmes have been found most helpful. This led to the establishment of both the database and the *Autism Treatment Evaluation Checklist* (ATEC: described below) which is used to measure changes following the treatment programme. The third type of research (C) is drawn from the written accounts of individuals who describe their own or their child's process of 'recovery' and the method/s they used to bring it about. These biographical narratives usually reflect the desire of parents (or others) to illustrate hope and, as a part of this, to establish that a particular programme worked for them For example, the Kaufmans, who designed the Son-Rise programme, first found they could recover their own son and then began to help other parents do the same. Their organisation is based on attempting to train as many parents in the specifics of Son-Rise as possible because they themselves cannot be personally available to help every child whose parents contact them. There are also two published narratives by recovered individuals: Temple Grandin and Donna Williams (both described in Chapter 4).

DATA TYPES

These different methods of research collect different types of data: quantitative research and qualitative research. Quantitative research aims to measure general trends across groups of similar individuals to give a statistically likely result. They may therefore use diagnostic assessments and other standardised measures to screen and diagnose, and/or decide the level of autism in the individual. Some of the more common of these are outlined below. In contrast to statistically based data, qualitative research is more interested in each individual's experience, although it may also collate statistical data as well. It can tell us more about the real life of the individual, including how and what they do to help themselves.

DIAGNOSING & SCREENING CHILDREN WITH AUTISM

As will be seen from the research cited below, a range of diagnostic and screening assessments have been designed for use in establishing the presence of the *triad of impairments* and in making a formal diagnosis of autism. Some of the best known and/or frequently mentioned in the recovery narratives are the *Autism Diagnostic Interview-Revised* (ADI-R: Rutter, LeCouteur and Lord, 2003); *Autism Diagnostic Observation Schedule* (ADOS: Lord et al., 2000); *Childhood Autism Rating Scale* (CARS: Schopler et al., 2010) is a widely-used measure which can both diagnose autism and discriminate between autism and other cognitive problems; *Gilliam Autism Rating Scale* (GARS-2: Gilliam, 2005); The *Checklist for Autism in Toddlers* (CHAT: Baron-Cohen, Allen & Gillberg, 1992) now improved to the *Q-CHAT* and the *Autism Behaviour Checklist* (ABC: Krug et al., 1980). Professionals will show preferences for which measure they use and why they use it.

INTERVENTION EVALUATION OVER TIME

There are also number of measures used specifically to test treatment programmes and their effectiveness over a span of time. Two of these are:

THE PDD BEHAVIOUR INVENTORY (PDD-BI)

The Pervasive Developmental Disorder Behaviour Inventory (PDD-BI; Cohen & Sudhalter, 2005) is used to assess responsiveness to interventions in children aged 18 months – 12.5 years diagnosed with a pervasive developmental disorder (PDD) – a category diagnosis which includes autism/ASD. The standard form of the assessment focuses only on those aspects associated with autism and takes 20-30 minutes to administer.

THE ATEC

The *Autism Treatment Evaluation Checklist* (ATEC) was developed in 1999 by Bernard Rimland and Stephen M. Edelson of the ARI to help parents determine if their children are benefiting/have benefited from a specific treatment intervention. The ATEC is a one-page form (see Appendix I) designed to be completed by parents, teachers, or researchers, consisting of four sub-tests: *Speech/Language Communication* (14 items); *Sociability* (20 items); *Sensory/Cognitive Awareness* (18 items) and *Health /Physical/ Behaviour* (25 items). Responses can be entered online and results directly supplied by ARI. Until its introduction there was no test or scale specifically designed to measure treatment effectiveness, so researchers used diagnostic scales such as the CARS, GARS -2, or ABC. Rimland suggests that using autism diagnostic scales to measure treatment outcomes is not ideal because most are not sufficiently sensitive to changes within the individual. The ATEC itself gives only an external perception of functioning in each scale and cannot provide subjective data. Nevertheless, it can offer some indication of current status on the diagnosable difficulties of autism/ASD. Published studies have shown the ATEC to be sensitive to changes as a result of a treatment. For example, Jarusiewicz (2002); Lonsdale, Shamberger and Audhya (2002), and Klaveness and Bigam (2010) demonstrated the ATEC is able to measure behavioural improvements following a gluten-free/casein-free diet. Further research is underway to compare the ATEC with other outcome measures (ARI, 2010, *Website).*

RELIABILITY OF THE ATEC

The reliability of an assessment is the degree to which it measures what it purports to, each time it is used and by anyone who uses it. This must also take into account whether the child was having an 'off day' when tested. The internal consistency of the ATEC was examined using a Pearson split-half coefficient (where a score of 1 equals total consistency) on over 1,300 completed ATECs. Table 2, below, gives the results (May 2007):

N = 1,358	Uncorrected r
Scale I Speech	.920
Scale II: Sociability	.836
Scale III: Sensory/Cognitive Awareness	.875
Scale IV: Health/Physical/Behaviour	.815
Total ATEC Score	.942

Table 2 Reliability of the ATEC

These figures show the ATEC is a highly reliable measure for its purpose, with the Total Score (.942) being almost totally reliable.

SECTION A: THREE QUANTITATIVE STUDIES

a.) A study by Zimmerman and colleagues in 2012 was published in the journal *Pediatrics*. This surveyed 1,366 parents of children with a past or current diagnosis of autism, aged 17 or younger in 2007 and 2008. Of these, about one third (453 children) no longer retained their original autism diagnosis. Parents were asked if their children had been diagnosed with other developmental problems such as hyperactivity, depression, speech, or learning problems (conditions which may impact on the likelihood of outgrowing the autism diagnosis). The researchers also adjusted their results to account for the influences of known effects on autism/ASD, such as race, gender, family income status, education level, health insurance coverage, and whether the children where enrolled in a personalised education plan at school. They found that, in some cases, autism does not appear to be the 'lifelong condition' it is usually considered to be. The suggestion was made that these children may have been originally 'misdiagnosed' (e.g. In James, 2012). However, Zimmerman cautions against drawing this conclusion, stating:

"It's not unusual to see a child start out with more severe autism and then become more moderate and even mild as the years go by...A lot of the kids are improving, and we don't really know why, except we know there's a lot of moldability of the developing brain....We think that earlier treatment is essential and there are reasons to think that we can improve the kids. I'm very optimistic."

(In: James, 2012)

The reference to the brain being 'moldable' refers to the innate 'plasticity' and ability of the cortex to compensate for trauma and grow new pathways (see Chapter 4 of Poole, 2017). The potential for this is particularly high in young children: hence early intervention is important. Zimmerman's view that autism may 'become milder' is not something that is generally stated, and most individuals are not told this when they are diagnosed. Parents certainly are not yet given this type of advice in place of the 'lifelong' message. However, it is becoming clearer to researchers that various degrees of recovery are possible.

b.) A joint observational research study has been undertaken between US and Canadian universities with children who had previously been diagnosed with an ASD but no longer had this diagnosis. The researchers compared 34 'optimal outcome' (OO) children, with 44 'high functioning' Asperger (HFA) individuals and 34 typically developing (TD) individuals. The groups were matched for age and gender. For this study, 'optimal outcome' (OO) indicates:

"...losing all symptoms of ASD in addition to the diagnosis, and functioning within the non-autistic range of social interaction and communication. Domains explored include language, face recognition, socialisation, communication, and autism symptoms."

(Fein, et al., 2013)

The research was published in 2013 in the *Journal of Child Psychology and Psychiatry*. It found that the mean group scores did not significantly, statistically differ between the OO group and the typically developed group on socialisation, communication, face recognition or most language subscales, although three OO individuals showed below-average scores on face recognition. The researchers conclude:

"Although possible deficits in more subtle aspects of social intervention or cognition are not ruled out, the results substantiate the possibility of OO [optimum outcome] from autism spectrum disorders and demonstrate an overall level of functioning within normal limits for this group."

(Fein, et al., 2013)

Optimum outcome (OO) in this context appears to be a euphemism for 'recovery'. Face recognition is something which requires expertise (practice over time) as Schulz (2015) has suggested. This may reflect lack of practice, and can therefore improve. A point of interest is that the OO group had originally displayed milder ASD symptoms in the social domain than the high functioning Asperger group, but equally severe difficulties with communication and repetitive behaviours. These researchers are now examining possible reasons for the difference between those who 'lost the diagnosis' and those who did not. Children in the OO group had received early, intensive therapy – 40% with ABA (described in Chapter 5) – between the ages of two and two and a half. This compared with only 4% of those who did not lose their diagnosis. Some commentaries by 'experts' have suggested that the OO children's symptoms were merely 'masked' (Lawrence, 2013) and they did not in fact 'grow out of' their autism/ASD. This is probably because their genetically determinist view point does not allow for recovery.

c.) A study by Anderson and colleagues (Anderson et al., 2014) examined 85 children with autism from the ages of two to 19 years. By aged 19, eight of the children (all boys) equating to c9% of the study population, no longer met the criteria for a diagnosis of autism, requiring no additional support. Six of these boys had retained their diagnosis until they were at least 14 year of age but had lost it by the end of the study period. This suggests progress towards recovery can continue over adolescence and beyond. Lord referred to these children as gaining a 'very positive outcome'. Neither Fein nor Lord suggest reasons for these outcomes and do not use the term 'recovery'. In this study all eight boys who no longer met the diagnosis criteria had received early intervention by the age of three years of age, compared with only half of those who did not (In: Carpenter, 2017).

d.) Greenspan and Wieder (1997) analysed the recovery rates of 200 children previously diagnosed on the autistic spectrum, and subsequently treated with their DIR/Floortime programme (described in Chapter 5). The children were re-assessed on the *CARS* measure, two to eight years after commencing the programme. Results are shown in Table 3, below:

Good to outstanding	58%
Medium	25%
Ongoing difficulties	17%

Table 3 DIR/Floortime Intervention Outcomes.
From: Greenspan and Wieder (2006) p381

Of the 58% in the 'good to outstanding' group, Greenspan and Wieder write:

"… these children became warm and interactive, relating joyfully with appropriate, reciprocal preverbal gestures; could engage in lengthy, well organised and purposeful social problem-solving and have attention on various social, cognitive, or motor-based tasks; used symbols and words creatively and logically, based on their intent and desires, rather than using rote sequences, and processed to high levels of thinking, including making inferences and experiencing empathy. Some children in this group developed precocious academic abilities two or three grade levels above their ages."

(Greenspan & Wieder, 2006, p379)

They conclude:

"On the CARS, they shifted into the non-autistic range, although some still evidenced auditory or visual-spatial difficulties (which were improving) and most had some degree of fine or gross motor planning challenges."

(p381)

The second group of children with ASD, comprising 25% (50) of the original group:

> "…made slower progress but still made significant gains in their ability to relate and communicate with gestures, entering into long sequences of purposeful interaction but not necessarily a continuous flow."
>
> (Greenspan & Wieder, 2006, p381)

The third group forming 17% of the sample was formed of those who originally had the most complicated neurological pictures, including other disorders such as seizures. This group made slow progress. Most eventually learned how to communicate with gestures or simple words but they continued to experience poor attention, avoidance and self-stimulation. Of this group eight children were wavering or losing abilities. All the children in the study were brought by their families who had clearly chosen DIR and were motivated to use it. The authors point out that this self-selecting sample cannot be said to be representative of all children with ASD.

DIR LONG-TERM FOLLOW-UP

Sixteen children from the 'good to outstanding' group in Greenspan and Wieder's 1997 study were followed-up 10-15 years later. The authors report: 'The core deficits and symptoms of ASD were no longer observed' (Greenspan & Wieder, 2006, p387). On the *Achenbach Scales of Social Competence* (Achenbach, 1992/1992/1997) 96% were in the normal range; 88% were in the normal range for activities and school competence, and 75% in the normal range for clinical symptoms, such as anxiety, depression, withdrawal and/or aggression. In addition 87 of the original 200 children were no longer diagnosable on the CARS measure.

PLAY PROJECT

A second DIR study was undertaken in the USA by Richard Solomon as the *Play and Language for Autistic Youngsters Project* (PLAY). Here, monthly home visits by PLAY consultants videotaped parents in DIR activities, and recommended activities and techniques to increase social interaction with their child. Of 68 children evaluated (the measure used is not given) 52% were assessed as having made:

"…very good clinical progress over the study period, with a further 14% making good progress."

(BPS, 2007, p410)

B   THE ARI DATABASE RATINGS (QUANTITATIVE DATA)

ARI began researching promising treatment methods for autism, largely of a biomedical nature, following positive reports of parents removing milk and other allergens from their children's diets. Table 4, below, shows the percentage of parents who rated autistic behaviours in their children as 'better' following different biomedical treatments:

Treatment	% of Parents
Heavy Metal Detoxification: Chelation	75%
Gluten-Free/Casein-Free Diet	65%
Vitamin B12 Supplementation	62%
Food Allergy Treatment	62%
Risperidal (anti-psychotic medication)	55%
Diflucon (anti-fungal medication)	52%
Vitamin B6 Supplementation	51%
Removing Dairy Products	50%
Nystatin (anti-fungal medication)	49%
Rotation Diet	49%

Table 4 Parent Rating of the Behavioural Effects of Biomedical Interventions
From: Edelson and Rimland (2006) pp382-3

Parents assess their chosen treatments using the ATEC (Appendix I) and submit a simple rating scale (online) which is then scored and the information added to the database. There are separate result tables for autism and Asperger children. From this it can be seen that 75% of parents rated heavy metal detoxification (chelation) as producing beneficial changes in their child's autistic behaviours. The second most highly rated method was the gluten-and-casein-free diet (65%) with both Vitamin B12 supplementation and food allergy treatment closely following (62%). Various medication ratings ranged from 49%-55% improvement.

C   BIOGRAPHICAL NARRATIVE: QUALITATIVE DATA:

This qualitative data is drawn from the personal experiences of individuals who have found ways of improving or, in some cases, completely recovering from autism/ASD. Each is a unique 'individualised package' of treatment methods with many using a 'pick and mix' combination. The child has usually been given a formal diagnosis of autism, although they may not have received a follow-up assessment. Therefore the degree of recovery itself is not always measured. Sometimes, however, following some time on a programme, a child is formally re-assessed and found to no longer register as 'autistic' on the particular measure used. Narrative data provides a rich and valuable description of the changes and differences in the individual over time. Often this outlines how a child begins to behave in a developmentally more typical way, such as gaining speech, eye contact and social skills, being able to sleep, becoming confident and making friends. It is often these personal elements that provide the most insight into *how* recovery occurs. Indeed, a true picture of recovery can only be fully understood by reading these individual, biographical narratives, (as presented in Chapter 4) or viewing narrative videos. Gaining an awareness of the wide variety of such experiences also tends to mitigate against false assumptions such as that the child was 'wrongly diagnosed' to start with.

EMILY

The following is an example of a personal narrative, from the NAS website, by Andrea Spinks, whose daughter Emily has followed the Son-Rise UK home programme:

> "Since February 1998 I have been working with Emily for two and a half hours each morning with our Son-Rise program. She has also had one-to-one tuition from Hilary since June 1998, taking her

hourly therapy to four and a half hours a day. We began working with Emily on her second birthday. She is now almost three and a half years old. The Son-Rise idea is based on working with your child on their terms but being careful to set goals and achieve the desired outcomes without confrontation. It basically suggests that to accept and work well with your child you must initially understand them so completely that you try to get into their world. It is more to do with the simple idea of working from their side towards ours rather than forcing a world of terms and conditions upon people to whom it simply makes no sense. I was surprised at how, given time, it is possible to read situations through your child's senses if you are present with them on this one-to-one basis. All the time we spend with Emily is in a room that we have made to the Son-Rise specifications. This is a converted bedroom with blank walls, a lino floor, a few shelves out of reach with toys on and large mirrors. This blankness enables Emily's concentration levels and eye contact to rise to a much higher pitch than in any other environment. There is nothing to distract her, nothing to filter out – just you, the child and the endless possibilities of communication. It really is good fun! The only stimulating thing about this environment will be you.

Emily's autism, we feel, is quite severe. She has very little language and I suspect no receptive language as yet. However, she continues to make remarkable progress in this learning environment and her concentration level and eye contact have vastly improved, thus giving her an opportunity to learn. Emily is more happy and confident than we could have imagined at this stage in her development. Her sociability is remarkable and she now mixes very well with her peers as well as adults. She has developed many self-help skills and a very real ability to use her learned imagination in extremely appropriate ways. Eighteen months ago Emily was totally self-absorbed, swaying and staring into space with a fixation about dummies. Due to these incredible changes in her trust in people none of these traits exist in her any more. I strongly believe that the one-to-one child-led therapy has suited our family and provided Emily with a very real and permanent foundation on which to build her millions of potential goals and achievements."

(NAS, 2010, *Website*)

It is heartening that the NAS now includes the Son-Rise programme on its website.

TREATING AUTISM WEBSITE

The *Treating Autism* (TA) website (TA, 2017) contains a number of personal narratives of the same type as *Emily*, above. As described earlier in this chapter, TA is a UK charity which offers research and discussion on many alternative and innovative programmes, including nutritional research, hyperbaric oxygen treatment, stem cell therapy, anti-fungal treatment, antibiotic therapy, psychological approaches, educational therapies, IV immunoglobulin therapy, biofeedback, somatic therapies and also play and music therapies.

SOURCING NARRATIVES

When researching recovery stories for this book a decade ago, I was surprised at just how many published accounts there are. Not all of these provided sufficient information to be included in this study: a similar limitation of the many video presentations encountered. The starting point was reading more than 30 personal biographic narratives written either by a parent of an individual diagnosed with autism/ASD, or the individual themselves (see Bibliography in Appendix II). Each of these was essentially about how they had 'recovered' and/or improved to a better state of health and/or wellbeing: even in some instances to no longer being diagnosed with autism/ASD. For this reason the personal meanings of these recoveries varied between writers – some not using the term 'recovery' at all – while the outcomes also varied considerably. The narratives chosen for analysis in Chapter 4 represent a variety of approaches to recovery; span several decades and illustrate different outcomes along the recovery spectrum. They were selected to provide a wide range of programmes and outcomes and gain understanding of what may be helpful for different aspects of autism/ASD. Information and available research on the various methods recovering individuals have found helpful in the narratives is presented in Chapter 5, to form a 'recovery resource'.

THE FRAMEWORK USED IN EACH NARRATIVE

This research study examined the biographical narratives of individuals who have lived through and described a process of personal recovery, or of working towards recovery, from autism/ASD. Clearly, to learn from the recovery experiences of others, and to study them from a psychologist's viewpoint, it was necessary to reduce the narrative data which was frequently of book length to a manageable format, whilst embracing the essential qualities of each story. This necessitated considerable editing of the data. Each narrative in Chapter 4 is therefore presented as a *Summary*. Following the *Summary* further information under five sub-headings is presented in each narrative:

1. The Diagnosis of Autism Given
Different assessments and measures for autism/ASD were used in the narratives. In some cases the individual received this retrospectively. This is especially the case with older individuals such as Temple and Donna. Diagnoses now tend to occur at a younger age.

2. What is Meant by 'Recovery'?
As the word 'recovery' is used to mean different things by different people and in different contexts, the specific meaning in each narrative is described.

3. Attitude Towards the Idea of 'Cure'
Where given, attitudes towards 'cure' were noted separately from 'recovery'. This is largely because 'cure' is referred to in much of the literature on ASD and by many autistic people writing about themselves and their autism. It is also the term used by one of the parents of a fully recovered child (Max: Narrative 5 in Chapter 4).

4. The Programmes Used
The narratives featured in Chapter 4 were chosen to give as wide an exploration as possible of the different programmes used. Each programme or treatment method mentioned by a narrator is described in detail in Chapter 5, together with any related research found, to form a 'recovery resource.'

5. The Outcomes

Following the summary, an ATEC assessment based on the final narrative data provided in the published account is given. This is not intended to be taken as a reliable measure of the individual's recovery, as it is not based on a full interview, but is able to highlight differing outcomes on the four sub-scales of the ATEC, and where further work may benefit the individual.

THE NARRATIVES

The personal biographical narratives included in Chapter 4 (with their published sources) are:

1. Alex (Stone, 2004)
2. James (In: Edelson & Rimland, 2006)
3. Campbell (In: Edelson & Rimland, 2006)
4. Temple (Grandin & Scariano, 1986)
5. Max (Lansky, 2003)
6. William, (In: Edelson & Rimland 2006)
7. Mark (In: Stehli, 2004)
8. Donna (Williams, 1992/1994/1999/2004)

CHAPTER 3

PARENTS AS RESEARCHERS

The role of parents of children with autism/ASD has traditionally been that of struggling to access services and, where there were none suitable, to establish their own. The latter has generally taken place alongside lack of help and even positive resistance from the establishment of the time. In 1962 Lorna Wing, the psychiatrist who with her colleague Judith Gould defined 'the triad of impairments' (Chapter 1, Figure 7), helped set up the *National Autistic Society* (NAS) with 11 other parents in the UK. She was inspired by Clara Claiborne in the US, whose book *The Siege* was published in 1967. Both were mothers of girls diagnosed with autism. Following her daughter Jessica's diagnosis at about 3 years old, Claiborne had initiated a strong parent-led 'campaign' for better understanding of autistic children. Wing describes how:

> "Park's experiences with professionals were distressing and unhelpful, and she decided to help her daughter herself, by experimenting and finding out what worked best for her. Park helped many parents feel that they knew what was best for their own child."

> (Wing, 2010)

At the same time, Bernard Rimland, an American psychologist whose son was diagnosed with autism, proposed a neuro/biological theory (Rimland, 1964) and helped found the, then current, *Autism Society of America*. It was Rimland who first used the term 'developmental derailment' in connection with autism. All these parents rejected the Freudian 'refrigerator mother' explanation and were particularly concerned about the long-term care of their children. The NAS opened the first residential schools for autistic children in the 1960s with Sylvia Edgar, who specialised in this work. Such boarding schools continued in the UK until Margaret Thatcher's Conservative Government *Care in the Community* (1989) legislation resulted in a change of emphasis from institution to inclusion.

INSTITUTIONAL DENIAL

Although initially designed to liberate parents from an oppressive establishment viewpoint, the NAS in particular became composed of individuals with fixed ideas of what care was best for all autistic children. Ironically, this led to them replicating the situation they had themselves rejected, and in denying the experiences of those parents who did not agree with them, or who wanted a better way to help their children. Wing particularly objected to any suggestion that the child might be able to 'recover' and was joined in this view by major figures in the research field (e.g. Frith, 2009). As was seen from the comments at the beginning of Chapter 2, remnants of this inflexibility remain. Evidence from parents of recovery tends to be either doubted or frankly denied, and biographical narrative data dismissed as 'anecdotal' – an expression commonly adopted to enable those working in laboratory research to ignore the experiences of those living in the 'real world.' This collective, institutional denial resulted in parents having little relation to their autistic child. For example, in NAS educational institutions the child had group contact with teachers and carers but very little with their mothers/parents. This change in the mother's role from 'cause' to 'irrelevant' can be clearly seen in the writing of Ann Lovell, mother of Simon (cited in Chapter 2) who was offered a place at the Sylvia Edgar School in Ealing:

"Gradually I saw Simon adjusting to the new efforts required of him. He began to settle down, and to make unimaginable progress. By the end of the second term, Mrs Elgar was very pleased with him. I was amazed at the improvements in his writing and number work – the two subjects the teachers had despaired of at the ESM [educationally subnormal] school. The only drawback, as far as I was concerned, was the difficulty I found in visiting the school. Ealing is nearly thirty miles from our home, separated from us by heavily congested roads. With the three younger children to care for, and a large amount of ferrying to and from to be done, the journey could only be fitted into daily routine with great effort. I never attended any school function and regretted and missed this greatly. It meant that I no longer felt involved in Simon's life to the same extent, and this was hard."

(Lovell, 1978, p103)

She goes on to describe how Simon went further afield to the point where he hardly ever returned home:

> "As a caring parent, I thus find myself pinned between two opposing forces, *which should not be opposing*: the one which decrees [by the NAS] what is best for Simon, both socially and emotionally, and the one which decides what is best for the rest of the family. It seems to me that our modern Welfare State, for all its liberal attitudes, is, when it comes to basics, as Victorian as any of our asylum building fore-fathers. It is more convenient, and economical, to isolate the mentally handicapped [how autism was interpreted at that time]. As I see it, from a parent's point of view, Simon and his like need both the emotional experiences of a loving family life as well as support and training as members of a larger community....I think that parents have some rights....I have had to give up my rights as a mother."
>
> (Lovell, 1978, p126)

This 'decree' was probably not so much due to the 'welfare state' as NAS policy, however. Simon was considered lucky to have gained a place at the long-term community, but both he and his mother exhibited doubts about this provision:

> "...in the eyes of everyone else, he *is* lucky. He is safe, safe from my death or his father's, safe from murderous cars, rapacious men, or disorientated thugs. He is leading a useful life with his plants and his animals. He need not feel a total parasite, if he were capable of formulating such a concept, for he costs the taxpayer less than he would if he were in a mental sub-normality hospital....But inside me, I cannot silence that other voice that quietly, continuously mourns his loss. I do not just mean his loss to me. I mean also his own loss in terms of his own identity, his personality, which is moulded by his membership of an ordinary human family. A little of it still remains, as when he immediately asks: 'Where's Joanna' [his sister] when he arrives home, with a flash of his old smile. But nowadays he no longer looks us in the eye as he once did, at least, not until he has been at home for several days. He looks persistently

away, leaving me to guess uneasily at his feelings. Then after a while
he seems to relax with us all again, to become once more his old self,
the self which went cheerfully off to ESN school every day."

(Lovell, 1978, p128)

Following the break from his family Simon appears to display more 'autistic'
behaviours than before he started at the school. He also appears less happy.
In addition, Simon was a very gifted musician (as was his sister) with perfect
pitch, and he loved music. Music is often of considerable therapeutic benefit
to children with autism, but it fell away completely when he went to boarding
school, and then an independent community for adults.

A SHIFT TOWARDS PARENTS

From the 1960s-1990s the role of parents in the relevance and (usually)
practical care of their autistic children beyond primary school age was
diminished to zero. A child might be 'normalised': that is taught to fit into
an adult community of other similar individuals, but no other improvement
and certainly not 'recovery', was considered possible. The general assumption
(at least in the UK) appeared to be that, as mothers are not to blame for their
children's autism because it is a genetic/biological condition, then parents
have no role at all. As mentioned previously, in the UK the implementation
of *Care in the Community* (1989) as a budget exercise shifted emphasis away
from institutional care towards policies of inclusion. This led to the closure
of many NAS and other ASD boarding schools. An indirect impact of this
was that it effectively freed up parents to reclaim their children and set up
their own services for them. In some cases this took the form of local day
schools (such as the *Tree House* in London) or integration into special units
in state schools. In other cases it has enabled parents to adopt a home-based
social interaction programme (such as ABA: described in Chapter 5). Social
interaction is the core difficulty in autism/ASD. It is therefore somewhat
strange that, despite a diagnoses on Wing's 'triad', in which the social aspects
of development are considered 'impaired', the NAS-preferred treatment for
autistic children was 'normalisation' through residential education instead
of a programme of enhanced social interaction.

Theirs was not an inevitable policy direction, however, as an educational setting can be flexible in this respect. This can be seen if we contrast Simon and Amy Lovell's experience with that of Amy, mother of a boy in the 'optimum outcome' group of Fein's study, cited in Chapter 2:

> "When he was 3, he entered a therapeutic preschool that emphasized social interaction, and he blossomed there. One day Amy took him to meet a classmate at a playground. When they arrived, [he] couldn't immediately see the child in the crowded park. I remember him saying, 'I lost my friend. That makes me sad'. Amy says, 'that was an early revelation that he recognised and cared for another peer'. By the end of second grade, the director of [his] elementary school, a therapeutic school for children with language-based learning problems, assured Amy she thought he was ready for a mainstream school. Later he joined a regular education classroom at a public school with strong special needs programming. A Monday afternoon socialising group strengthened skills such as initiating conversations and compromising with teammates."
>
> (Carpenter, 2015)

The schools Amy's son attended focussed heavily on the actual difficulty in autism/ASD. His degree of 'autism' decreased as a result, in contrast to Simon's which appeared to increase in favour of literacy skills. Simon's mother wrote her narrative in 1978; thirty years ago, and 25 years before Fein's study uncovered Amy's evidence of her son's recovery. It has taken psychologists this long to learn to listen to personal experience through such biographical narratives. Of course, we all learn over time to find better ways of addressing problems; yet a single reading of Ann Lovell's 1978 narrative reveals just how unsuitable for an autistic boy was the type of educational treatment he received. *Normalisation* remained the policy in NAS boarding schools until they were closed. And, in such an institutional setting, anything even slightly suggestive of parent involvement, such as altering diet or trying a new therapy, was extremely difficult to enact. Those working in the field at that time who attempted to break into a more relationship-based approach, or who felt similarly to Simon's mother, experienced repeated frustrations from NAS policy. In the US, thanks in large part to Bernard Rimland, a slightly different situation occurred. While equally rejecting the Freudian 'refrigerator mother' explanation for autism he developed a viable alternative theory. And by establishing the *Autism Research Institute* parents became free to explore non-established treatment options. Hence, it is no surprise that the first research to fully address recovery originated in the US. Since Wing's death in 2014, the NAS has begun to include examples of recovery on its website (as with Emily's Son-Rise programme cited in Chapter 2). This is helpful as parents will continue to seek solutions for their own children, regardless of established views. It is therefore to be welcomed that some psychologists are now listening to parents' own experiences at last.

COMING UP TO DATE

In the past, the 'brain/gene flaw' theory of autism held great appeal as, compared with the Freudian assumptions of the time, it was 'blame-free' (of mothers). Hence it is understandable that some parents of autistic children clung to it fiercely. We now know there are 'no genes for autism' and that genes alter their expression in the presence of various environmental factors: a field of study known as *epigenetics* (Rossi, 2002). This must inevitably lead us to a new, ecological perception of autism (see Chapter 1 and also Poole, 2017). But it is one which in no way implies blame to parents. Indeed, as Rimland demonstrated, it has always been entirely possible to accept that no parent is to blame for their child's autism, and the fact that parents seek help for their child does not imply that they are in any way 'to blame'. Mothers and infants have evolved as a *dyad* with the mother's role that of preserver and enhancer of their child's life and the father as protector of both mother and child. Parents (especially mothers) are therefore *evolved* to seek solutions for their children's problems and to refuse to accept anything that does not serve this end as they see it. When undisturbed by cultural interference, 'caring' is a result of the natural birth process. In relation to autism/ASD this means that parents will continue to seek optimum ways to help their child's health and welfare, regardless of the views of 'experts'.

PATRICIAN ATTITUDES

Sadly, vestiges of a patrician attitude towards parents remain. A good example is found in: *Defeating autism: a damaging delusion* by Michael Fitzpatrick.

Supported by individuals such as Paul Offit (a vaccine manufacturer) and Roy Richards, (an anthropologist), Fitzpatrick, a general practitioner (not a psychologist or autism researcher) writes:

> "Modern scientific knowledge in any discipline is complex and highly specialised. The professional understanding of research scientists and clinicians is the product of long processes of study, training and experience. Such knowledge and expertise cannot be acquired through reading papers, downloading information from the internet and attending occasional conferences. At best, parents can acquire what has been called narrowband competence… familiarity with one small aspect of a subject. This may allow them to select information that supports pre-conceived conviction and presenting this may be effective for campaigning purposes. But a narrow and selective approach can lead to the sort of dogmatic outlook expressed by advocates of the biomedical approach."
>
> (Fitzpatrick, 2009, p51)

Fitzpatrick's statement clearly requires further examination. The assertion made is that parents are: a) unable to understand 'specialised knowledge'; b) able to take in only a small amount, or 'narrowband' of information; c) will already have an opinion they are seeking to 'prove' as part of a campaign; are d) dogmatic, and e) are erroneously/naively using a 'biological approach' as a result. As a scientist/researcher myself I know that most researchers only concentrate on a very small area of their own field of interest. This is one of the major problems of science: that it is not in any way 'joined up'. Also, as a GP, Fitzpatrick, must be in a similar position to most parents when it comes to learning about autism, in that a general practitioner is not an expert in autism. Autism is not a medical condition and so is not taught at medical school: the GP has to rely on 'research papers' and the 'occasional conference' and, therefore, on the opinions of others in general for knowledge. In fact, all researchers use existing research papers to learn from – what else is the point of research if not to disseminate its findings? Further, unlike a busy GP, parents have only their own child/children to be concerned for so must be in a better position to do the necessary research, and decide between options, than any GP. And much of this information is now available on the internet as original documents, making it readily accessible to them. Parents are also, arguably, in the best position to choose what would suit their own particular child and family. In addition, their only loyalty is to their child and not, as with most scientists and experts, to their organisation's funding body or particular credo. Further, as can be seen from the narratives in Chapter 4, many parents of autistic children are themselves scientific researchers, doctors and/or 'experts': a fact repeatedly ignored or overlooked by those who dismiss their experiences and views. Finally, in relation to the 'biomedical method' (described in Chapter 5), this treatment effectively repairs the chronic inflammation of gut and/or brain frequently present in autism/ASD: something one would expect any GP to be aware of and support. Based on the ARI parent-ratings shown in Table 4 of Chapter 2, it has done a great deal to free children from pain and discomfort. In short, Fitzpatrick and colleagues' assumption that parents will, through their naiveté or some other mechanism, be dragged into 'quack cures' and delusional thinking, and should therefore do what 'experts' tell them is entirely misplaced.

Evidence from the 'real world' does not support the view of parents as gullible fools. For example, Turnbull describes how Charlotte and Graham, parents of Sam, researched their own solution and took him to the US only when they were unable to obtain support in the UK for the treatment they had chosen:

> "Since last year when Sam was diagnosed as autistic, [his parents] have read everything they can on autism, consulted medical experts and researched avenue upon avenue to find constructive treatment. 'In this country it is sadly lacking' Charlotte said. 'Each of the authorities is totally restrained by financial cutbacks and the onus is on the parents to accept…or to fight.'"
>
> (Turnbull, 1996)

Theirs was a long and considered search for help, and this appears to be the case generally. As Karyn Seroussi states:

> "We are not stupid…we are educated, informed parents who had done thousands of hours of research into autism."
>
> (Serrousi, 2000)

Similarly, outside of autism/ASD, a US mother helped find the correct diagnosis for her 13-year old son, Bobby, who had been suffering from severe stomach pains since the age of nine. Having been diagnosed with dysautonomia (autonomic nervous system malfunction) his mother doubted this could account for all of his symptoms. After many hours of searching the internet she found a paper published by the *Cohen Children's Medical Center* in New York which described exactly her son's health problems. The author of the paper, Dr Harold Rekate, a neurosurgeon at the *Center*, identified the child's condition and operated on him with his own unique surgery developed for this problem. Bobby stated that he 'could not believe' the unbearable pain was gone after so many years of suffering (Campbell, 2015). A more tragic case occurred in 2013 when Bronte Doyne died after doctors in the UK told her to 'stop Googling' her symptoms following treatment for a rare liver cancer. Bronte (19) had correctly predicted the disease would return but 'was repeatedly dismissed by medics'. One doctor ascribed her dramatic weight loss of two stone in a month to being 'part of a skinny family'. In her final text, two weeks before she died, Bronte wrote that she was 'fed up of trusting' doctors after one had told her this form of cancer was rare in teenagers, when in fact is was common (Robinson, 2015). These stories indicate that doctors are only human and are not necessarily the only (or best) person to provide advice, and that there is an important role for the individual concerned in their own health care. Parents have the time and motivation to search for those approaches which have not been 'approved' by the establishment (and consequently for which there is no funding) and to decide for themselves the treatment they want, based on practical outcomes and not theoretical limitations. And, far from being a 'delusion', children can recover physically and psychologically from autism. Contributions such as Fitzpatrick's therefore achieve nothing but to deny the reality of parents' experiences and the positive potential for those with autism/ASD.

'QUACK' PROGRAMMES?

Due to the tendency of parents to seek their own answers outside of 'approved' treatment, a UK charity was set up in 2005 purporting to 'stamp out quack interventions for autism and similar disorders' (BBC, 2005). But do 'quack' programmes for autism actually exist? And/or are parents in danger of falling for them? Over the course of this study I found two therapies with documented concerns. One was holding therapy. Although this was designed as a no-blame treatment some of its US practitioners had adopted a Freudian basis, blaming the mother for her child's autism. (The parent who wrote about this subsequently swapped to an ABA programme). There was also one recorded case of child abuse by US parents professing to be using the method. Both of these examples represent a complete misuse of the treatment, now re-named PPCE in order to distance itself from this malpractice (see Chapter 5). The other example was in relation to chelation: the removal of heavy metals from the body. Here, a medically trained doctor accidentally gave the wrong medication (with a very similar name). An error of this sort can happen in any general medical setting and has done so quite frequently. For example, a report commissioned by the *Policy Research Unit in Economics Evaluation of Health and Care Interventions*, which examined prescription errors in the UK, NHS, concluded there had been up to 22,000 deaths due to errors when prescribing or dispensing medications. The researchers who undertook the study at the University of York considered this to be 'worrying' but "probably typical" for a developed country (EEPRU, 2018). Examples of such errors are easy to find. For example, a four month old baby died in the UK when she was given the wrong prescription. Her father committed suicide following harassment by the public who wrongly blamed him and his wife (DM, 2010). A 62-year-old grandmother also died after receiving the wrong prescription (Collins, 2014) and in the US a man died in hospital after being given a paralytic medication instead of the antacid he was prescribed because the packages were similar (Caron, 2011). In relation to interventions for autism, nothing remotely 'quack' has been found when applied as intended. And chelation itself received the highest rating given by parents on the ARI database, with 75% stating it made significant improvements to their child (see Chapter 2, Table 4).

HOPE AND 'FALSE HOPE'

From reading the narratives it becomes very clear that the most important thing anyone can do for a parent of a child with autism is to offer them hope of a positive life expectancy. Parents themselves state that this is what they want. For example, in William's narrative (Chapter 4, No. 4) his mother writes:

"We made great sacrifices and incurred great costs… but we never lost hope. We have returned to William the gift of health and speech… and those gifts are priceless. With each passing day, the hopelessness of regressive autism is being challenged and overcome."

(Edelson & Rimland, 2006, p233)

The value of hope is indisputable but, as the opening quotes in Chapter 2 illustrate, has been frequently denied by narrow expectations. This resistance to what may be possible has already been proven to be misplaced, as one establishment writer observes:

"At one time, it would have seemed inconceivable for a person on the autism spectrum to write this [poem]….The prototype of the person with autism for many years was that of a profoundly disabled individual, with very limited powers of communication."

(Roth, 2010, p270)

It is perhaps worth noting that this was not the 'prototype' of many parents of their children, but of established 'experts'. Roth's surprise should therefore serve as a warning not to hinder, but to help parents who have a wider vision for their child than they do. And, as Raun Kaufman states, the concept of 'false hope' is itself false:

"The only reason I can write to you today is because my parents believed in me when no one else on earth did….I am continually flabbergasted at some people's sincere and strenuous concern about parents of children on the autism spectrum being given 'false hope'. I continue to be befuddled as to what they think hope will do that is so harmful to our children. Who decided that a life sentence was better than an open heart and an outstretched hand? The bottom line is this: hope leads to action. Without action, none of our children can be helped."

And

"I hear people complaining about 'false hope', but I never hear anyone worrying about false pessimism….Why is it that telling a parent all the things that will not happen for his or her four-year-old or ten-year-old or fifteen-year-old over the next six decades is perfectly sensible, but giving every one of these kids a chance is deemed false hope?"

(Kaufman, 2014, p20)

This view is entirely supported by parents' own comments. For example, a parent feedback summary of TA states:

"When you get your child's diagnosis you can be told there is no future to look forward to for them. Everything appears bleak. *Treating Autism* completely turns that on its head. It has changed not only my son's life but our whole family life. The conferences give so much information for a parent to start helping their child back to full health. The support I have had from fellow parents who attend these conferences is priceless. I have life long friends and a support network that completely understands mine and my son's life. I know my son wouldn't be the healthy 12 year old that he is today without them and I would not have the support that I do without them."

(TA, 2017, *Website*)

It is clear from all of this that parents and their supporters have now left the established 'experts' in autism far behind them. It appears fortunate for their children that this is so.

HOPE FOR THE ESTABLISHMENT?

Recently, there has been a move towards honouring parent-led expertise. For example, research into programmes which aim to assist parents is gaining ground. One recent example is the parent-mediated social communication therapy (PACT) programme led by Professor John Green from the University of Manchester, UK (Pickles, et al., 2016). In this study 152 families were enrolled from the time their child was diagnosed at about three years of age. Half of the parents were given 'the usual therapies' for autism and half PACT. Over the six-year period of the study in the non-PACT group the percentage of children diagnosed as 'severely autistic' increased 13% (from 50% to 63%). However, in the PACT group this figure reduced 9% (from 55% to 46%). Despite some residue autistic symptoms in the improved group, Green states that these results are 'extraordinary' (In Gallager, 2016). How was this reduction to milder autism achieved? The PACT 'super-parenting' programme was based on enhancing mother/child interaction. Practitioners showed parents film of themselves playing with their child while the therapist gave precise tips for helping their child's communication. One mother states:

> "Several years ago it was largely a silent interaction, but now he will be so chatty, 'Mummy, Mummy, look they've gone on in a different order.' If you told me four years ago he'd come out with a sentence like that then I'd be crying."
>
> (Gallagher, 2016)

Chapter 5 illustrates older parent-led initiatives (such as DIR/Floortime, Son-Rise and ABA) in which parent/child interaction is the centre of the work. These programmes have previously shown positive results but have tended to be ignored. Fein, whose study was cited earlier, began studying the therapeutic background of 'optimum outcome' (OO) children when she noticed some had recovered beyond their diagnoses (Fein, 2013). Credit is due to her team that they are now pursuing this work. Changes are also slowly occurring across the UK, NAS. In a recent conference in Winchester, UK, Tony Attwood (a UK autism/ASD figurehead) stated that the triad of' impairments' is no longer an acceptable term. Rather it is to be replaced with the concept of 'neuro-diversity'. This was driven by the autism/ASD community themselves, rightly rejecting 'brain flaw' and/or 'genetic flaw' interpretations of autism/ASD in favour of embracing difference (see Chapter 8 for a discussion of neuro-diversity). Welcome though such changes are, it is time established 'experts' moved further in support of those parents seeking more positive outcomes, and of those practitioners offering them.

'REAL WORLD' EXPERTS

Partly because of the historic, collective derogation of interest in them from the establishment, it is now parents rather than professionals who are the 'experts' in autistic children and their recovery. Parents are not so much interested in statistics as in what will help their particular child, with the child's health and welfare as the 'measure' or indicator for treatment choice and continuation. Their questions are likely to be simple such as: 'is my child better on this?' and/or 'does the benefit outweigh any possible harm?' The latter is the same criterion used in all medical research, such as the UK, children's cancer drug trials (for example). In a similar way (but clearly safer) a parent may change their child's diet, adopt therapeutic holding or massage, or introduce supplements after having read positive reports from other parents in the same situation as themselves. This parent-led initiative is one huge 'real world', empirical experiment and the outcomes are often collected more systematically than for most medications dispensed in local surgeries and pharmacies. Consequently there is now a wide and rich bank of autism recovery data for us to study and learn from. That this is the case is due to parents ignoring professional limitations and low expectations; and to the bravery of the individuals who work towards recovery, in the face of not much help from the expected quarters. This then is the continuation of a parent-led determination to move the establishment of the day away from a hopeless and rigid viewpoint about autism/ASD towards a brighter future. And, in addition to parents' own accounts, it is invaluable to hear what ASD individuals themselves have written (such as Temple Grandin, Naoki Higashima and Donna Williams) and who are able to explain to others what is 'going on inside'. Certainly, Donna William's first book (Williams, 1992) and Temple Grandin's personal accounts have changed perceptions of autism for good. (Donna and Temple's narratives are included in Chapter 4 for this reason). The narratives in the following chapter illustrate the varied struggles and successes of a range of parental and personal experiences. They are followed in Chapter 5 by all of the programmes and methods mentioned in each of the narratives, to form a 'recovery resource'.

CHAPTER 4

PERSONAL NARRATIVES OF RECOVERY

For this study of recovery, I read over thirty personal narratives of parents and/or individuals with autism (Appendix I), although there are many more than this published including online and in articles. For illustrative purposes I have chosen eight to describe in detail for this book. They show a variety of definitions and attitudes to recovery, as well as differing degrees of progress. They also illustrate a wide range of programmes and interventions (which are described in detail in Chapter 5). For each narrative I present an initial summary, followed by a more detailed account, including of the five main aspects of recovery outlined in Chapter 2. I have also used the ATEC to assess each individual's final (or current) outcome. In doing so, I have relied entirely upon information provided in their own written account which, although not obtained in person, provides a rough measure of 'recovery' along the four subscales it entails. As each individual was diagnosed with autism by a professional – either when young or as an adult – the ATEC provides a measure of recovery, and is designed for that purpose. After scoring, each ATEC was submitted online to be scored by the Autism Research Institute. Where information was not available, or was unclear from the account, it was scored 'in favour' of an ASD/PDD so as not to over-estimate the ATEC score. Quite apart from what the ATEC might suggest, much can be learned about the nature and elements of recovery from these personal biographical accounts.

NARRATIVE 1   ALEXANDER

The source for this recovery story is the book: *Autism – The Eighth Colour of the Rainbow: Learn to Speak Autistic,* By Florica Stone, (2004) Alexander's mother.

SUMMARY

When her son Alexander was 3 years and 8 months old he was diagnosed as autistic by a doctor. He had made his first attempt to speak at 18 months, used certain words but then lost words he had appeared to know. At the time of the diagnosis he was repeating phrases in 'echoed' way. He counted by rote without apparent understanding of the significance of number. The diagnosis concludes:

> "Alexander shows wide discrepancies in his cognitive functioning. He is a bright little boy in the non-verbal areas and has good understanding of small toys and functional play. His language is well behind for his age. He shows very little social interest in others and does not use much gesture for communication. His social interaction shows many characteristics of autism."
>
> (p131)

The doctor told Florica that Alex 'could not be cured' because 'we don't know what (autism) is'. She writes:

> "I was advised there was little I could do for him and to focus on my normal children."
>
> (p17)

Florica decided the prognosis could be challenged even if the diagnosis could not. She believed then that the only way to reach her son was 'through a cure' but also wondered: 'Could an autistic child adapt to a non-autistic world without being cured?' The 'maze of advice' offered her varied from passive acceptance of his ASD to behaviour modification techniques. Florica rejected all of this advice, largely because it failed to explain the reason why her son 'needed to behave autistically'. In 1993 she read about the *Options* Son-Rise Programme (S-R) and travelled to the USA to attend a course. While adopting their basic techniques she ultimately rejected this too and turned to autistic people themselves for insight into how to relate to the 'autistic reality'. Gradually, Florica came to believe that autism was not something 'which could be removed from my child, but part of who he was'. This enabled her to accept him as he really was. She now recommends this as the best way to help an autistic child. Florica continued to read medical books in the search for a scientific solution to her son's autism, accepting her child's state as genetic. She also invited many autistic adults to stay with her. After spending 'thousands of hours' relating with them, she decided: '…the only way we can truly understand (autism) would be to experience it' (p23). To achieve this, Stone set up an S-R inspired playroom at her home, but with some differences. At the same time she continued to talk with the many autistic people who were guests in her home. Over a period of nine years she came to the conclusion that their reality is not the same as a non-autistic person's. She: 'grieved and gave up grieving' for the type of relationship she had wanted with Alex, and began instead to appreciate the love he and other autistic people gave her in its own form. Stone writes that her desire to see Alexander 'normal' caused her to make many mistakes in her developing friendship with him until she gave up thinking of cure as relevant. Accepting the 'literal thinking' of her son also opened the way for more meaningful communication and for helping him understand the non-autistic world. 15 years later she is a consultant and author on autism. Her book is a manual for parents/adults on how to understand and learn to interact with autistic people.

MILESTONES

Alexander was 3 years and 8 months when he commenced the S-R programme. Two months later he named all the parts of his body, greeted his friends with a big smile, screamed less and slept longer. He had initially had no meaningful verbal communication. At five years and nine months, two years after the playroom was adopted:

> "…we sat down to our first joyful dinner around the table.…If nowadays we talk about the old days, Alexander laughs in dismay'. Did I really do that Mum?'…and then, with curiosity, 'What did you do when I did that?'"
>
> (p44)

On his first day of school, Stone describes how:

> "…I hugged my smiling son as he ran to me. Our hug and our thoughts were interrupted by his shouted-out words. Pointing at a

girl he said, 'That boy pushed me!' My first thoughts were: 'Couldn't he see that the child was a little girl?'…My son spoke, but his words did not reflect reality. I wondered why."

(p219)

The age at which Alex realised the difference between literal thinking and other forms is not given, but one day:

> "Alex ran to say 'Mum, I am hungry'. The play helper, David, followed 'Alex, I am Thirsty, how do you do?' and shook his hand. Alexander paused for a minute and giggling said, 'Not that. I am Alex and I want to eat. I am not Hungry!" (p182)

At eight years old Alexander stopped lining up cars obsessively. He had habitually lined up his collection of over 100 cars until then. As a result of the work Stone and colleagues did with Alexander he also gained a sense of self (p16). Until this, Alex had believed his name changed from *Alex* to *Frightened* when he was frightened, for example. Between 1991 and 2000 Alexander transformed from non-verbal and exclusive into an interactive and verbal child, as well as a mainstream student. But two-three years later there was a relapse. His mother writes:

> "I really thought he was overcoming his autism (a myth) until once more our world fell apart. At the end of living in the 'rat race' for three years, towards the end of year six in junior school he became unable to keep up with the pressures and became depressed."

(p242)

Stone received an email from school to say Alexander's autistic behaviour had increased there. He had tried to strangle a child who was bullying him. Stone writes:

> "Alexander ran to me and in one long breath said 'Mum you must help me! I need your help! I strangled a child X…only for a second…I had enough! He kept picking on me. I told the dinner ladies but they told me to ignore him. I can't ignore him! Now I am being punished."

(p242)

Although this situation was dealt with, the family emigrated. Alex continued with his 'autistic behaviour' for six more months:

> "Eventually his anger levelled out and the communication channels opened once more. What he had to say, share, tell and wish for is a story in its own right."
>
> (p244)

Stone does not elaborate on this. But, with some bitterness, she concludes:

> "Contrary to what I had been told, my non-judgemental love could not cure autism and my child's autism would not miraculously disappear. Society wasn't prepared to make allowances for him and he couldn't catch up with the normality to meet the demands that come with living in a 'rat race' social set-up. My despair was triggered by his newly developed depressed behaviour. Seven years after Alexander's diagnosis, I panicked and felt worse than the day when I was first told he had autism. I resented my moment of weakness that led me to choose to believe in miracles. What a waste of time and emotion! The belief, and the lack of understanding of autism, clouded my judgment."
>
> (p222)

Florica concluded that she would have to change the way she related to Alexander, rather than expect him to change. This entailed accepting her child's autism and learning to communicate in a way which was meaningful to him: 'If the help makes sense the changes in his behaviour become long lasting' (p43). Her perception of autism and her autistic child altered. Rather than being something separate, which affected her son, and which could therefore be 'cured', she identified her son as from a different culture – one of autism – in the same way one would be Japanese or English, with beliefs and communication systems specific to each. By doing this, and learning to understand how he thought and what he believed, she was able to draw up a method, which Alex could understand, to help their two cultures communicate. This alteration in her perception is illustrated in Figure 13, below:

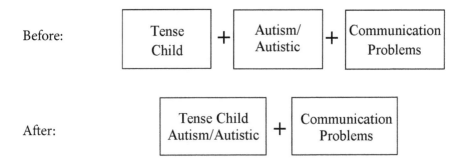

Figure 13 Florica Stone's Perception of Autism. From: Stone (2004) pp40-1

As can be seen, in this perception, the child and the autism become compounded, i.e, they are inseparable. In tune with this, Florica shifted from trying to help her child be 'cured' to trying to communicate with him and with other 'autistic people'. That is, 'trying to find a shared system of meaning so that he could – interact with society at large' (p133). She had read the writing of other parents (such as Jim Sinclair) who expressed the same suggestion; that it was necessary to stop grieving for the child they could not have, and change the way they perceived autism. But there was no guidance on exactly how to develop this into a practical strategy. Her own book is largely a manual for how she achieved this, and how other parents can do the same. Eight years after the diagnosis, Florica describes a quarrel between Alexander and his brother in which Alex expresses an entirely lucid and self-aware set of feelings and behaviours:

> "'I thought you were going to tell me off', said Alexander with tears
>   in his eyes.
> 'Why did you think that?'
> 'Because I called Sebastian names'
> 'You were angry, that is why you called him names…'
> 'I know that, but he is good at this game now. I was the one that
>   taught him how to play it. It isn't fair that he can beat me at
>   it now. I asked him to give me a chance but he wouldn't. So I got
>   angry.'"
>
>   (p194)

The boys found a compromise and later continued playing together. Alexander had more questions, reflecting some insecurity and concern:

'Mum, how can we make a kinder world?' – 'and wiped two tears from the corner of his eyes. He was concerned with global warming and even had an idea for an invention to prevent it (p194-5). Nine years after his diagnosis, Alexander:

> "…has reached the ability to do two or three things at once. By three things at once, I mean that he is able to effortlessly listen to a question, process the reply and ask his own follow-up question/s…. We all know if we have lost his attention. His behaviour lets us know. We also know that if Alexander says 'Never mind' it means 'I need time to think' or 'I am not sure I understand your question'."
>
> (p89)

Ten years after his diagnosis his mother writes:

> "Alexander can't remember not wanting to share time with us (he wasn't aware). He can't remember screaming or the reasons why he chose not to wear clothes…."
>
> (p54)

During this ten-year period Stone found meanings for all the apparently 'autistic' behaviours he displayed, which no longer occurred once the underlying cause (such as his confusion over the meaning of a word or request, or his fear over losing his 'self') was addressed. At the time of Stone's writing, aged eleven-twelve, Alexander's sleep is still not ideal. He goes to bed but then:

> "…talks to himself in whispers apparently in order to process all that has gone on that day. He denies that he is talking to himself, and wants to be left alone to do this."
>
> (p95)

Afterwards he goes to sleep. At eight years he would fall asleep only if his mother kept him company. Florica describes this as an 'unnatural fear of abandonment' but stayed with him because if she left him he screamed for 2 hours, or woke up and screamed. He suffered nightmares four nights out of seven for years. After aged eight this seems to have stopped. In conclusion she asks:

"What changed between the time Alexander was diagnosed with autism and today? Not a miracle cure, just love and empathy. First of all, Alexander's autism is just as present today as it was the day he was born and he is no less autistic today than ever before. Because he learned to express himself verbally, he can teach us about his autism as well as present us with a new perspective on things in general. I can talk to him and he can talk to anyone. It is easy."

(p196)

ATEC OUTCOMES

Based on a final assessment of the narrative given in Stone's book, I assessed Alex using the ATEC. The ATEC includes four sub-scales including one for physical health, not usually assessed in a diagnosis of autism, but experienced by many individuals with an ASD. A low ATEC score is indicative of few characteristics of autism. For Alex, the following scores were obtained:

I. Speech/Language/Communication:	0
II. Sociability:	1
III. Sensory/Cognitive Awareness:	1
IV. Health/Physical/Behaviour:	9
Total ATEC Summary Score:	11

Table 5 ATEC Scores for Alexander age c 12 years

Using this measure, Alexander had only 2 points on the *triad of impairments* which form the basis of a diagnosis of autism, including one point on the Sociability Scale (he sometimes needed time alone) and one for Sensory/ Cognitive Awareness (he was sometimes 'spacey'). Alex's main score (9) was on the scale for Health/Physical Behaviour. This assessment suggests that Alex no longer appears to be classifiable as 'autistic' (although his mother would not agree) but retains some physical/sensory problems (or 'differences' from Florica's point of view). Only by compounding his sensory/thinking style with his autism could he be classified as autistic. In an ecological theory of autism, these remnant sensory difficulties are the result of the initial trauma that resulted in his autism, and they could themselves be treated as such (for example using one of the interventions in Chapter 5). Whether having a 'different thinking style' in the manner of dyslexia or left-handedness, is itself necessary and/or sufficient to be considered 'autistic' – as his mother suggests – is questionable. Dyslexia itself may be the expression of an, underlying sensory disorientation, to which left handed individuals may be more susceptible (Poole, 2008). In both cases (autism and dyslexia) sensory integration can help. (See Chapter 5)

DIAGNOSIS OF AUTISM

The diagnosis of autism was made by a medical doctor when Alexander was aged 3 years and 8 months. The measure used is not named in Stone's book. Stone also provides her own model of her understanding of the autistic child:

> "This way of being stems from a genetic make-up that tampers with the sensory system. Because the sensory system feeds the brain 'false' information, the body responds in an unnatural way."
>
> (p85)

She writes:

> "Accepting autistic to mean belonging to a nationality other than ours helped me to understand our differences and our common grounds. From those, meaningful communication emerged."
>
> (p42)

Therefore Stone accepts a biomedical, genetic determinist diagnosis of autism as 'difference', not 'deficit' or disease. Her own diagnostic criteria are therefore those of the established 'experts' in the field. But whilst accepting these, and the triad of impairments, Stone also asserts:

> "Every child communicates his needs to you, even if he communicates them through what we perceive as unacceptable, repetitive or senseless behaviour."
>
> (p31)

Florica concludes that communication and emotion in autistic children is not lacking but 'slowed down' by 'poor comprehension' and an 'autistic sensory system'. That is, a different way of processing sensory information or of thinking (such as with a spatial rather than a verbal thinking style). Over a period of ten years, and from interacting with about 20 autistic people who were mainly resident guests in her home, Stone's conclusion is that the autistic child's behaviour is dictated by his mind which tells him to behave a certain way to protect himself – according to his sensory nature. This is actually not quite what Frith or Wing imply, and has more in common with the Tinbergens' *Motivational Conflict* theory, (see Chapter 1). We can understand this easily within the ecological theory presented in this book, as the need for security and self-protection in the absence of a 'mother' in this role following the initial trauma, and which Florica's work gradually provided.

WHAT IS MEANT BY RECOVERY?

In this account, recovery from autism is conflated with cure, which is stated as 'impossible'. For Stone, the autistic child/individual will always possess the unique thinking style which Stone believes is the autism itself. Overall Stone advocates an acceptance of what we have in common as people rather than 'managing behaviours':

> "There is no autistic behaviour left to manage when the use of understanding and unconditional love leads to meaningful interactions, shared understanding and friendship."
>
> (p12)

The process by which Stone 'learnt to speak autism' appeared to help re-integrate Alex's sensory system and prevent the 'overload' he experienced. It entailed understanding how the autistic individual perceives the world and then finding meaningful ways of communicating with them through that medium. Stone suggests that when an autistic child becomes distressed, his behaviour will become 'more autistic' (p122). She describes 'autism' as:

> "…a way of being with which we can empathise even if we don't understand all its implications. – I refused to think about my child's

autism in terms of an illness or a disease....I wanted to hear my child speak to me, and now he does....Science can or is trying to cure most illnesses. A way of thinking and learning cannot be cured, but it can be worked with."

(p295)

For Stone, 'autistic' is:

"...an individual way of being. It describes the combination of a visual, spatial and literal learning style of a person. In this sense I compare it to left-handedness or dyslexia."

(p295)

ATTITUDE TO CURE

In answer to the question: 'Can autism be cured?' Stone writes: 'No. I believe that the genetic differences between an autistic person and a non-autistic will always remain. Autistic people dislike the fact than normal people (NTs) want autism cured'. She states of her own book:

"This book is not meant to teach you how to 'cure' autism or how to 'behaviour modify' your child. It wants to show you how to connect with your child's soul, enjoy his love, make allowances and become his guide."

(p210)

And by accepting the child as he is:

"You will discover and enjoy his 'added' ability that only autism brought about."

(p221)

For Stone, as for many, autism is not an illness and therefore it cannot be 'cured'. Largely influenced by 'Feather', an un-recovered autistic friend, Florica eventually abandoned 'cure' as irrelevant:

"It took me two more years and the writing of a book to clearly separate autism from autistic and to stop hurting. Without realising this clear distinction I would never have been able to – shelter my son from doing harmful things to himself; teach him language so that he may talk to me about his problems; provide him with comfort through a hug; stop chasing this non-existent 'miraculous' cure. Alexander did want a hug, but not the easy physical thing we all do. He needed a room, volunteer friends; a change of attitude on my part; my friendship and acknowledgment of his perception of reality; my knowledge about how his mind works and where my understanding failed me. He needed my acceptance."

(p223)

On interaction (in the playroom) she writes:

"The reason why interaction is not a therapy per se is that your child is not looking for you to provide him with a cure; nor is he aware of why you feel so much pain. Unlike cancer, autism doesn't hurt him. Therefore your child is not actively looking to you for a cure. Instead he is looking to you…for love, acceptance, understanding, help and protection."

(pp221-2)

An autistic child can grow to develop communication skills, social skills and interdependent skills. For Stone, that doesn't mean his autism is cured or that he is faking normality, but rather:

"…that he is able to translate his visual thinking and learning style into words (cognition) and that he is able to contain various discomforts and confusions arising from his sensory perceptions of environmental stimuli."

(p253)

When an autistic child began to communicate with gestures such as blowing a kiss, Stone refused to interpret this as 'curing' autism, but 'just as shared understanding and human bonding' in which the child learns though copying like a 'normal child' and is driven by emotion to return the gesture. Ultimately 'cure' is perceived here as a rejection of the person with autism:

> "Autism describes the essence of a human being (not an alien living in a bubble). A way of being cannot be 'cured', which is why some of my friends find the word 'cure' so offensive. For the autistic, autism is not a weed to be pulled out; on the contrary, autism is something to be proud of."
>
> (p12)

Stone accepts the belief of one of her autistic friends:

> "She [Bexxy] taught me that talking eloquently doesn't mean autism has gone (because the sensory side remains unchanged and the working memory gets tired of talking or gets 'clogged' up by too many words). The inner fear of not being able to live up to someone else's expectations and the tiredness stemming from confusion can be surpassed only if the 'rat race' is taken away from the autistic person."
>
> (p241)

Stone makes it clear this does not mean the person with autism cannot be helped. Her book is packed with the practical help she could not find for Alex and herself:

> "Whilst your love and understanding cannot cure his way of learning, it can prevent your child from feeling lonely, will protect him from physical pain and can inspire him to communicate. It can also inspire you to create an autistic-friendly environment designed to meet his sensory and learning needs and a sanctuary for you."
>
> (p31)

THE PROGRAMMES USED

Stone states that it was the Son-Rise (S-R) programme run by the *Options* Institute in the USA which was the catalyst for her work with Alex. This 'seemed like the most loving approach towards autism I had yet encountered.'

However, although Stone fully accepts and recommends core elements of the S-R programme, such as loving, unconditional acceptance and 'joining' (see Chapter 5) she frequently does not credit them and appears to transfer much of her earlier (misplaced) 'guilt' at wanting a non-autistic child onto them. Some of her hostility appears to stem from an argument she had with staff about the strict time boundaries in the play room. She was initially advised by the S-R team that she could choose to be happy herself, even if her son remained autistic, through acceptance of him 'as he is': (a central strand of their approach). Florica appears to have agreed with this as, despite her rejection of S-R, acceptance is now the essence of her own approach.

THE PLAYROOM

For Stone, the playroom is a sanctuary for both the child and parent adult 'where you will notice how, of his own volition, your child replaces some repetitive behaviours with other activities and the violent behaviour vanishes.' (p57). Her decision to abandon the compulsory 'rules' of the S-R playroom stem from an occasion when a child became distressed:

> "The therapist left the room and the child pulled me towards the toy shelf. He pointed to a farm toy and smiled. As I reached to bring it down the therapist returned and said, 'X, your time is up. You had the time to play with it but you chose not to. Next time play with it when it is given to you.' The child continued to look into my eyes and tears fell as his grip on my hand grew stronger. I had his attention. His eyes connected with mine. His body language showed me his willingness to explore a new toy, yet I couldn't do anything to help him."
>
> (p79)

This does appear somewhat uncompromising (and more akin to the more rigid behavioural programme ABA than S-R's philosophy). Another significant alteration Stone made to the S-R playroom was retaining the presence of the child's mother throughout. She writes:

> "I realised that children are more relaxed (adults too) when their parents are present during play sessions. All the children looked at their parents for reassurance and wanted their parents to understand

them. They had fun playing with me and kissed their mother for a reward. Fantastic! If they didn't like what I did they hid behind their mother or father for comfort."

(p84, note)

Here, play is not therapy, but interaction:

> "The role of playful interaction is that of helping the child to assimilate a shared system of meaning so that he may communicate and interact with society at large."

(p133)

Stone gradually devised her own adaption of the S-R method utilising a playroom with a door she did not lock, (unlike in S-R) and a similar team of volunteers, while seeking to understand what made her own son behave the way he did. She stresses that the playroom: 'is not necessary in order to improve the quality of interaction between you and your child' and that:

> "It doesn't act as a cure catalyst."

(p71)

However, it formed the core of her later success, including with adult autists.

CONTAINMENT

The playroom has a containing role in both S-R and Stone's use of it although Stone rejected locking the door. In fact Stone did decide to lock the playroom door as a last resort, with one child, Brandon, with his mother and herself inside. Interestingly, after crying for three consecutive days – each time for a shorter period – Brandon voluntarily locked the door himself and cried no more. Stone describes how:

> "After using the playroom for less than two weeks we benefited from Brandon's first signs of willingness to compromise. He stopped blocking the television with his toy and sat down with us on our lap, or on a corner of the same sofa (at arm's length) when he needed space. Instead of pouring out the contents of his Battleship Command

toy, he brought it to me and we played. We played our own game and followed our own rules. But as opposed to him emptying the contents and his mother and I tidying up…we *played together*. He learned numbers and acquired more meaningful language. When he had had enough he went to play quietly on his own as opposed to screaming for attention."

(p77)

It is noteworthy that several times Alexander refrained, when in the playroom, from behaviours he otherwise engaged in when outside it. For example, he drew a line on the walls round the whole house except the playroom. He liked to study train books, tearing the corners of pages to mark them. (Alexander taught himself to read unbeknownst to his mother). But:

"In the playroom we gave him books he could rip apart if he so wished. He never did."

(p61)

Also, Stone describes how Alexander used to cover every wall in the house with pictures. After their work in the playroom, this habit ceased except for on one occasion following a two-week holiday. The playroom was also a means of introducing other people into Alex's life in a controlled setting. As with S-R, some mild behaviour-modification techniques were in fact used, such as offering a child a toy he wanted to play with, in exchange for being tickled. The playroom also enabled Alex to physically remove from situations which created 'sensory overload':

"This was not aloofness, but quiet, thinking time in which he absorbed what had occurred. Alexander then returned with plans for the next day's events and shared with his family what he found fun to do and what was not."

(p54)

The playroom therefore provided some control over the environment and Alex's fears:

"After he relaxes around you he will seek interaction."

(p52)

It was also a place to repetitively play the game of his choosing until he chose to stop, leading to the ability to trust (p52). Overall, Stone's use of the playroom gives more autonomy to the child than the S-R programme. It enables a child to come and play/learn when they are ready rather than when they might not feel like it, and to leave when they have had enough.

'JOINING'

As described with Ryan, in Chapter 2, this is another fundamental aspect of the S-R programme (described in more detail in Chapter 5). In joining (mirroring), the child takes the lead and the adult simply 'joins' with them in the activity the child has chosen. For example:

> "I watched and joined a child watching the traffic. If I spoke or tried naming the cars going by, he pulled his body away from me or covered his ears. I understood that my input wasn't welcome so I stopped talking. Half an hour later, he looked at me, smiled, waited for my smile and returned his attention to the traffic. I'd never seen him so peaceful before….In another corner of the same room a 22 year old autistic friend made the following remark: 'He looks so cool and peaceful. I wish my mum allowed me to take time out and do my own thing from time to time."
>
> (p141)

THE ROLE OF THE ADULT

'Joining' highlights a specific way of working with autistic children. As Stones writes:

> "Your role is best described as translator and mentor. As you read the various examples and work your way through the exercises (in the book) I hope that you will understand that it is *in your power* to help your child, understand his reality and to empathise with him, thus helping him to communicate with you. As his communication skills develop he will be in a position to explain what is in his power to change by telling you why he doesn't like being touched, why he

doesn't eat soft foods, why he is afraid of a noise, or any other 'why' question you might have. You can cherish him so he may feel he belongs, prevent him from feeling lonely, as well as help him develop a sense of self-worth and personal value. The rest is up to him."

(p265)

And of the role of the adult/helper:

"Their aim was not to help Alexander overcome what we suspected to be *avoidance of interaction*, but to help him *make sense of interaction*. The adult player/help should be patient and try reaching out to Alexander when a child of his own age hadn't the patience to make sense of Alexander's behaviour."

(p53)

Ultimately:

"The only person who can integrate Alexander is Alexander, not me, not someone else!"

(p246)

Here, integration means in a social sense, such as at school.

LEARNING STYLES

Stone is clearly influenced in her thinking by the concept of learning and thinking styles. This plays a core role in her belief that the child/individual will always be autistic and cannot be 'cured'. She cites Donna William's first autobiographical book *Nobody Nowhere* which was published at this time. Florica writes:

"Donna helped me become aware of the existence of a 'different reality.'"

(p111)

Williams wrote at that time of the experience of being autistic from the 'inside'. Stone's writing on sensory-overload and different thinking styles reflects a large element of Donna William's writing. For example, she explains the benefits of using a learning styles approach in school. This means adapting the methods used to the thinking (sensory) style of the individual child, which she suggests for Alexander is visual. (Donna William's narrative is No 8 in this chapter.)

NARRATIVE 2   JAMES

This narrative is taken from Edelson & Rimland (2006). James is the second of triplets born in 1998 to Clare, a medical doctor now living in the UK (see Chapter 1 for his example pathway). In 2002 she writes: "He is severely autistic but has two normal sisters." This account also gives follow-ups from 2003 and 2005.

SUMMARY

Clare's pregnancy was uncomplicated although she requested oral steroids during pregnancy:

> "…to assist foetal lung maturation in case of a premature delivery."
>
> (p77)

James's birth took place in the presence of a large medical retinue, all known to his mother. She underwent an elective caesarean at 36 weeks gestation. However:

> "25 minutes after delivery, while I was still being stitched, a midwife most apologetically said she had rung for one of the paediatricians to return to the room because James was having some respiratory difficulty. She asked if I would like to hold him until the paediatrician arrived. Of course I wanted to; until then no one had even thought to let me see my children. What I saw horrified me because James was definitely cyanotic [blue from shortage of oxygen]."
>
> (p77)

Although it was clear to her that too much time had already been lost, James's mother, 'did not want to make a fuss' and so did not say anything to the doctors. She says she is 'haunted' by this now:

> "I have come to believe/hope/pray that perhaps it was James's underlying autism…with an associated enzyme deficiency…that caused his respiratory disorders and not the hypoxia that caused his autism. Certainly James's blood gases were never as bad as those of some babies who go on to develop normally."
>
> (pp77-8)

She adds:

> "I know I am enormously lucky to have two normal daughters from the same pregnancy. I guess it makes it much easier for me not to blame myself for any imagined thing I may or may not have done in the pregnancy, which is a fear that I know haunts many mothers who give birth to a handicapped child. I am sure James is a 'victim' of a genetic flaw that lies within my family, which contains an astonishing number of atopic (allergic) individuals."
>
> (p78)

James's mother was struck immediately on leaving the hospital at how different he was from his sisters. But she attributed this to the fact that he had been traumatised at birth, and was a boy. She felt:

> "Even if I had voiced my concerns about James being somehow different at birth, I know my colleagues would have brushed them away as simply being the result of postnatal depression on my part."
>
> (p78)

James would avert his eyes when feeding, as if to look over his shoulder, and would occasionally projectile vomit mucus after his bottle. He had a perpetually blocked nose and a distended, swollen abdomen. When his mother consulted their paediatrician, he had not heard of milk allergy. James was growing well and he did not give these symptoms any consideration. Shortly afterwards, James started refusing milk except as yoghurt or cheese.

From birth onward, James would have about five dirty nappies in 24 hours, and this continued until digestive enzymes were introduced in 2000-1, when he was about 2-3 years old. James 'reached all his developmental milestones' (despite the poor eye contact) until he was 14 months and would interact with his sisters in baby walkers, chasing each other round and round. James could become terrified of some 'normal' situation, such as a next-door neighbour suddenly saying hello to him in the garden, and when he was six months old it was a neighbour who noted that James would not look her in the eye. However, she assumed she had scared him. It was common for those around to comment on how 'good' James was as a baby, being much more placid than his sisters. He loved cuddles but would not demand them. He was a dreadful sleeper, but his sisters were 'worse!' so that this did not cause concern. Although his mother berates herself for missing these signs, she knows they were also missed by the two mother's helpers they employed. One had 30 years experience working with children and the other had three normal daughters of her own.

VACCINATIONS

At the time, James's family lived in Italy where triple Hepatitis B is given with the other routine childhood vaccinations. His mother accepted this:

> "While I frowned a little at the idea of giving such tiny babies Hep. B, I decided to go along with the practice, believing at least it was one less lethal disease to potentially threaten them as they grew up. Only much later did I discover that it was the worst decision I could have made for James because blood sulphate levels fall even in normal, healthy adults after Hep. B immunization."
>
> (p80)

(This refers to Rosemary Waring's findings on low sulphate levels in autistic subjects). However, it was the Meningitis C vaccine which proved:

> "...the 'final straw' and which catapulted James from a gradual descent into autism into a frenzied free-fall."
>
> (p80)

While she confirms that her daughters will receive their boosters, she states that James will not. And:

> "If I had known what I know now about diagnosing autism, James would never have been vaccinated."
>
> (p80)

Once a 'beaming, happy little boy' James stopped smiling. His 'healthy, glowing face became pale, with panda shadows around his eyes'. James began tearing at the skin on his arms and upper chest, and would claw his face, resulting in ugly scratch marks.

> "He lost the few words he had learned, stopped humming his favourite tune and making clip-clop noises for a horse."
>
> (p81)

James stopped finger-pointing or making any eye contact. He stopped playing altogether. When his mother saw him lining up his vehicles in a semi-circle round him, she realized something was seriously wrong. His diet went from excellent to eating only about five different foods: bread, biscuits, apples, cake and dried fruit, plus 14 bottles per day of diluted blackcurrant juice. He refused to sit at the table, eating only on the floor. James started to experience 'appalling nappy rash'. However, he appeared to have a very high pain threshold as he never cried if he fell over and hurt himself. James's mother realised she had to 'bite the bullet' and gain a diagnosis for him. She writes:

> "It may seem ludicrous, but my training actually delayed me from seeking a diagnosis. Because I knew how little hope was offered to autistic children and their parents in England, I truly believed it was a diagnosis without hope, as at the time I had never heard about Dr Bernard Rimland, Dr Paul Shattock, or Dr Ivar Lovaas."
>
> (p81)

A 'kind paediatrician' diagnosed James as autistic, and then told his mother to 'enjoy my son': the only other suggestion being that she could put the family in contact with another autistic family for 'mutual support':

"Even the Professor of Child Psychiatry whose main research interest was autism could not advise me on any specific treatment other than attending a Hanen More Than Words course to help me to find ways to communicate better with my child. I did not find the experience beneficial for either of us. It only increased my sense of anger and frustration, and my belief that there must be a better way to help my son."

(p82)

At this point by chance, James's mother met an old friend, Elaine, whom she had not seen for some time and who asked after the triplets. She was the first person to whom his mother felt able to confide her fears about James. The friend had a nephew who had been diagnosed as autistic and suggested a gluten-free, casein-free diet (GF/CF). Elaine suggested Paul Shattock (Sunderland University Autism Unit) who with his college Paul Whiting, specialises in gut problems in autism, and researches dietary approaches. The suggestion to remove dairy foods from James's diet, which Shattock made, was relatively easy to implement by this time, as James was only taking milk as porridge. But he now couldn't even eat this and would wretch mucus on the sight of it at breakfast time. While the gluten-free diet had seemed daunting, James's mother states that she had no choice:

"He was scratching his chest and arms until they bled, and he had two or three bald patches at the back of his head. His eyes were lack-lustre, and his five dirty nappies a day were indescribable. The perinea candidiasis was getting even worse; and when I gave him paracetamol (acetaminophen) for a fever at New Year 2000/2001 he became very aggressive towards us all, biting and scratching and hitting his head repeatedly against the wall."

(p82)

DIETARY HELP

Paul Shattock explained that some autistic people cannot tolerate paracetamol, as they cannot break it down and excrete it, possibly due to problems with sulphate metabolism. James's self-injurious behaviours stopped once the paracetamol was discontinued:

"…a further dramatic improvement occurred the moment I excluded casein from James's diet. Overnight he looked healthier; he stopped retching; he looked happier and seemed calmer."

(p83)

After three days of this 'amazing transformation' his mother realised the porridge oats themselves had probably been aggravating James's health. She removed gluten from his diet as well as dairy products, with additional vitamin and mineral supplementation. At this time, they also commenced a programme of applied behavioural analysis (ABA: described in Chapter 5), but:

"I think if we had not embarked on the diet and vitamin and mineral supplementation, we would have made little progress with ABA."

(p83)

And:

"Very soon after implementing the diet, James started sleeping better and no longer squealed, babbled or giggled like a maniac Bertha Mason in Charlotte Bronte's novel *Jane Eyre*. Or at least if he did, it meant he had eaten something that he should not have."

(p85)

Within a couple of weeks, James's face had completely healed with no signs of scratch marks, and he stopped tearing at his skin. It took a further five months or so for his hair-pulling to stop. James's mother had only two disappointments with the diet:

"The first was that his range of 'acceptable' foods did not broaden within a few months as most commentators suggested it would. If anything, the reverse happened which, given how little he would accept to begin with, was hardly conceivable. However, after 15 months on the diet he is at last starting to broaden his range of foods just a little bit. On the positive side, James never seemed to suffer a withdrawal reaction when I removed gluten from his diet."

(p83)

CANDIDA TREATMENT

Secondly, the diet did not sort out James's bowel problems as hoped. This was, in his mother's opinion, due to the Candida infection. To treat it, all dried fruit was removed from his diet and a digestive enzyme, *(Bio Kult)* a probiotic *(Culturelle)* together with *Fructolite,* to nourish the beneficial bacteria present in these supplements. In addition he received *Biocidin*, a herbal product for bowel health:

> "The results were dramatic. James has never again suffered from candidiasis (at least clinically) and his bowels now open only once per day."
>
> (pp83-4)

The *Bio-Kult* was increased and then decreased (according to the manufacturer's guidance) and the *Culturelle* was given for one month before stopping. The herbal Biocidin too was discontinued. The improvements remained with a maintenance dose of Bio-Kult retained. A wide range of supplements were also continued, including: DMG, Super-Nu-Thera, CoQ10, Lecithin, Ambrose, Seacure, cod-liver oil, MSM and homoeopathic secretin. His mother writes:

> "Yes. I spent a fortune and still spend a lot of money on these supplements, but it is so worthwhile. Which of the supplements helped the most? Super Nu-Thera and DMG have both helped greatly. James had better eye contact and was calmer, more focused, more verbal and more sociable."
>
> (p84)

After an experiment at withdrawing the DMG, his mother writes:

> "I will not do that again! James started crying again with minimal provocation and for prolonged periods. I am sure it is not a placebo effect."
>
> (p84)

James was also taking a supplement of TMG, (trimethylglycine) which raises the stomach acid to aid digestion, and reduces the risk of infections. A stool analysis showed his acidity was now at the lower end of normal. Evening Primrose Oil improved his skin and the cod liver oil led to marked cognitive improvements and sociability, (omega 3 for brain function). However, James's mother felt N-acetyl cysteine, lipoic acid, and homoeopathic secretin worsened his symptoms. Removing blackcurrant juice was considered essential by Paul Shattock, but James was addicted to it. His grandmother suggested substituting real blackcurrant juice for the 'aspartame-rich (a carcinogenic substance which is in many flavoured drinks) sugary, tooth-rotting kind.'":

> "The results were astonishing. Within 24 hours, James was no longer addicted. Quite literally overnight, he went from craving bottle after bottle to actively rejecting it in favour of water, drunk in normal amounts from a normal glass, not a bottle."
>
> (p85)

James had been sweating heavily on his head and had 'panda eyes' occasionally. This was improved with homoeopathic *Silicea* which palliated the problem but if stopped the sweats returned. His mother writes:

> "…after all my glowing recommendations for following a GF/CG diet, multivitamins, probiotic and enzyme supplementation, perhaps one would think that James must be just about cured. Sadly not. James remains severely handicapped by autism, but the quality of his life and, therefore, our own lives has undoubtedly improved beyond measure. It has given me enough space to go on hoping, searching, and praying for a 'magic bullet'. And, to return to my previous comment, without these biological interventions James could not have embarked so successfully on his ABA programme."
>
> (pp85-6)

THE UK MEDICAL PROFESSION

James's mother has this to say about the UK medical establishment:

> "The attitude of the medical profession in England, even among those who claim to be experts in the field of autism, remains arrogant, ignorant and, above all, negative. It is a sad irony that most parents, when they are most vulnerable and desperate to help their autistic children after a diagnosis is obtained, will never hear about the biological interventions or ABA from the mainstream medical profession."

Adding:

> "…how useful I have found both osteopathy and homoeopathy for James. Most of my colleagues would want to have me struck off the medical register for voicing such heretical beliefs!"
>
> (p86)

She praises Bernard Rimland for his pioneering work, which saved her from being labelled a cold, dysfunctional mother, and for befriending her and offering hope where no-one else had done:

> "It must have taken enormous personal courage to overturn the perceived wisdom of the aetiology of autism."
>
> (p86)

UPDATE MARCH 2003

Early in March 2003, James had suffered an upper respiratory tract infection which set back his progress for six weeks. He became 'absent' somehow and refused to take his Super Nu-Thera. The fever appeared to 'throw a switch' in James's brain from which he took a considerable time to recover. He benefited at these times from cranial osteopathy and 'relishes' his sessions with them. He appeared to take no interest in his own 5th birthday party and had to be taken home early as he cried so much from the noise:

"Everyone does describe James as a most gentle and affectionate child and I am lucky that he is not at all destructive. Unlike a normal 5-year old boy, he carefully steps around the towering edifices that his sisters build with wooden blocks and he is mortified if one gets knocked down, which occurs very rarely as he has cat-like powers of negotiating spaces…not your usual autistic picture…"

(p87)

At that time James had virtually age-appropriate gross and fine-motor skills and was 'very affectionate with reasonable eye contact most of the time.' However he did not speak and was 'flatly refusing' any attempts at toilet training. A speech analysis showed James was following a 'normal' pattern of development, and that the range of sounds he could produce should, ultimately, combine to form speech. James did once actually request to sit on the toilet 14 months prior to this update. But:

"My biggest disappointment is that despite being on the GF/CF diet for two years, James remains as fussy an eater as ever….I fully believe that James's supplements are worthwhile and have been responsible for allowing me to again have an affectionate, happy little boy who is calm enough to benefit from ABA. And, while I cannot prove it, I genuinely believe that osteopathy and homeopathy do produce beneficial effects."

(pp87-8)

FURTHER UPDATE OCTOBER 2005

James was no taking any supplements, having stopped just after the last update. His mother writes:

"James is a lot happier; he is eating better; and he continues to make painfully slow progress. I have also abandoned the gluten and casein-free diet, and he is now eating very well and a fairly broad range of foods."

(p88)

James would no longer take the Super Nu-Thera, omega 3 and 6 or DMG supplements so these were discontinued. He still did not speak, and was not yet toilet-trained. He would put off going to sleep until very late (after midnight). But was very affectionate and calm, with no tantrums or self-injury, and was sociable and tolerant of social events, not being upset by disruptions to his routine or rooms full of strangers:

> "…including sitting silently in church and at a table of 10 people in a room full of 160 strangers."
>
> (p88)

ATEC OUTCOMES

Using the ATEC with the data given in the most recent update of James's narrative, I registered a score of 36 for James, broken down as shown in Table 6, below. The majority of the total score falls into the Speech/Language/ Communication sub-scale because of James's lack of speech. Without these James would score only 16 points overall with 11 on the Health/Physical Behaviour scale. These latter are largely due to toilet and sleep problems. The score of 5 on the Sensory/Cognitive sub-scale reflects his sensitivity to noise which may or may not still be present (it was not mentioned in the final summary) but which I have included so as not to under-score the outcome. It is also not known if toilet training has yet been successful, or if James has started to speak since this summary, and so these are also included in this assessment. James scored 0 on the social scale (the triad):

I. Speech/Language/Communication:	20
II. Sociability:	0
III. Sensory/Cognitive Awareness:	5
IV. Health/Physical/Behaviour:	11
Total ATEC Summary Score:	<u>36</u>

Table 6 ATEC Scores for James age c 5 years

DIAGNOSIS OF AUTISM

This was made quite late, because James's mother felt her concerns would have been disregarded by her medical colleagues. Eventually, a paediatrician informed her James was autistic shortly after his meningitis vaccination at 20 months of age.

WHAT IS MEANT BY RECOVERY?

Recovery is here synonymous with the idea of progress towards cure. However, recovery is not a word James's mother uses.

ATTITUDE TO CURE

'Cure' is used once in this narrative. It represents a total loss of autism and/ or autistic behaviours. James's mother does not comment on whether she thinks 'cure' is possible, but simply gives the progress – or lack of it – James made.

THE PROGRAMMES USED

Programmes mentioned in this narrative include:
    Adoption of the Gluten Free/Casein Free (GF/CF) diet
    Enzyme supplementation
    Probiotics
    ABA – James's mother does not mention this other than in passing
    Homoeopathic *Silicea* and other unspecified remedies
    Cranial Osteopathy

NARRATIVE 3   CAMPBELL

This narrative is taken from the account given by Dr Natasha Campbell-McBride in *Recovering Autistic Children* (Edelson & Rimland, 2006). She does not name her son so I refer to him as Campbell throughout.

SUMMARY

In February 2003 Campbell was 10 years old. When he was born his mother was a trained neurology MD with seven years experience. She writes:

> "When it comes to your own child, you are just as prone to denial and blindness as any other patient. Apart from that, as all the parents of autistic children discover, doctors know very little about autism."
>
> (p89)

She continues:

> "They are taught how to diagnose it, but when it comes to treatment, official medicine has nothing to offer. On the contrary, they are hell bent on convincing you that there is nothing you can do and that any other opinion is quackery. So, being a doctor has given me no advantage at all."
>
> (p89)

At three years old, Campbell was diagnosed as autistic. His parents began to find out all they could about autism. And, although there was not so much information available as there is now, someone gave them the contact details of Dr Rimland at the Autism Research Institute (ARI):

> "We had a long conversation with him and as a result our son was on an ABA programme by the time he was three and a half. At the same time he started taking DMG."
>
> (p90)

DMG (Dimethylglycine) is a non-toxic nutritional supplement. Of Dr Rimland, she writes:

> "This conversation was like a ray of sunshine in our lives. Here was a person who knew so much about autism and who was prepared to share his knowledge with us and help us. Here was a parent who did

not accept the official position on autism and who had devoted his life to changing that position."

(p90)

She describes the ABA programme as: 'performing absolute miracles with our boy'. Campbell had no speech and his understanding of language was 'questionable' but after three months he was speaking in short sentences. His parents meticulously documented his life on video, and after three months of ABA were able to have 'quite a sensible conversation with him' (then aged three years and nine months old).

NUTRITION

While the ABA programme was in progress, Campbell's mother devoted her time to learning all she could about nutrition, biology and biochemistry. Campbell was extremely fussy with food and, as a result, ate a very poor diet. Convinced that this had a lot to do with his autism, his mother felt his digestion, which 'almost never functioned normally,' was possibly key. However she became disappointed with orthodox medicine which:

> "Apart from symptomatic drugs with lots of side-effects…could offer my boy nothing to help with his digestive problems, constant fungal nappy rash or tremendous feeding difficulties. At the same time it was clear to me that his immune-system was in disarray due to his poor nutrition."

(p90)

Like many autistic children, Campbell experienced ear infections, chest infections, impetigo and fungal thrush and each time was offered more and more antibiotics. His mother changed his diet dramatically:

> "Our ABA consultant helped us work out a system of introducing foods into our son's diet. Without that system it would have been impossible to change his diet, as he was finicky with food. Having examined diets that have been successful for children with severe digestive problems, such as ulcerative colitis, Crohn's disease and chronic malnutrition, I realised that just introducing a gluten- and

casein-free (GF/CG) diet would not be enough for my own son. So I worked on a far more natural and focused approach, which also excluded gluten and casein. The result was amazing, as if somebody had lifted a toxic fog off his brain."

(p91)

As a result, Campbell:

"…was calmer, and much more able to learn. His eye contact improved on its' own and a lot of self-stimulation disappeared."

(p91)

His parents also introduced a therapeutic probiotic aimed at restoring the bowel flora in the gut, which had been lost through repeated antibiotic use. They tried a variety of different products until they found one which worked for Campbell:

"It was powerful enough to heal his digestive system to such an extent that we could cheat on the diet on an occasional basis without any problems. At the same time it gave his immune system such a boost that I don't remember how when he last had a cold. Now he looks a picture of health with rosy cheeks and bright eyes and he is full of energy."

(p91)

His mother went on to develop her own formula, *BioKult*.

NETWORK OF SUPPORT

Campbell's mother writes that it is impossible to overestimate the role of the family in the struggle against autism:

"I have seen quite a few sad situations, where one parent is trying to help a child without the support of the other parent. Treating an autistic child is a huge undertaking and united families usually succeed much better."

(p91)

She describes how important it is that parents of autistic children can talk together, as:

> "That is where we get our strength and inspiration to carry on. Our success became an inspiration for many other families, who were calling me and who were willing to try what we did."
>
> (p91)

It was through other parents ringing for help that Dr Campbell-McBride started her clinic for autistic children in Cambridge, UK, and subsequently wrote her book. She and her husband now work to help other families. She believes every autistic child has a chance, given help, and says:

> "Don't let anyone tell you that autism is incurable!"
>
> (p92)

In February 2003, when Campbell was 10 years old, he was in mainstream school and doing well. His academic achievements were within normal range, although he struggled with maths:

> "He can be clumsy, as far as social-skills are concerned, but he has friends and children generally like him. He can be naïve and hyperactive at times, but amazingly mature at other times. His language is excellent, with a wider-than-usual vocabulary, and he likes to write poetry and short stories. He is learning to play piano and is doing well, particularly composing his own music. No one would suspect what this child and his parents have been through. Nobody who meets him now would ever think of autism in connection with this boy."
>
> (p89)

In November 2005, when Campbell was 13, his mother writes:

> "He is tall and handsome and he is a delight."
>
> (p92)

His parents have not told Campbell what happened to him in his younger years, preferring to wait until he is older:

> "There are no traces of autism in him now, and he is leading a normal life. He is doing well at school and started playing rugby on his school team. His digestive system works like a clock now, though we still adhere to the diet."
>
> (pp92-3)

ATEC OUTCOMES

Campbell's scores using the ATEC are shown in Table 7, as follows:

I. Speech/Language/Communication:	0
II. Sociability:	0
III. Sensory/Cognitive Awareness:	0
IV. Health/Physical/Behaviour:	0
Total ATEC Summary Score:	<u>0</u>

Table 7 ATEC Scores for Campbell age c 13 years

According to the ATEC, Campbell would not be diagnosed with autism today. He retains no residue physical problems, and although his social skills were sometimes 'clumsy' this appears typical of a 13 year old, and insufficient to rate on the ATEC.

DIAGNOSIS OF AUTISM

A formal diagnosis of autism was made at three years old. The measure used is not given.

WHAT IS MEANT BY RECOVERY?

In this narrative, recovery means no longer being considered autistic or displaying autistic behaviours.

ATTITUDE TO CURE

Dr Campbell-McBride states that autism is not 'incurable' (p92). This suggests cure and recovery are synonymous for this writer.

PROGRAMMES USED

ABA and nutritional changes were the two main approaches used for Campbell. In addition to the GF/CF diet, probiotics and digestive repair work were important. The diet devised for Campbell is the Specific Carbohydrate Diet, outlined in Chapter 5 and, in more detail, in Dr Campbell-McBride's book: *Gut & Psychology Syndrome: Natural treatment for autism, ADHD, ADD, dyslexia, dysphasia, depression and schizophrenia.*

NARRATIVE 4   TEMPLE

This narrative of Temple Grandin is from her autobiography *Emergence Labelled Autistic* (Grandin & Scariano, 1987/96/2005). This is drawn from Temple's memories and she also quotes journals kept by her mother. The book was updated several times with some edits and a new introduction. However, I have used the original as the most authentic version.

SUMMARY

Temple describes herself as 'a bizarre kid'. She did not talk until she was three and a half years old and until then would only scream, 'peep' and/or hum. She was diagnosed autistic by a neurologist, using a Rimland checklist in 1950. At that time autism was a relatively new phenomenon and her mother was told there was nothing that could be done. Temple writes:

> "There are still those who believe once autistic, always autistic. This dictum has meant sad and sorry lives."

(p9)

Temple was the first child of four, none of her siblings were autistic, but her father displayed some mild similarities with Temple. Her mother was 19 when she was born: 'a normal, healthy baby, quiet and good'. At six months, however, she was 'no longer cuddly', would stiffen when her mother tried to hold her, and clawed at her, 'feeling trapped'. Over the next few years she began to demonstrate the 'usual autistic behaviours': a withdrawal from touch; spinning and fixating on spinning objects; a preference to be alone; destructive behaviours; temper tantrums; inability to speak; sensitivity to sudden noises; an appearance of deafness and intense interest in odours. She urinated on the carpet and used her faeces as clay. She chewed up puzzles and spat them out and broke objects, screaming all the time. At age three her mother took her to a neurologist who found nothing physically wrong. An EEG reading was normal. However, she was assessed as autistic using a checklist for Kanner's syndrome. A speech therapist was recommended. At first Temple's vocabulary was limited and, when she first met Bernard Rimland, her voice was flat in a way he describes in the forward to her autobiography as 'typically autistic'. She did not make eye-contact until well into adult life. 'I wanted to but couldn't.' The spinning behaviour, she writes, made her feel 'powerful, in control of things'.

LANGUAGE EXPRESSION UNDER 'STRESS'

A curious aspect of Temple's early language was that she found it easier to articulate in stressful situations. Examples are when she was in a car accident where glass fell on her and she yelled: 'Ice. Ice. Ice.' She writes:

> "Although I could understand everything people said, my responses were limited. I'd try, but most of the time no spoken words came. It was similar to stuttering; the words just wouldn't come out."
>
> (p22)

But during the car accident, she reports not being scared, but excited. In this instant her inability to respond verbally was overridden by increased adrenaline from the excitement.

ENCLOSURE

As a child, Temple and her sister were looked after by a nanny/governess. She writes:

> "Since the governess, who lived with us from the time I was three until I was ten years old, never hugged or touched my sister or me, I craved tender touching. I ached to be loved…hugged. At the same time I withdrew from my overweight, overly affectionate 'marshmallow' aunt. Her affection was like being swallowed by a whale."
>
> (p28)

At five years Temple began kindergarten – 'a small private school for normal children'. This was difficult but she made it to second grade, where she first began:

> "dreaming about a magical device that would provide intense, pleasant pressure stimulation to my body. In my imagination this wonderful machine would not be a substitute for Mother's hugs, but would be available at any time to soothe me."
>
> (p28)

She continues:

> "Tactile stimulation for me and many autistic children is a no-win situation. Our bodies cry out for human contact but when contact is made, we withdraw in pain and confusion…It wasn't until my mid twenties that I could shake hands or look directly at someone."
>
> (p29)

In third grade (about eight to nine years of age) 'while daydreaming' Temple visualised a different sort of 'coffin-box' with an open end she could crawl into, in which she could lie and control the amount of pressure she applied to herself from a plastic lining. She spent much time at school designing different forms of enclosures for this – some heated, providing warmth and pressure together. For Temple, this was not a substitute for her mother's affection, but to help her accept love from those who loved her, such as her father and aunts. When she was about nine Temple went to summer camp. She was unaware of the sexual nature of much of the teasing by the boys there, which she herself did not really notice, but which embarrassed the staff as she repeated things they had said to her without understanding what they meant. Her mother felt the staff at the school camp panicked over Temple's behaviour: 'largely because of an archaic view about sex'. Temple had had a painful urinary infection, but the staff had attributed this to masturbated and sedated Temple for a week. On her return she was taken to visit a psychiatrist, who, in keeping with the Freudian theory of autism held at that time, believed she had suffered a 'psychic insult'. Neither of her parents felt this really addressed Temple's problems. In a letter to him, while not debating the possible cause of her various behaviours, her mother writes:

> "…The same characteristics turn up to some degree in all children, but it is the same compulsive quality of her behaviour that is the problem. It has also been the point of greatest improvement. When Temple is in secure surroundings where she feels love above all, and appreciation, her compulsive behaviour dwindles. Her voice loses its curious stress and she is in control of herself. At home there is no problem. In the neighbourhood with a few close friends she manages better all the time. She and two other little girls have been great pals. She appreciates them and they her. They play together as Temple could never have played last Summer and last Summer these two little girls did not like her at all. Their whole relationship has been that of three normal, happy little girls. At school her behaviour improves. Difficulties occur when she is tired or when she returns to school after vacation and has to adjust again. Large, noisy groups confuse her….She wants someone near her in whom she has confidence. Her improvement is tied in, I'm sure, with appreciation and love. Until she is secure in her surroundings, knows the boundaries and feels accepted and actively appreciated, her behaviour is erratic."
>
> (pp43-4)

Her mother believed Temple needed to feel loved in order to make up for not being able to give or receive love in her earlier days. She describes how, when Temple felt happy, she would say, 'I love you Mummy' and behave well, like tidying her room, as if the two: love and happiness, were synonymous.

LACK OF ORDER

Temple describes how her often unusual behaviour, as with many autistic children, was an attempt to give order to her world:

> "Today my childhood memories are like a rich tapestry. I can still picture some parts of the fabric quite well. Other parts are faded. The incidents I recall tell a fascinating story of how autistic children perceive and respond in unusual ways to the strange world around them…the world they are desperately trying to give some order to."
>
> (p12)

She writes 'an autistic child is unable to bring order to his world' (p145). Temple describes how she 'wanted to control things' and drove her family mad with her obsessions with the election of the state governor, and election posters and stickers. 'Making things real' involved talking aloud. If a story wasn't read aloud, it wasn't real (p31). A character she made up was Brisban, who was able to control things: 'I wanted to control things and Brisban was my alter-ego'. At 11 years Temple had included the school bully in her stories, and was able to laugh at him in these when he got caught. She described uncontrollable laughter, constant talking and obsession with one topic as typical of her behaviour at that time, as with other autistic children. Temple was poor at 'sportsmanship' and organised games. She needed to know the boundaries of any situation and to be responded to with affection. Her teachers were all attached to Temple, and other children liked the fact that she had lots of ideas and was fun to be with. Her mother noted that Temple either lacked the instinctive desire to pattern her life around others in order to please them, as most people do, or else her 'nervous impulse is too great for her to overcome'. She told the psychiatrist not to feel sorry for them as parents, as there was 'nothing morbid or difficult' in caring for Temple which was 'frequently exciting and inspiring'. Her mother felt that Temple herself gained from her own insights about every experience she had, and would 'turn it over in her mind' considerably after any event, often with strangely mature insights. Temple attended the psychiatrist once a week. She describes how she did not tell him certain things as he would have spoken to her mother about them, including her desire to build a hug-machine. Whilst rejecting the then current Freudian theory of autism, she says Dr Stein was helpful in that he advised Temple's mother how to work with her. She valued her mother's practical help far more than 'expensive private psychiatric help'. Reading was Temple's best subject at school and, with the help of her mother, established a reading ability two years above her age. This and the hot tea which she gave Temple made her feel 'grown up' and 'increased my self-esteem'. Temple also describes art as the one subject 'that made school bearable'. She also helped make all the costumes for the school play, creating them herself. In sewing and embroidery and in making things generally, she excelled. Temple believes she and other gifted young people:

> "…often score high in 'fluid intelligence' and nonverbal thinking as opposed to crystallised intelligence, which requires previous training and education. Crystallised intelligence makes use of verbal mediation, sound inference and sequential steps of logic in problem solving. Crystallised intelligence is rewarded in our educational system in which regurgitation of knowledge is accorded value."
>
> (p34)

As a result Temple suggests many gifted people who possess 'fluid thinking' don't fit into the education system.

THEORY OF MIND

Lack of a *Theory of Mind* (TOM) is considered one of the major 'deficits' in autism/ASD. TOM is the awareness that another person's assessment of a situation may differ from our own, and the ability to take this into account. Temple clearly exhibits this capacity. She several times lied to get herself and her best friend out of trouble as children, blaming other children or the dogs for things they had done, and being believed due to her sincerity. Temple was teased at school for her jerky movements and odd speech. Her reaction was to throw temper tantrums. She describes her father as also 'noted for his bad tempers'. He too experienced nervousness and a tendency to become totally engrossed in one subject, such as 'mutual funds' or details of a planned trip. Despite her temper, Temple always appeared to have at least one close (female) friend. At the end of Grade 5 her mother wrote again to the psychiatrist that Temple was improving all the time, being more independent and outgoing.

She was well behaved at home, neat and helpful. Her school work was 'adequate'. But her mother was worried about how Temple would cope in the wider world and felt they had little time to prepare her for this beyond school. She feared she had been 'too much of a rudder' for Temple who at aged 10, now had only two more years before secondary school. She felt home discipline and boundaries helped Temple, even though she complained, and was concerned about boundary-setting in a new school. Temple's habit of copying the 'panty talk' of boys also troubled her as she did not seem to understand what it meant and yet continued it, encouraged by the boys. Her mother felt there was 'so much maturity combined with babyishness – all mixed together'. At 12, Temple attended a large, private, day-school for 'upper class' girls with 30-40 girls per class. She describes this as:

"…a confusing, traumatic experience."

(p56)

After her behaviour deteriorated there, the psychiatrist wrote to the school:

"Temple is one of those unusual children who had a very disturbed early childhood and was at the time, unfortunately, wrongly labelled as having brain damage. In 1956 she obtained a full scale I.Q. of 120; in 1959, a full scale I.Q. of 137. She does not function quite up to this very superior level."

(p57)

He describes her as unable to 'free her affect' at this time in order to live up to this high intelligence. He concludes:

"Temple is not now psychotic, or close to it. One could call her a neurotic child…She has come an amazing distance since last seen."

(p57)

The psychiatrist felt Temple had huge potential and was in the process of developing 'the healthier aspects of her personality'. Temple was voted to a school committee and this acted as a spur to 'clean up my act' behaviour-wise. She also invented a 'flux valve' years before one was patented, through her interest in flying objects, building planes and science fiction. She nevertheless 'lacked the ability to get along with people' and her grades were 'deplorable'. She was ultimately expelled from the school two and a half years after starting there, because of her temper, in response to being called a 'retard' by another girl. In this incident the head teacher rang and told Temple not to come back to school without even asking her what had happened. Her mother 'as usual stood up for me'. Temple's mother had by this time become a successful writer for television and recently researched a school for an award winning documentary. This was a small boarding school with only 32 students. Temple writes:

"I was known as Temple…not some girl who was different from the many other students….a smaller school with individual attention made it much easier for me to deal with my problems. But in the attic of my mind I dreamed of a magical machine that would sooth me and make me less different."

(p61)

When she left her mother at the start of each term, Temple wrote:

"I ached to be enfolded in her arms, but how could she know? I stood rigid as a pole trapped by the approach avoidance syndrome of autism. I drew back from her kiss, not able to endure tactile stimulation…not even loving, tactile stimulation."

(p65)

With this school, Temple's behaviour improved but her fixations worsened. These had for several years been much diminished. Here, Temple's nerves began to disturb her with anxiety attacks due to her difficulty adapting to change…She wore the same jacket and dress for days, so as to preserve sameness, and refused to move to a bigger, better room. With the onset of menstruation her panic attacks increased. These did not respond to *Librium* or *Valium,* both of which were prescribed:

"These nerve attacks, complete with pounding heart, dry mouth, sweaty palms, and twitching legs, had the symptoms of stage fright, but were actually more like hypersensitivity than anxiety….The panic would worsen as the day progressed and the afternoon hours from two to four in the afternoon were the worst. By nine or ten o'clock at night the anxiety subsided."

(p68)

These were cyclical and connected both to menstruation and to the length of the day, being worse in autumn when the days were shorter. The anxiety attacks were trigged by the phone ringing, collecting the mail ('what if I didn't get any?') and school social trips. From age 7-16 Temple also had pinworms which became intolerable to her after menstruation 'like being mugged'. She writes:

"Perhaps if I had received more tactile and deep pressure stimulation as a child, my hypersensitivity would have been reduced at puberty."

(p69)

She felt she was:

"...caught in a maze of physiological symptoms that distressed, destroyed and defeated any gains I had made earlier."

(p70)

At 16 years the attacks were accelerating. Temple found temporary relief from them by chance on a 'Rotor Ride' during a summer visit to an amusement park. This threw the occupants to the outside of a barrel via centrifugal force.

"After the ride I was at ease with myself for the first time in a long, long time."

(p80)

She describes how:

"Again and again I rode the barrel, savouring first the over stimulation of my senses and then the quiet surrender of my panicky, anxious nervous system. Recent studies with hyperactivity children indicate that stimulating the vestibular system by spinning the child in an office chair, twice weekly, reduced hyperactivity."

(p72)

Back at school Temple had more anxiety attacks and attempted to have them install a Rotor machine. Writing to herself as her alter ego *Alfred Costello*:

> "Respect his letter. It is your only hope for getting help. Our school needs your Shadow representative, Temple Grandin."
>
> (p73)

These letters said the school would fall into a 'force field' if the Rotor was not built – and the advice was coming 'across the time barrier' from Alfred to Temple at school. Temple writes in her autobiography:

> "Now, even in my frenzied state, I knew the Shadow Alfred Costello was a figment of my imagination, a throwback to my childhood story-telling days, but I felt driven by panic and anxiety to act. In re-reading these letters as an adult, I find it hard to believe that I wrote them. It was necessary to tell the story aloud in order for it to be real."
>
> (p75)

Temple's campaign to get the Rotor Ride at school failed. Shortly afterwards she had an experience in which she became convinced that she could find 'a door' which would lead 'to heaven' and out of her situation. She viewed each door as potentially *the* door and eventually, climbing to an extension that was being built in the school, she found a 'Crow's Nest' with a little door leading up to it:

> "It was a little wooden door that opened out onto the roof. I stepped in to a small observation room. There were three picture windows that overlooked the mountains. I stood at one of the windows and watched the moon rise up behind the mountain range to meet the stars. A feeling of relief flooded me. For the first time in months I felt safe in the present and hope in the future."
>
> (p76)

In the following days and months, Temple visited the Crow's Nest often:

"Once I entered the small room, I became calm and felt enriched with ideas and self-discoveries."

(p77)

Temple came to understand what her mother had told her: 'Every person needs to find her door and open it. No one can do it for her.' She wrote:

"...the little wooden door leading to the roof and the world beyond symbolised my future. I just had to walk through it."

(p79)

Temple found that she could go onto the roof from the Crow's Nest and 'drawn by the beauty of the night sky' she did, pulling the door shut behind her. 'I had walked into a new life and I would never spiritually go back through that old door'. The school psychiatrist tried to prevent Temple from her visits to the Crow's Nest, but she refused to comply. Temple was now at peace, but not until she discovered psychology – and the psychology of animals – did she begin to enjoy studying and learning. Following one psychological experiment, she built a replica 'distorted room', channelling her 'fixation' into something of interest. She made costumes for the school play, rode horses and participated in shows. She continued to be teased and. finding that communication continued to be a problem: 'I often sounded abrasive and abrupt. In my head I knew what I wanted to say but the words never matched my thoughts'. While visiting the Crow's Nest she wrote her feelings in her diary.

HELPFUL PEOPLE

Temple describes several helpful people without whom she believes she would have ended up in a 'school for the retarded'. Her mother was one of these; the psychology teacher is also mentioned, while another teacher, Mr Carlock, was 'my salvation':

"Mr Carlock didn't see any labels just the underlying talent....He didn't try to draw me into his world but came instead into my world."

(p92)

Mr Carlock channelled Temple's fixations into constructive projects and was almost the only teacher who believed she could make it to Technical School. She learned from him 'humanistic attitudes' by modelling his social behaviour. He also gave her philosophy books to read as he recognised the symbolic nature of much of her thought. After a while her flat voice improved:

> "I puzzled about this for several days. After a while I decided that as I became more socially perceptive, the tone of my voice must have improved. I guess I was no longer needing it as a defence against the world."
>
> (p83)

Mr Carlock gave Temple increased self-esteem and self-worth in all areas of her life. Her aunt Amy also helped when she stayed at her ranch. To help Temple, her aunt suggested all sorts of manual building and mending jobs, including repairing the cattle squeeze chute – a device for holding cattle for branding, vaccination or castration. Channelling her fixation and nervous energy into this physical labour eased Temple's nervous attacks and she became fascinated by the workings of the squeeze chute (which somewhat approximated the 'hug machine'). The school psychologist was uneasy about the model chute she built on returning to school, not knowing if it was a 'womb or a casket'. Temple told him it was neither. But the school found the chute 'weird' and persuaded her mother she should not be allowed to indulge her obsessive interest with it. This aggravated Temple's nervous problem, and also made her even more determined to show that there was something genuinely important about the chute. If not, she asked:

> "Why did the pressure of the cattle shute calm frightened calves and soothe nerve-driven me?"
>
> (p99)

Temple decided she had to trust in herself, before others could trust in her and her thoughts. She came to see that the squeeze chute was her own creation, and made of her own thoughts, and that therefore 'the same feelings and thoughts (she) had in the chute could be had outside of it'. When in the chute she felt closer to people:

"It broke through my barrier of tactile defensiveness, and I felt the love and concern of these people and was able to express my feelings about myself and others."

(p92)

BEYOND SCHOOL

Following her graduation, Temple attended a small college near to her school. She stayed in touch with Mr Carlock who, when told of the 'flack' she had received over her cattle chute, encouraged her to build a better one and use it to test her theory scientifically. This entailed learning maths, reading scientific articles and researching the subject:

"He aroused my interest in science and directed my fixation into a worthy project. I spent hours in the library looking up everything I could find on the effect sensory input had on sensory perception…"

(p99)

This interest in sensory interaction became the basis of Temple's later undergraduate thesis, the result or her findings being that the pressure stimulus affected auditory thresholds (the seat of the vestibular system). Temple also learnt to 'get along' with people as part of her need to communicate her ideas and defend her machine from people, in particular, the Freudian psychotherapists who imbued her interest in the chute with sexual implications, and which 'made me feel guilty'. Temple describes how she learnt that gentleness is not weakness and attributes all the improvements in her social skills to her 'much maligned' squeeze machine. The pressure of the machine was more powerful by being gentle. Temple became able to endure 'brief physical contact' like a pat on the shoulder, through learning to accept the gently but enforced pressure from the squeeze machine, which was nevertheless under her own control. Test results using the machine on other people showed it had a calming effect by lowering metabolic rates. Out of 40 normal people, 62% relaxed and liked the squeeze machine. Interestingly, some liked it for 10-15 minutes but then found it annoying. It was less effective on hot summer days or if the room was cold. It was being used (at the time of writing in 1986) at a clinic for hyperactive and autistic children in Arizona. During the summer following her first year at college, Temple worked at a home for disturbed children. For this work she realised that fixations serve a purpose for the child and the 'way in' to them is through the fixation. After two years of college, Temple worked on a review at school which helped her to relate better to her peers as it enabled them to accept her creative ability – designing and building sets. She used the symbolism of the door once again to commit herself to increased self-improvement, taking responsibility for her lack of social understanding and attempts to improve. As part of her final exams Temple had to write an essay for the Marriage and Family class. In it she writes:

> "In a marriage the girl is subservient. I have not seen one marriage yet that could be a model one for me. The only way I could marry would be if my husband and I worked as scientists."
>
> (p110)

And including the squeeze machine in the essay:

> "One point I want to make clear is that the purpose of the squeeze machine is not to make a person submit to some doctrine put out by society but rather to enable the person to completely search his soul and come to terms with his intellect…"
>
> (p110)

At graduate school, Temple experienced the same anxiety and nervous attacks that she had when first in the new environment of school, and realised she might have to find an alternative route. One of these difficulties was an obsession with a sliding door. The sliding door represented another transition for Temple. With support, she was eventually able to walk through the sliding door without cringing:

> "I simply walked through like a normal person. I decided that getting along with people was like a sliding door. The door has to be approached slowly; it cannot be forced; otherwise it will break."
>
> (p120)

The evening afterwards, at a party, a friend remarked that Temple seemed different: 'you actually visited with your classmates and seemed interested in them'. Thinking through her previous problems, Temple realised she really was 'different' and had always been 'a special individual'. She accepted this and her differences. Of obsessions, she states:

> "A certain amount of fixation is required to reach any goal."
>
> (p129)

With her mother's support Temple continued to work with cowboys, using the cattle chutes and developing her thesis. At the end of her second year she switched from psychology to animal science, visiting a slaughter house and continuing to refine her squeeze machine based on what she had seen. She still experienced difficulties when in a new environment, or when she returned home (due to the lack of sameness and the short winter days) or if she did not have her own squeeze machine with her. But, at her mother's suggestion, she started to write down her thoughts. This she did 'like a newspaper assignment'. Temple describes wanting to be closer physically to her mother:

> "I wanted to touch her…tell her she was special."
>
> (p125)

Temple also discovered that touching to-be-slaughtered cattle at the abattoir where she was working seemed to calm them and showed respect for their feelings. Temple completed her Master's thesis on the design of cattle chutes in feedlots – one of the first animal behaviour research projects in the United States. This was despite the fellow veterinary college advisors thinking cattle behaviour during handling was not a 'proper academic subject'. In her late 30s – at the time of writing her autobiography – Temple Grandin was:

> "…a successful livestock handling equipment designer, one of very few in the world, I am called upon by firms throughout the world to advise and consult and to design special equipment for them. I contribute regularly to the professional journals in my field and speak at professional conferences across the country. Presently I am

completing my PhD in Animal Science. My life is normal and totally independent with no financial worries."

(p9)

In addition, Bernard Rimland, who wrote the foreword to her book, writes:

"I was impressed with how much less-autistic sounding she is today than she was when I first met her. She has continued to grow and develop. She has accomplished a great deal not only in her profession but also in her vocation which is represented by this book. She has also accomplished a great deal as a human being. The indomitable spirit which shines through the pages of the book makes one proud to be human."

(p4)

ATEC OUTCOMES

Table 8, below, shows ATEC scores on the outcome data from Temple's 2005 updated biography:

I. Speech/Language/Communication:	1
II. Sociability:	2
III. Sensory/Cognitive Awareness:	0
IV. Health/Physical/Behaviour:	11
Total ATEC Summary Score:	<u>14</u>

Table 8 ATEC Scores for Temple age c 39

Using the ATEC on this data, Temple no longer appears to be classifiably autistic. Indeed, Temple has referred to herself as 'a recovered autistic person" (1987, p1). Her score of 11 on the Health/Physical Behaviour sub-scale relates mainly to her nervous problems, for which she found an anti-anxiety medication helpful. William Carlock writes that when he met Temple again after 20 years:

"Some of her autistic qualities were still there, but were redirected

– or even put to good use: her intense involvement in her doctorial research in animal psychology, her still strong handshake; her functional Western clothes; her adamant resistance (relayed to me) to her mother's suggestion that her hair be 'redone'. Clearly Temple hadn't emerged from autism by becoming a different person, but had taken and reworked what she already had."

(p6)

Because of the 'intense involvement in limited subjects' the ATEC is marked accordingly: but it is an interesting assumption that this is 'autistic' behaviour. Following a lecture Temple gave, a therapist friend remarked:

"What a contrast with your speech in Chicago! (12 years previously). You seemed quite at ease and sprinkled your talk with humour, which the audience really appreciated. And handled questions easily, rubbed shoulders with the crowd during breaks, shook hands without hesitation and generally seemed calm and self-assured. Your old tendency to perseverate seems to be gone. You used to have a lot of trouble dropping one subject and going on to another…and I know that even though you were aware of it, you couldn't help it. Now that seems a thing of the past."

(p139)

REMAINING DIFFICULTIES

In 1986, Temple's gait remained 'masculine' according to some contemporary accounts, and she found it hard to 'hug' some people. She herself reported that loud noises, such as a car backfiring, would make her jump and panic. Loud, high-pitched sounds such as a motorcycle were still painful. She also found it hard to synchronise: (rhythm was always difficult). For example, if clapping, she took her lead from the person sitting next to her. Of her recovery, Temple writes:

"As an adult, I have overcome some autistic tendencies…I no longer hit people or 'peep', but I still have deficit areas. When I went to Vienna to present a paper on livestock handling I was frustrated by my inability to communicate in German. I found myself reverting to the simplified one-word speech I had used as a child. When I became lost in the foreign city, it was all I could do not to scream. I was under a great deal of stress and got shingles during the meeting….It would seem that maturation might cloak autistic characteristics, but they are still there."

(p130)

These physical signs of stress, such as shingles and eczema (evidence of immune system dysregulation), are attributed to her autism and her reactions as autistic. Use of medication to control nerves and anxiety was on-going at the time of writing her original autobiography (1986). Again, interpreting these symptoms as 'autism' depends upon whether the triad of behaviours is used as the diagnostic criteria. If it is, then Temple is no longer 'autistic' but may have some sensory difficulties which make her (or are themselves) vulnerable to stressful events. In this respect she resembles Alex and Donna (see later narrative). In the later edition of her autobiography, written in 2005, Temple suggests she was originally too hard on her nanny who spent long periods of time playing 'to and fro' games with her as a child. This is an interesting observation which appears to reflect her improved development. Temple describes several steps she made in her 'emergence'. One of the most interesting is with her voice. This altered of its own accord after she began modelling her teacher in being more social. Temple suggests the 'defence barriers' were coming down socially and this was then reflected in her voice development. Years later she realised she still had some flat tone to her voice, which appears from her account to have also eventually gone. Temple quotes Kanner's own observation and research on recovery, in which some individuals 'become uneasily aware of their peculiarities and begin to make a conscious effort to do something about them' (p84). She notes this as a self-motivated change which she herself made following the belief and trust shown her by helpful adults. Temple now travels all over the United States, Europe and Canada designing livestock handling facilities for ranches, feedlots and meatpacking plants. Her thesis written at the time of her book, 20 years ago, was on the effect of environmental enrichment on the nervous systems of animals and her interest in brain plasticity. Temple has researched the neurology of autism in order, not only to understand herself, but to help to put her experiences into a scientific perspective 'that might be helpful to others'. She has also become a speaker at workshops designed to help therapists, parents and teachers of autistic children.

DIAGNOSIS OF AUTISM

This was undertaken in 1950 by medical personnel using an older Rimland checklist for Behaviour-Disturbed Children: Form E-2, (the results of this assessment are given in detail in the Appendix of Temple's biography). The E-2 was designed to differentiate cases of early infant autism (also known as classical autism or Kanner's syndrome) and childhood schizophrenia. By this more classical definition of autism, Temple was 'labelled autistic':

> "I scored +9 (only about 10% of children described as autistic fit in the narrow definition of Kanner's syndrome because there are metabolic differences between Kanner's syndrome and other types of autism). Although my behaviour patterns were definitely autistic, the beginnings of basic, infantile but nonetheless meaningful sounds by age three and one half lowered my Rimland checklist score."
>
> (p16)

Temple's view is that autism is 'a developmental disorder':

> "A defect in the systems which process incoming sensory information causes the child to over-react to some stimuli and under-react to others. The autistic child often withdraws from her environment and the people in it to block out an onslaught of incoming stimulation."
>
> (p9)

Temple 'overreacted' to sounds, smells, movement and spinning. On causation she writes:

> "What causes autism? Therein lies a mystery. Is it neurological? Is it physiological, intrauterine trauma, rejection by the mother, or lack of trace minerals? Is it brain damage? Is it psychogenic? The opinions of many eminent professionals vary. Research indicates that certain parts of the central nervous system may not develop properly. For some unknown reason the many millions of neurons which are growing in the developing brain make the wrong connections."
>
> (p10)

This is a medical model of autism centred on a 'defective brain'. Temple ascribes this to damage 'in the womb' (p15), but is unusual in giving brain *connections* rather than 'genes' as a possible 'cause': clearly a developmental perspective. In a later book (Grandin, 2014) Temple describes her developmental differences in more detail (see also Temple's Pathway in Chapter 1 of this book and also Poole, 2017, Chapter 11).

WHAT IS MEANT BY RECOVERY?

In this account 'recovery' represents the extent to which the individual approximates 'normality' or can live a 'normal' life. The word she uses is 'emerge'. Temple 'emerged' from her autism as if it had been a cloud or confusion obscuring her. Indeed, her autobiographical book carries this title. Temple believes that where there is meaningful language before the age of five years, much can in fact be done to help the child 'emerge'.

ATTITUDE TO CURE

The word 'cure' is never used in Temple Grandin's account. However, although she believes she has emerged from autism, based on her return of stress-induced physical and emotional states when under pressure, Temple suggests the 'autism' never goes away completely. Nevertheless:

> "My story is different and I offer hope to parents and professionals who deal with autistics because I was labelled autistic. Some clinicians may look at Mother's notes in my story and say that there is too much 'normal' behaviour…that I was misdiagnosed…. Lorna Wing at the Institute of Psychiatry in London states that an autistic child may be socially responsive in one situation but not in another.…In 1950 I was labelled autistic and groped my way from the far side of darkness."

> (p11)

PROGRAMMES USED

For her mother the best therapy for Temple was 'love' (p44). At about aged 9 she was taken to a Freudian psychiatrist once per week. Temple believes:

> "…instead of psychiatry I should have received more psychotherapy. Practicing with a tape recording and playing it back would have done more for my social life than trying to ferret out the dark secrets of my psyche. I wish one of the psychologists would have told me about my speech problem instead of worrying about my Id. I was aware sometimes people didn't want to speak to me, but I didn't know why."
>
> (p83)

Carlock describes how the 'way out' of Temple's autism came through one of her own obsessive interests – the cattle shute. He encouraged her in this interest and then drew her into more constructive channels. Contrary to the more established attempts to divert or break autistic children from these interests, he used her interest to establish a relationship which enabled further ideas to be explored. The same situation occurred with her aunt who owned a cattle ranch, and with whom Temple stayed at times. It was here that she discovered the cattle-holding machine which became the 'Squeeze Machine'.

THE SQUEEZE MACHINE

This device played an important part in helping Temple. She discovered it while staying at her aunt's ranch, where it was used to enclose cattle securely on all sides, but with their heads free. Once inside, Temple was unable to withdraw from the chute, although she directed her aunt as to the amount of squeeze she needed:

> "The effect was both stimulating and relaxing at the same time."
>
> (p87)

Temple subsequently spent a considerable amount of time designing her own squeeze machine and experimenting on herself. She writes:

"Recent research indicates that certain stimuli and stereotypical behaviour seem to reduce arousal. Warmth and pressure tend to lessen arousal, especially in a damaged nervous system. Perhaps if I had had a magical comfort machine, I could have used its warmth and pressure instead of throwing a temper tantrum. My imaginary designs were a fixation…an obsession that was refined and improved with each imaginary, magical machine."

(pp30-31)

Of this interest, her aunt wrote to her mother:

"…far from being an unhealthy sort of thing, I feel it is simply part of the way in which her unusual mind works out its unusual problems. I am proud to have had even a small part in freeing that good brain for the constructive work I know she can do…."

(p90)

ANTI-DEPRESSANTS

Temple also found a low dose of the drug *Tofranil* (50 mg a day) controlled her nervous problems. This adjusts the sensitivity of B-adrenergic receptors in the *locus ceruleus* of the brain, which process sensory input. As a result, Temple's nervous system is no longer flooded with adrenaline, and:

"Gone are the frenzied searches for the basic meaning of life. I no longer fixate on one thing since I am no longer driven. During the last four years I have written very few entries in my diary because the anti-depressant has taken away much of the fervour. With the passion subdued, my career and livestock equipment design business is going well. Since I am more relaxed, I get along better with people and stress-related health problems, such as colitis, are gone. Yet if medication had been prescribed for me in my early twenties I might not have accomplished as much as I have. The 'nerves' and the fixations were great motivators until they tore my body apart with stress-related health problems. Autistic and dyslexic traits are probably normal traits that become excessive in certain individuals.

A certain amount of anxiety and fixation is needed to motivate a person to get things done."

(p138)

And:

"People on the Kanner end of the spectrum (Classical Autism), like myself, have responded very well to antidepressants such as *Tofranil, Norpramin, Prozac* or *Anafranil*. I have been on the same low 50 mg of *Norpramin* for eleven years. The effective doses for people with autism are much lower than the doses recommended for treating depression. Too high a dose will cause insomnia, aggression and restlessness. If these symptoms occur the dose must be lowered."

(p179)

NARRATIVE 5   MAX

Amy Lansky, Max's mother, had degrees in mathematics and computer science, and a PhD in computer science, before her son Max was diagnosed with autism. Her book *Impossible Cure* (Lansky, 2003) contains the story of his recovery and is also updated in *Recovering Autistic Children by* Edelson & Rimland (2006). This account is taken from the later source.

SUMMARY

Max was 2.5 years old when his autism became clear. He had about 10-20 words but did not appear to understand language at all. His mother observed:

"On some level he seemed to be slipping away."

(p186)

Max knew the alphabet, numbers 1-10, and was manually dexterous. He could build intricate structures easily, use the computer and play a 'concentration' pattern- matching game, better than his parents:

"He enjoyed television and danced rhythmically to music. Indeed, for the most part, Max was a happy, though distant, toddler at home. He usually had a smile on his face and liked to play with his older brother Isaak… but when we all sat around talking and laughing in the evening and on weekends Max would prefer to be off on his own – and retreat into himself….Although he never pushed us away, he never reached out for affection."

(p186)

Max 'exuberantly' started nursery school at two years of age but had never settled in. He didn't interact with the other children and the teachers greeted him with hesitation. He had his milk bottle for comfort, and could not sit still during story times:

"He was antsy, as if there was a motor running inside him. It wasn't like classic hyperactivity…he didn't run about. He just wasn't paying attention. It was if the story the teacher was reading was in a foreign language. Left to his own devices Max would just wander off and play quietly with toys in the classroom that interested him. He wasn't disruptive; he just wasn't really 'there.'"

(p187)

One of the teachers told his mother that he manifested self-stimulation activities – spinning in a circle – and had poor eye contact. Max's eye contact was better at home, though still poor, but he did not spin there. The teacher suspected autism:

"Increasingly, there were noticeable oddities. One morning while driving to school, I asked him, 'Do you know where we're going now?' No response. Max just stared into space."

(p187)

Max was unable to sit and listen to stories at night – standing on his head and fidgeting, or running his fingers up and down his legs, the table, or wall. He would poke his finger against other peoples' chests, or butt his head against them:

"...not to hurt them, but as a kind of contact."

(p187)

By the end of the school year Max was just three years. The preschool called his parents in for a conference, telling them:

> "Max will never be able to attend the private school that Isaak goes to. He will always need special education."

(p187)

His mother could not rest easily while Max had a problem like this, feeling the whole family would be affected. They embarked on a 'quest' to do everything in their power to find the 'key' to Max:

> "I felt instinctively that Max's entire future hung in the balance and that I had to do everything in my power..."

(p187)

For Amy this was one of her 'worst nightmares', as she and her mother had been 'deeply affected' by her own brother's struggle with mental illness. A fact which added increased motivation to the search for help.

ACTION

On the advice of a speech-therapist friend, Amy and her husband decided to care for Max themselves at home, rather than place him in the local child-development clinic. This clinic had been recommended to them as it was affiliated with Stanford University:

> "Our friend told us that they'd just label Max and create a sense of hopelessness in us. Instead we took him to a highly respected speech and language therapist who runs a clinic in Palo Alto: Donna Dagenais."

(p188)

Max had private sessions with Donna and also group sessions with two other children. One of these also had a Pervasive Developmental Disorder

(PDD) and, of the three, Max was the least verbal and the most 'spaced out'. The family made dietary changes next and adopted the Feingold Diet for improving children's behaviour. This involved removing cow's milk – 'to which Max was addicted', some days drinking nearly eight bottles (half a gallon). Max had surgery for pyloric stenosis when he was an infant, and his attachment to his bottle was thought to be connected to this. He had violently thrown up breast milk during the first month of his life. Removing milk had a dramatic effect:

> "Before, it seemed like Max was behind a curtain, living in a different world. Now, the first veil lifted. He finally began to talk and build two-to-three word sentences. And he was clearly more present, more aware of his world. His behaviour and language were still by no means normal, but it was a start….Certainly cutting down on Max's intake of milk did create a dramatic change in him. But it did not cure him."
>
> (p188)

On the Feingold diet, all artificial colourings and flavourings were also now removed.

EDUCATION

Max continued in speech and language therapy and after testing qualified for special education benefits. He made slow progress, and despite now being able to talk he had:

> "…a decidedly autistic style. For example, he could only answer questions of the most literal kind and only about objects directly in front of him….He had another autistic symptom, echolalia…"
>
> (p189)

Echolalia, as the term suggests, indicates when a child repeats words or sentences that have just been said to him. The family changed Max's play-based nursery school to a highly structured Montessori one which focussed on reading, mathematics and manipulatory skills, all of which interested Max. Children here were encouraged to work on their own, which suited Max:

"The school did not see him as disabled but simply as quiet."

(p190)

Max's parents had been employing a nanny three days a week. They decided to change this arrangement and instead of a nanny, each parent worked a 4-day week so that each of them could stay at home with the children on 'the other two days':

> "Our nanny was a somewhat distant young woman with health problems of her own. Fortuitously, she left the area at just around this time, and we were able to find a new nanny who was extremely sweet and loving. We encouraged her to focus a bit more on Max than on his highly verbal and engaging brother....We realised we had to make a concerted effort to spend more concentrated and focused time with Max. It was often easy to 'forget him'...he was always wandering off to be by himself. So we decided to take turns, each spending intensive time with one child or the other."

(p190)

Finally, they examined their own feelings for Max. Amy realised that she felt feelings of rejection for Max in his current state:

> "I instinctively knew that I had to cultivate a state of unconditional acceptance and love towards Max, and that this acceptance was critical for his recovery. Coupled with this attitude, I also knew that I had to truly believe, to have true confidence, that she would recover. Steve went a long way towards helping me in this respect. Somehow he always knew things would turn out all right."

(p190)

HOMOEOPATHY

In January 1995, when Max was almost three and a half, Amy read an article by Judith Reichenberg-Ullman, a homoeopath, on treating autistic children with individualized homoeopathic medicine. They consulted a local professional (non-medical) practitioner and Max commenced treatment. Changes in Max were noted two days following the homoeopathic prescription:

"Max was using some phrases he had never used before and was somehow a bit more socially aware. It was subtle, but something definitely had shifted. We also noticed that his speech was slightly more fluid. Usually he spoke in a kind of 'cogwheel' fashion – as if he had to think about each word he said. Over time, we found that noticeable and sudden improvements in speech and social-awareness became Max's earmarks for the effect of the remedy upon him."

(p193)

Soon after his first prescription, Max had a session with Donna, his speech therapist, whom they had not told of his new medical treatment:

"She quickly noticed that something had changed; 'What did you do?' she asked….Suddenly he was able to perform two commands consistently."

(p193)

After a few months, the changes in Max had become more noticeable. His parents were initially sceptical:

"…being scientists, Steve and I were naturally a bit sceptical of the whole affair….We decided to conduct a simple and, admittedly, not totally rigorous test."

(p194)

Without the other parent knowing, over a period of two weeks, each parent noted when Max had his increased dosage (the time differences would be more obvious). They found a direct relation between his treatment and jumps in improvement. This scepticism over the effects of homoeopathy is extremely common:

"Because 'Max's cure seemed so natural and proceeded fairly gradually, it seemed to many of our friends and family that Max just grew out of his autistic state. But those of us who saw him almost daily – Steve, Isaak, our Nanny, our housekeeper, Donna and I – saw the direct correspondence between changes in dose and improvements in behaviour. Donna, who is extremely experienced with children like Max, repeatedly assured me that what happened to Max was atypical. When he was clearly better (after a year of treatment)… at which point we discontinued the remedy altogether – she confided in me that Max had been autistic. She said that she had seen autistic kids improve before, but not lose their autism like Max did. In fact, our paediatrician made the same confession. Once he was better, she admitted that he had been autistic. She was quite surprised by the change in him. Many years later…she had commented that she was still amazed at what had happened to Max."

(p195)

OSTEOPATHY

At the recommendation of the homoeopath, Max also received traditional osteopathic treatment commencing six months after his homoeopathic medicine programme. Although his ability to speak and understand language and his social awareness had improved, he was still restless, and retained some social distancing. Max received three osteopathic treatments in a month followed by an occasional treatment once every few months. The osteopath diagnosed signs of cranial compression, which were corrected:

"…Max's initial reaction to treatment was striking. While the homoeopathic remedy had its primary effect on his language production, comprehension and social awareness, osteopathy created the first major shift in Max's desire for physical affection. It also seemed to create a calming effect in him, quelling the sense of internal restlessness. The night after his first osteopathic treatment, Max crawled into my lap and said, 'Mommy, sing Rock-A-Bye-Baby.'! Although he did not usually push me away this was the first time he directly asked me for this kind of physical loving attention. From that point on, Max did."

(p196)

Soon Max began crawling into bed with his mother in the mornings and running after his dad or mum when they left the house for an extra kiss goodbye. After nine months of homoeopathy, Max began his second year at Montessori preschool. His speech was now more complex, spontaneous and fluid. He tested as 'approaching age level' by his speech therapist. Speech therapy was discontinued, but Max remained eligible for special education. Socially, Max wanted to join in with other children but was behind in his social interaction skills:

> "…he was stubborn and cried too easily when he didn't get his own way."
>
> (p197)

While his mother was delighted at Max's progress and attempts to socially integrate, school did not like this change. A teacher asked his mother:

> "Max was such a nice boy before. Can you put him back the way he was?"
>
> (p197)

His parents changed school once more, this time to a more socially orientated one which followed Montessori principles, but not so strictly:

> "His new teachers had no preconceptions or biases toward him and they easily helped Max adjust. Within a few months he knew everyone at school, was interested in what was going on around him, had a couple of friends, and was having play dates."
>
> (p197)

Other changes took place at home. When their nanny decided to return to her home town, Max's parents chose not to replace her, adopting after-school child care three days per week instead:

> "This change had many beneficial side effects for our family. For one thing we finally began to eat dinner together every night as a family. Given the hectic schedule of families with two working parents, the institution of the family meal has gone by the wayside in many American homes. Returning to it created a feeling of greater coherence and stability in our lives. It also assured a better diet for our kids."
>
> (p197)

In 1996 a leap in language and social ability, which had continued over a four month period, evened out and Max's full personality began to emerge:

> "He is an entertainer. He is sociable and sensitive. Although he was still immature at this point, he was ahead of his peers academically. He was respected and liked by both his teachers and classmates. In May 1996, Donna tested Max once more. He was testing above age level! On the day Steve and I joyfully signed letters releasing Max from eligibility for special education, Donna told the county social services representative that it was not her therapy that had done the trick for him; it was homoeopathy. She also invited John (the homoeopath) and me to present Max's case to her clinic, which we did that summer."
>
> (p198)

'CURE'

Max was now five years old and his parents were tempted to believe that he was 'fully cured'. But his homoeopath felt there was still some way to go. Max retained some vestiges of his former autism; for example his language was occasionally awkward and in times of stress or illness he would retreat into himself and use echolalia:

> "But overall, Max was functioning extremely well. He engaged in real discussions with family and friends. He asked for explanations about his body and environment. He related stories about his day at school and about TV shows. He was also fascinated with fantasy play and dress up. Max was even becoming popular at school, with children running up to him and greeting him. He was able to adjust easily to new social situations the summer of 1996, readily adapting to two new summer camps. Max had become an avid reader... Before he began kindergarten he could already read simple Dr Seuss books."
>
> (p198)

At the end of the summer of 1996, Max's parents noticed a slight decline in his speech and social awareness. It was the time of his five-year check up and they chose to omit the routine childhood vaccinations: DTP, MMR and polio. Their paediatrician concurred, but persuaded them to give Max the TB test that is legally required for kindergarten entry in California.

> "Unfortunately, this injection led to a marked aggravation and deterioration in Max's state. For the next week, he became increasingly sensitive, crying for no reason. The teachers at his camp and at school remarked about the change in him. He had become more withdrawn and fearful. He was not his usual self. This reaction made us wonder if, indeed, vaccination was the root cause of Max's problems in the first place."
>
> (pp198-9)

Max's mother records how, years later, she went through his medical records, and realised that at aged 18 months Max had been given a dose of the MMR vaccine only one week after recovering from rosella – an ailment related to measles. She wondered if he had been 'in a compromised state'. After a couple of different homoeopathic remedies, the homoeopath returned to Max's original prescription:

> "After a single dose, Max was back to his normal self within hours."
>
> (p199)

Since this time, Max has not needed regular visits to the homoeopath or osteopath. He visits – as does all the family – about twice a year, or when necessary. In autumn 1997 Max left the Montessori school and entered first grade of the same school as his brother Isaak:

> "Since then he has done well both academically and socially. He is an open-hearted, sensitive and somewhat comedic fellow who loves drawing and art, (he is especially fond of the quirky and enigmatic paintings of M.C. Escher), playing computer games, reading fantasy and science fiction books, and writing and illustrating his own works of science-fiction."
>
> (p198)

When in second grade, his teacher noticed Max was still having some auditory processing problems. He sometimes missed oral instruction or key points in stories, especially when read aloud to the class. Being sensitive to disapproval, Max tended to cover up these deficiencies and did not ask for help in clarification from teachers. He might then write an excellent essay on the wrong subject. His teachers had not been told about Max's autism, but at this point his parents decided to make them aware of it. As a result they tried to provide visual or written instructions for him when necessary, and by third grade, Max's auditory problem had disappeared. His teachers no longer reported any problems with Max.

Writing in 2002, when Max was about 12 years old, his mother reports:

"Today, his behaviour, demeanour, and day-to-day interactions with friends and family are not in any way autistic. He's a sociable fellow with many friends, and an excellent student working at his age and grade level. He takes piano and tennis lessons. He attends summer camps, including a month-long slipway camp. He is resilient within his peer group, always able to defend himself with a kind of entertaining humour and charm. He is also a gentle soul, loved by his teachers. Of course he still has issues, like any other child. But we continue to work on them and Max continues to improve....Max is no longer autistic..."

(p200)

SEPTEMBER 2005 UPDATE

"Max is now 14 years old and a Freshman in high school. He remains completely autism free...no teacher or friend suspects his past. I still try to keep him away from cow's milk, corn, and food colourings. But when he goes to sleep-away camp in the summer, he eats all these things with no problems....Max, like the rest of our family still sees our homoeopath about twice a year. He gets remedies to help with acute ailments or with the stresses of being a teenager. I would still classify him as a bit more on the spacey or forgetful side – especially in comparison to my older son, who is much more Type A. Max can tune out conversations easily if he wants to, gets a bit lost in his thoughts, and sometimes does miss social cues. But by and large, he is a more resilient teenager than his brother. He is loving school, has many new friends there, is doing well with his studies… likes the artistic counter-culture image, and is most interested these days in girls, (he already has a girl friend or two), music and his passion: computer animation."

(pp207-8)

ATEC OUTCOMES

Scoring of the ATEC for Max is given in Table 9, below:

I. Speech/Language/Communication:	0
II. Sociability:	1
III. Sensory/Cognitive Awareness:	1
IV. Health/Physical/Behaviour:	0
Total ATEC Summary Score:	2

Table 9 ATEC Scores for Max age c 14

The two points given in this assessment were for his ability to be 'spacey' (dreamy). Again, as with Temple's 'obsessions' it is questionable whether this aspect of 'personality' can be attributed to autism. (Personality in autism/ASD is explored in Chapter 8)

DIAGNOSIS OF AUTISM

Max received a diagnosis of autism from his paediatrician only after he had recovered. She had not wanted to tell his parents at the time. He was not tested on any standard measure, but his autism was recognised by both his doctor and his speech therapist, an experienced practitioner used to working with autistic children. It is interesting in this narrative that, despite the child's recovery, his doctor did not deny his original autism. It is more common for a recovered child's parents to be told that they did not have autism after all.

WHAT IS MEANT BY RECOVERY?

In this narrative the word 'recovery' is not used.

ATTITUDE TO CURE

Amy Lansky's book is titled: *Impossible Cure* partly because she was told that there was 'no cure' for her child's autism and that he would always need special education. The attitude of this narrative is that this is not at all the case. As scientists, she and her husband were both sceptical of homoeopathy initially but, having come to understand the science behind it (explained fully in her book), she now lectures on this subject. Her belief is that it was probably the MMR vaccination, given when Max was already suffering from a measles-type disease, which compromised his immune-system and 'caused' his autism. 'Cure' is therefore used within a medical model to signify the result of successfully treating his 'illness'- with homoeopathic medicine. It appears from this narrative that where an individual believes or perceives autism to be an illness, the word 'cure' is used. But where autism is perceived to be the 'essence' of a person, 'cure' (rightly) becomes an insulting rejecting of their selfhood and/or difference. This terminology is discussed further in later chapters.

PROGRAMMES USED

The main programmes used by Max's parents were:
Dietary: (Dairy-free & Feingold diets)
Homoeopathic Medicine
Osteopathy (Cranial)
Montessori Education: two styles

NARRATIVE 6   WILLIAM

This narrative is taken from Edelson & Rimland (2006). William's father was an attorney who originally practiced in medical malpractice defending doctors and hospitals. His mother is an advocate for special needs children.

SUMMARY

William was nearly two years old in 2000, when he received his 'catch-up' vaccinations:

> "Since that day, our lives have been profoundly changed in a way that none of us could have anticipated."
>
> (p232)

William's mother describes how the local Starbucks displayed a notice giving the rates for autism in the USA (in March 2003, this was about 1: 5,000). She took out a pen and added:

> "In Oregon, autism strikes one child in 150!"
>
> (p232)

During the summer following his booster shots, William suffered from constant diarrhoea, unexplained bumps and welts, reduced speech, bloating, binge eating, bloody lesions, 'croup' attacks, and lost interaction and eye contact. These conditions progressed into rocking, teeth-grinding, eye squinting, spinning, hand flapping, gross motor problems and a total loss of language. Twenty weeks (less than six months) after his shots William was diagnosed with 'regressive autism'.

> "But this is not a story of grief, but of hope. Through a combination of medical and educational treatments, our son has made great strides."
>
> (p232)

William was a healthy nine-pound baby at birth, but he quite rapidly lost weight during the summer following his vaccinations and became progressively withdrawn and unresponsive. His parents first checked his hearing and were told that this was fine, but that they would need to go to the Oregon Health Science University (OHSU) autism clinic:

> "Until that day we had never heard of autism. We believe in a cause-and-effect universe. We did not believe that our formerly normal

child could be afflicted with a terrible psychiatric condition without an identifiable cause. Science can clone pets and splice the human gene; science should be able to tell us what is happening to our child."

(p233)

DIET

At the clinic, a doctor told them that some autistic children were being helped with a gluten and casein-free diet:

"We couldn't believe what we were being told: could this mysterious psychiatric disorder be remedied by a change of diet?"

His parents put William on a diet free from wheat, rye, spelt, oats, barley and dairy products. Within a few days his bowel movements improved, and within three weeks his self-stimulatory behaviours (stims) had dropped by about half:

"It was clear to us there was a cause-and-effect impact. We started looking for more answers."

(p233)

EARLY INTERVENTION

When they took William to the public education specialists, they were told:

"Autism is a lifelong disabling disease for which there is no cure." At his early intervention assessment, William was tested with an IQ of 55 and severe language paraxial – an inability to understand or respond to words....William was ranked smack in the middle of the DSM-IV psychiatric diagnosis of typical 'late-onset' autism, in which children lose their ability to communicate and interact socially. The early intervention experts told us we might have to institutionalise our son."

(p233)

DAN!

Shortly after this 'demoralising experience' William's parents attended a conference held by Defeat Autism Now! (DAN!), an organisation connected to the *Autism Research Institute* (ARI) established by Bernard Rimland. DAN! is a group of parents and doctors who have undertaken extensive research showing a biomedical component to autism. The conference focused on a variety of biomedical treatments being reported by parents as helpful with their autistic children. At the conference William's parents met a physician who offered to take him as a patient: 'and our world began to change'. The new doctor ordered laboratory tests of William's hair, urine and blood:

> "From these tests, we learned that something was terribly wrong with William's internal chemistry. While William's earlier doctors had simply told us that he had a mysterious and incurable psychiatric disorder, we now realised that something very physical and abnormal was going on inside him. He had seven times the reference range for mercury. He had an immune dysfunction and his body was devouring his nervous tissue. He had little IgC or IgA. He had terrible microbial infections from wheat and Clostridium in his stomach and his intestines were permeable. Most children with regressive autism are medically ill: they suffer from abnormal conditions that can be treated medically."
>
> (p234)

William's new doctor referred him to the Pfeiffer Clinic in Illinois for further tests. At this clinic Dr Bill Walsh had found in further studies that 95% of abdominally affected children with an ASD show significant deficiencies of metallathionein (MT), a protein that, together with glutathione, removes toxins such as mercury from the body. Many autistic children have reduced MT:

> "Whether this is genetic or the result of some environmental insult is still unclear."
>
> (p234)

William's mother cites research by the MIND Institute at the University of California, Davis, suggesting the 'epidemic' of autism in the USA is not genetically based:

"There may be a genetic susceptibility within a child, such as an autoimmune issue in the family tree, but the regression is environmentally triggered."

(pp234-5)

By this time William's parents had formed a 'logical, science-based, treatment plan' with a team of 'supportive forward-thinking doctors' to help them. William was placed on a 'yeast-free' diet, high in protein but low in carbohydrate and based on gluten and casein-free foods. In response to the medical tests showing William had a suppressed immune-system (and indicated by his yeast and fungal infections) he was given vitamin and nutritional supplements and a variety of drugs for dealing with any gut infections and 'leaking'.

In addition, his home was made allergen-free, and preservatives, excess use of hormones (e.g. in meat) and antibiotic use were avoided in favour of natural products. William's parents also began a home-based applied behaviour analysis (ABA) programme and added speech therapy, occupational therapy and auditory integration therapy to his schedule:

"Over time we noticed several clear indications of his recovery. William began to live in the present. He responded to his name and his interest in the world around him increased. He became more interactive and began to demonstrate imaginative play. Gradually, his sensory issues began to improve. He began to recover some of his early motor milestones and to walk normally. His vision improved. William is regaining speech and his cognitive scores improving as he continues to make slow but steady progress."

(pp235-6)

INTESTINE INFLAMMATION

As part of a collaborative study by Harvard University and Massachusetts General Hospital, (the Harvard-Mass General Study) William was tested by biopsy for inflammation of the intestines, and found to have 'nodular lymphoid hyperplasia', an intestinal inflammation affecting the lymph nodes (part of the immune system). His mother writes:

"This finding is consistent with inflammatory injury to the intestines and is a clear indication that William had an adverse biomedical reaction to a foreign environmental agent or toxin."

(p236)

Unlike many autistic children whose intestines 'look like Swiss cheese'. William's intestinal ulcers are now 'mild' and his lymph nodes are 'soft and healing'. His stomach acid had been found to be very low – a condition which promotes yeast-growth – and he was given Betaine HCL. At the Mass-General Hospital his stomach acid was now found to be Ph4 – very acidic. Secretin was found to be too low for his pancreas to function normally and several key enzymes: lipase, which digests fats, and amylase, which digests carbohydrates, were missing altogether:

"This information is vital in shaping his treatment options. The Mass-General Hospital team is successfully treating autistic children by replacing enzymes and probiotics suspected to be deficient. Left untreated, these gastrointestinal problems will continue to cause increased neurological problems and exacerbate other symptoms of autism."

(p237)

OUTCOMES

His mother describes their progress:

"When William was three (in 2001) we were told that he might never talk and that we should ultimately investigate medications to sedate him and institutionalise him for his long-term care. Today, William has over 350 words. He can say, 'I want more juice, please' 'I want to go outside' and 'See you later'. He plays with his sister, and he fights with her too."

(p238)

His parents say they have 'made great sacrifices and incurred great costs' but:

"…we have never lost hope. We have returned to William the gifts of health and speech…and those gifts are priceless."

(p238)

By the age of five (in 2003) William was attending a Montessori school with the help of an aid, and had progressed to a developmental age of three years:

"He is speaking six-word sentences, is potty trained, singing nursery songs, and drinking from a cup. He can read 15 words, and is learning more. He shows every sign of making slow but steady progress toward recovery."

(pp232-3)

She goes on to explain that, although it will be a long and arduous process: 'we have one thing denied parents before us: – hope'.

"With each passing day, the hopelessness of regressive autism is being challenged and overcome."

(p233)

In a 2006 update, when William was seven, his mother writes:

"The journey has been dark and at times terrifying….Who he is and what he will become has seemed at various points to be beyond reach and description. In 2003, William began or continued several therapies that have had dramatic effects on his recovery."

(p238)

These included vitamin B12 injections accompanied by folinic acid and TMG (Trimethylglycine). They adopted the specific carbohydrate diet (SCD) to heal his gut, (see Chapter 5) and chelation with DMPS (for toxic metal removal). His mercury levels after five years are now within the reference range. In 2004 William began Relational Development Intervention (RDI) as well as sensory integration therapy (see Chapter 5). His mother writes:

"Since we began RDI William has experienced a dramatic increase in (emotional) referencing and language. Most importantly, he has learned to enjoy the benefits of co-regulation and play with his siblings. William has continued to receive ABA therapy and has begun reading and is currently working on numbers. He is talking and tells us what he likes and doesn't like. He is very clear about what he wants."

(p239)

William is currently in mainstream first grade with a 'shadow'. He has significant verbal delays, and continues to improve emotionally and verbally. He plays with his brothers and sisters, is interested in the world: 'and tells us he loves us':

"He is continually emerging and growing up and developing. The wall is coming down. It may take a while before it is completely gone, but the wall is coming down."

(p239)

ATEC OUTCOMES

Based on this account, the following scores were obtained for William on the ATEC:

I. Speech/Language/Communication:	3
II. Sociability:	5
III. Sensory/Cognitive Awareness:	9
IV. Health/Physical/Behaviour:	6
Total ATEC Summary Score:	<u>23</u>

Table 10 ATEC Scores for William age c 7

As some information was missing from the final account, it was not possible to know how much enjoyment or inner emotional meaning William noted from his activities or the degree of stimulation or repetitive behaviour he may have retained. For this reason the ATEC was scored in favour of ASD, putting 'Somewhat' in places where 'Don't know' would otherwise have been attributed. As can be seen from this assessment, William has higher scores for Health/Physical Behaviour and Sensory/Cognitive Awareness. The latter is due to his remaining sensory difficulties and delayed development. The score of 5 for Sociability reflects his 'emerging' emotional and verbal development at the time of the summary.

DIAGNOSIS OF AUTISM

William was diagnosed with autism following a hearing test at aged c3 years. (Many autistic children appear to be deaf). His parents were told they 'would have to go to the Oregon Health Sciences University autism clinic' (p233) where they were told they would probably have to 'institutionalise' him.

WHAT IS MEANT BY RECOVERY?

Here, recovery is synonymous with cure – a complete reversal of the damage done to the child 'back' to where they would have been without the environmental toxic insult believed to have been responsible – assumed in this narrative to be mercury from vaccines.

ATTITUDE TO CURE

Cure is not mentioned except as part of the advice, that there was 'no cure', given to William's parents.

PROGRAMMES USED

Diet: G/C free – high protein low carbohydrates (yeast-free)

SPC – removal of specific carbohydrates

Nutritional supplements inc. Vitamin A, cod liver oil, Vitamin B, Super Nu-Thera, selenium, omega 3 fatty acids. magnesium, acidophilus probiotic and glyco-proteins.

Dramatic responses were found to *Vancomycin* and *Flagyl* to kill the intestinal bugs.

Saccharomyces boulardii

Clostridium (an AIDS drug)

Montessori

ABA

Speech therapy

Auditory integration therapy (AIT)

RDI – Relationship, Development Integration, is based on reconstructing the basic emotional referencing and co-regulation development, interrupted by the toxic insult suffered by the children.

Sensory integration (at The Sensory Centre) based on recalibrating the body's three basic sensory channels, vestibular, proprioceptive and tactile.

NARRATIVE 7   MARK

The story of Mark is taken from his mother's account in *Sound of Falling Snow*, edited by Annabel Stehli (2004). This book contains 14 narratives by parents on the recovery of their children from autism and related conditions (see Appendix II). At that time, Mark was in his early to mid 30s and he was diagnosed and so grew up during the 1970s.

SUMMARY

Pam Pritchard describes how, at six months of age, her son Mark happily played peek-a-boo with her from his crib. At one year he crawled to a newspaper on the floor and pointed at it, looking up and expecting to be read to:

"When he could speak in sentences he phonetically read the newspaper to me, not to mention reading from the *Physician's Desk Reference* (PDR) in his paediatrician's office. The doctor gasped in amazement and applauded the remarkable event."

(p1)

When he was two, his mother noticed that he had never uttered the words 'No' or 'Yes':

"If he didn't want spinach he would say 'Take it off, the spinach', and when I would say, 'Do you want a cookie?' he would echo, 'You want a cookie!' His meaning was clear…he did not eat the spinach, and he got the cookie. Nevertheless, unusual patterns were emerging."

(p2)

By the age of 3, Mark's attention wandered, his eye contact was intermittent and easily diverted, and he spent long periods of time on his own. He never asked questions or approached another child until one day he reached out to a little girl. This rarity made his mother cry. As a young and first-time mother, Pat found it hard to know whether his increasing tantrums were 'usual' for toddlers, or something else:

"What did I know of typical child development? Looking back on it, the only tools I had were love, tenacity, good instincts and an unshakable belief…born perhaps from naiveté…that my son would be okay."

(p3)

At about this time, Mark had an annual check-up with his paediatrician, who told his mother he 'had noticed for some time that something was wrong with the child':

"Wondering why he hadn't mentioned it before, I dutifully took my child to the psychiatrist he recommended. My husband, from whom I am now separated, also had a private appointment with the psychiatrist, as did I. She gave me her conclusion: The father is narcissistic and the boy has childhood schizophrenia. I was never told the contents of the file on me….No suggestions were made as to what could be done."

(p3)

At aged four, Mark attended a nursery school, 'staffed with lovely, caring people' where he sat all day with one of these, or stared at the corner 'making a high-pitched sound all his own'. Unlike the other children, he never came running out to his mother, but went happily with her nevertheless;

"Within a few months, he was gently but firmly expelled from nursery school. At that moment I learned two important things that would stay with me throughout the journey: 1, my son was decidedly not 'typical' and I had to face it and do something about it; and 2: there is a 'people factor' that is paramount in working with a special needs child. People – not 'placement' – make all the difference."

(p4)

In particular, a little nursery school helper impressed Pat with her loving kindness, while other people were 'downright harmful' to Mark. At home it was 'trial and error' to find ways to react with Mark:

"For example, the less eye contact Mark made, the more we played a game called 'follow Mommy's eyes'. The less related he wanted to be, the more games we played. With endless patience my mother rolled a rubber ball back and forth with him and never quit when he wanted to wander off....Had I known this was the thing to do to help him, we would have stayed in his face every waking moment."

(p4)

SPECIAL NURSERY SCHOOL

At aged four Mark attended a special nursery school for children with a spectrum of difficulties. It worked mostly with behaviour modification techniques, 'about the only modality available at that time':

"I recall Mark's enormous difficulty with putting on his jacket by himself. With patience and consistency such as I had never before seen, the teachers worked with him, teaching him step by step how he could encode in his brain the process of 'jacket donning'. It took the better part of a year, but, by gum, he was no longer 'the boy who couldn't put on his jacket.'"

(p5)

Mark was diagnosed with autism by Leo Kanner at the school:

"A kind grandfatherly man, he sat me down and told me he had no doubt that my son had what was known as autism, a word new to me. He gave me a brief clinical explanation of autism, little of which I retained, and finished by stating, (and with all due respect to Dr, Kanner; this is close to an exact quote: 'Unfortunately, autistic children never develop normally. Your son will never be able to function on his own in society. I recommend that you immediately place him in a setting that can care for him properly."

(p6)

Answering on pure instinct, Pat responded:

"I understand, but no. I'll find another way."

(p6)

These were the only words she was able to get out at the time. Dr Kanner remained sympathetic but told her she was making a grave mistake. Despite the diagnosis, other professions used different terms to describe Mark, including schizophrenia, emotionally disturbed, behaviour problems, all of which his mother rejected. Through trial and error again, they met a neurologist who after Mark had: 'hopped on one leg' prescribed a little-known drug called *Deaner,* which calmed and focused Mark. This was switched to *Ritalin*, which made Mark:

"...so high on the amphetamine, he literally dashed about the house for 8 or 10 hours, his little tongue occasionally darting in and out of his mouth....It was one of the worst days of my life, and my son's life I'm sure."

(pp6-7)

Deaner was banned for Mark, (reasons are not given), which his mother regrets, as it appeared to do him good, and not to harm him. This occurred after Mark was enrolled in a day school where the only drugs permitted were those prescribed by the psychiatrists at the school. They utilised behaviour modification, giving sugary-sweet rewards to the children (something Mark's mother found astonishing with hyperactive children) but in other ways 'were great'. Mark liked the school and began to interact with the others.

DIET

Mark's mother tried to 'calm down' his diet by modifying it to one of high protein with no processed sugar, 'pretty progressive for its time':

> "It worked well, except the school candy threw things off. Terrific things happened for my son during this time. He engaged in genuine play at home and school and loved his Tonka trucks and racing car track. All nice, typical 5-year oldstuff. He was excited about school's parent day for three weeks prior to the event, and on the big day came running up to me and my parents, showing us his classroom, and offering us refreshments."
>
> (p7)

Mark had weekly appointments with a psychiatrist at the school, as did his mother separately and also with a social worker:

> "At my first shrink appointment, a doctor with a slight smile (which he sustained for a whole hour) looked deeply into my eyes and asked what I thought had caused my son's condition. I babbled things like 'I have no idea' and 'nothing unusual ever happened', but the doctor just kept staring and smiling at me…waiting for the *real* answer."
>
> (p8)

Pat explains how the 'real' answer was that mothers 'caused' autism by being 'distant' with their children. Following a 3-4 minute stare from the psychiatrist, she describes:

> "…how much I wanted to say, 'Come to think of it, maybe it was the time I locked him in the closet with snakes.' No matter how much the psychiatrist believed I had 'caused' this condition, I and my instincts knew better."
>
> (p8)

She learned that:

> "…traditional psychiatry with five year olds with autism does not

work. One day my social worker informed me that my son, amid much crying, had told his doctor, 'We had a bird and it died. And then we got another bird and it died too.' It was obvious, she said, that he was dealing with feelings of loss in his life and questioned me about what had happened at home. The fact of the matter is that we had indeed bought two parakeets that died within a month. Not good for the parakeets, but I confess I very much enjoyed telling the social worker about it, although I was never certain she believed me."

(p8)

A new social worker arrived, however, who treated Pat 'not as a suspect, but as a mother dealing with life.' She:

"...offered practical mothering suggestions when I was 'at my wit's end' and personally counselled me when life was confusing. She was my confidant and advisor and I loved her. She in turn liked me and adored my son. She and her husband became 'adopted grandparents', inviting my son to their home for weekends with them and their teenagers, and later to their summer home in Arkansas."

(p8)

A TURNING POINT

Pat was called to a 'huge' meeting of numerous professions and experts. They explained to her that it was known that mothers were the cause of their children's autism, and that although she loved Mark, she had unwittingly been distant towards him:

"I had not related to him enough, touched him enough, played with him enough. Often, they told me, such mothers are clinical, intellectual, and uncomfortable with touching and playing with their children. They could not have described me more inaccurately: I made only one comment at the meeting. I asked: if that is true, why doesn't this happen to every child in an orphanage or to all children in dire poverty whose mothers have no time for them? The professionals smiled, mostly at one another, and did not respond.

My instinct and I knew they were dead wrong. I did not qualify. I was the mother who had been at risk of 'kissing the baby's skin off', and no one would have described me as intellectual, clinical, or distant....I breathed an internal sigh, but I knew enough not to mess with a good thing. I learned the psychiatry game early on and played along for the next three years. It was a good school. My son was happy there."

(p9)

By five years of age Mark had already been IQ tested, and despite his hyperactivity and inattention to the tests had scored 155. He was highly verbal and clearly intelligent so the professionals declared he could not be autistic. They chose to 'mainstream' him into public (open to all) school. Despite the resistance of Mark's mother and the head teacher of the school, he was sent, aged seven, into third grade. Soon after this the principal, a man who had protected Mark through the system, fell ill and retired. Without his support Mark deteriorated:

"The progress of the previous three years began to dissipate. I took him to a world-famous clinic, where I was told. 'We've observed your interaction with your son and we think you handle him too well.' To this day, I have no idea what that meant."

(p10)

On parents' night a teacher walked over to Pat and announced:

"Mrs Pritchard, your son is an emotional cripple."

(p10)

There were complaints that Mark's 'fuss' was upsetting the workmen doing renovations in the school, and after this his mother informed the staff that she would be finding a new school for her son, having been put off the idea of 'mainstreaming' (a new term at that time) and 'inclusion' – the current expression – for some time. Mark enrolled in a special education school that was still attached to the public school system, and with good teachers made progress. He began to take the bus, and developed a crush on a little girl who 'teased him endlessly'. Mark was experiencing tantrums, which were the biggest problem for Pat and Mark, largely because of judgmental reaction of adults in their environment, and he was bullied by many of the children:

> "...who took unspeakable advantage of him: Memories which remain to this day."
>
> (p10)

Despite these problems, they went bowling on Saturdays and to church on Sundays, Mark played with the other children, had a next door friend and made random phone calls with his pal. By nine, he could stay with babysitters and 'went to summer day camp, where he won a trophy for most improved camper'. After moving to a new state, another good school where the: 'special ed' was part of the whole school and the 'teacher was a saint', Mark continued to grow into adolescence. He could stay at home alone, had more than the occasional friend and flew by himself to Florida for long visits with his grandparents. He was taunted and bullied by other children and 'hated being on the 'special ed.' bus, something of which his mother was unaware for many years until Mark told her how the other children called it the 'retard bus'. Mark was doing well at school, but every afternoon his concentration appeared to wane. Every possible cause was considered, and again, it was years later that Mark, himself, explained that the chalkboard had looked like a whirlpool, to him, as the afternoon sunbeams hit it and he became lost in the vision:

> "He had and still has visual and other sensory perception so different from ours, we can't even conceive of how life looks to him and how distracting it must be. There are many, many parts of his life (even now) that I'll never know about..."
>
> (p12)

As an adolescent Mark was not 'typical' but he enjoyed pop music, 'cool clothes' and developed crushes on girls like other teenagers. By some mix-up his mother found she had enrolled him in 'a huge public school' for which both Mark and the school were ill prepared. A major meeting at school administration level was convened to organise an individual education plan (IEP) for Mark, including placement at a more appropriate school. Some of those suggested were boarding schools. Mark and his mother visited several and chose:

> "A pastoral, beautiful acreage, a stream on the property...a real country club Prep school for the 'difficult to otherwise place.'"
>
> (p13)

Mark made friends and brought his room-mate home on weekends. Unfortunately this placement went badly wrong for Mark when the headmaster, who had been on sabbatical, returned and lost his temper with Mark, screaming at him to 'Get out of my school'. This was following a 'frustration incident' – one of the reasons for which Mark had been sent to the school. Mark was found by his mother having run home from the school. After a talk together 'that neither of us will ever forget'. Mark returned and stuck out the school for six weeks, so that he could officially leave at the end of the year if he still wanted to, rather than half way. Six weeks later Mark left and after six months of home-schooling they found a small private school with 8-20 children per class, consisting mostly of 'ex-tough kids, drop-outs who were heading back in'. Here Mark blossomed, was awarded his diploma and went to college, with the support of the director of the school. Knowing Mark's history, the college accepted him. The college was:

> "...a quantum leap forward for him."
>
> (p15)

Mark was managing well, despite minor clashes with the landlord, 'a neat freak', and was exceptional academically. He was recruited to do his junior and senior years at Yale with a scholarship and grant funding. Mark was at home here, his confidence level soared and he was awarded his degree and cum-laude diploma. Personally, Mark continued to develop a sense of his own self – his favourite music, a girl-friend, and being upset when his favourite team lost. He preferred to leave university and seek his fortune rather than remain in post-graduate education. This proved more difficult for Mark, as with any young person seeking a niche. Being adventurous and fiercely independent, he worked in a variety of locations including Silicon Valley, not quite finding what he wanted:

> "He had the talent but didn't fit. As you might imagine the job interview process as we know it in corporate America does not allow for one with social and interactive difficulties and poor eye

contact. In the job search he took rejection after rejection, and in desperation, the Yale graduate took a job with the Postal Service."

(p16)

His mother writes of this time:
> "We didn't know he had autism….He only knew he felt like a failure, and the confidence level of the college years began to recede."

(p16)

After a job found with the help of the original social worker friend, in Chicago, Mark did well at manning the mainframe equipment. He then moved to New Orleans:

> "He truly loved New Orleans…it's laid back, nonconformist, and without snow. He had a lovely apartment in an old house where he could hear the street car clang. He was making excellent money, getting involved in political causes, going to Mardi Gras and Jazz Fest and best of all, friends began to appear…offbeat characters with names like John, The Tamale Man and Velvet, the hot New Orleans mama with a brood of children and her part-time husband, the cop."

(p17)

At this time, Pat heard an interview with Annabel and Georgi Stehli. Georgi had made a complete recovery from autism with the help of Auditory Integration Therapy (AIT: described in Chapter 5). The description of Georgi's difficulties – described as autism on the interview, rang bells with Pat, who immediately rang Mark to say that she thought he had been autistic all along. Mark read *Sound of a Miracle*, Annabel Stehli's book about her daughter's recovery. A short while afterwards he 'embraced the autism diagnosis as a partial explanation for the things that were happening to him'. Sadly, Mark had to leave his post in New Orleans because he 'behaved strangely' in the workplace, but remained for two years without employment living frugally. Eventually, his friends all moved away or moved on and at 29 years of age Mark unhappily returned to live with his mother. This was a difficult time for both son and mother:

> "As close as my son and I are, we don't make good room-mates…
> [I]…am amazed at how we got through that period. Mark's made

of stern stuff. Having recently 're-discovered' his autism and being at the low point in life's progress both came at him at once, but he didn't give up."

(p18)

AIT

Mark chose to undergo auditory integration therapy (AIT) for himself. He found this helpful, describing it as: 'a relaxation of the force field around him':

> "Mostly, I recall overhearing him say that after AIT he felt a lessening of the constant feeling that he was being chased by a tiger. That was the first time I had any idea that he had the 'fight or flight' response constantly colouring every experience."

(p19)

His mother continues:

> "It's a lot more difficult, though, to pursue therapies with a strong willed thirty year old than with a younger, dependent child. If only AIT had been available to us when Mark was younger – if only – if only. I could fill a book with 'if only' but I refuse to go there. We have so much else to focus on…"

(p19)

Mark 'climbed out of the hole' and moved on to his own apartment again, and then into New York City. He obtained a rewarding job in Hawaii working as a coordinator with a disabilities-related agency:

> "In his recent adult years, he does things that the books tell us autistic people can't do. I was gleeful when I learned he could dissemble a bit and tell a little white lie occasionally. He continues to amaze me sometimes with his observations of other's motivations, and he can often read me like a book."

(p19)

Mark also wrote his own summary to Pat's narrative in the book. He suggests that, because he wasn't acting as mentally retarded as well as autistic, his disability was not acknowledged. In the 1970s he was labelled 'emotionally disturbed' and perceived as a 'weird computer geek'. Mark underplays his own academic brilliance and attributes AIT with helping him understand and accept his autism as the explanation for his difficulties and his sense of isolation with employers, impressed with his ability but disappointed with him as a person.

RETURN TO YALE

In 2004 Mark returned to Yale, working in their autism unit. He writes:

> "Since then I have spent most of my career in the fields of psychiatry and disability. I have even spoken to groups of several hundred at autism conferences. Is this a success story in autism: That depends on what the meaning of the word 'success' is. I have a tendency to measure myself not against other people with autism, but against other members of my Yale graduation class, many of whom are doing things like writing for network television, working for political campaigns or, in the case of Jodie Foster, piling up Academy Awards. The irony is that some say Bill Gates himself exhibit's the traits of autism, which begs the question: why is he the world's richest man while I'm a cubicle rat? Then again, one might ask why I live independently and hold down a professional job, while so many other people with autism, including many with a college education, languish at home or even in a 'setting' such as a group home. Yes, I suppose this is, after all, a 'success story' in autism."

(p21)

Mark's mother adds:

> "I never thought undue modesty was one of Mark's traits, but he has only touched on his years of speaking engagements and neglected to mention how good he is at it. He was, and still is, a sought after speaker at local, national and international conferences on autism and related topics. I've seen him hold an audience of 300 people

spellbound, after the doctor/researcher speakers had all but put the crowd to sleep....When I...speak to parents of children with autism, I remind them that 'in our day' there was almost no help. Even today, there is precious little assistance of any kind for the high-functioning adult with autism. My son is a gifted writer, a genuine wit, intelligent and knowledgeable and conversant about almost everything, and has a social conscience. He's good company, fun to be with and in general, a good and decent person...ask anyone who has had the pleasure of knowing him....Mark's life is not where he'd like it to be and he still has some overcoming to do...don't we all? He's a bit eccentric and sees himself as a tiny bit different with what he calls a low sociability quotient. Well many said that about Einstein."

(p22)

ATEC OUTCOMES

Using the ATEC the scores in Table 11, below, were obtained:

I. Speech/Language/Communication:	2
II. Sociability:	4
III. Sensory/Cognitive Awareness:	6
IV. Health/Physical/Behaviour:	3
Total ATEC Summary Score:	<u>15</u>

Table 11 ATEC Scores for Mark age c 30

This was a very difficult ATEC to score as there is not a lot of information on how Mark feels, for example, in rooms of people. But based on what information there is, the above figure supports the low-ish Sociability Mark himself noted. The higher sensory/cognitive score was initially surprising, but refers to ATEC questions relating to interactions with, and relationship to, the environment (work or social) and so support his own assumption, and that of his mother's, that he does not 'fit in'. Mark is clearly not a 'rat' designed for the 'rat-race' and was much happier in the New Orleans, non-conformist and more relaxing society.

DIAGNOSIS OF AUTISM

Mark was diagnosed as autistic by Leo Kanner who recommended institutionalising him. Despite this, his diagnosis was not followed up because he was high functioning. In the 1970s autism was still considered an emotional disturbance for psychiatric reasons. This caused Mark and his mother to reject the medical and psychiatric opinion. It was due to another mother that Pat recognised Mark's problems and the diagnosis 'resurfaced.' (p6)

WHAT IS MEANT BY RECOVERY?

Recovery is not itself referred to in this account. Mark's mother continues to refer to Mark as 'overcoming' his autism, which she perceives as an on-going process, partly made more difficult by the lack of understanding and of help offered in the 1970s. Mark himself uses the word 'success'and questions if he is a 'success story'. Clearly in many ways he thinks so, but as a young man who has expectations equal to those of any other person of his age and education, he feels less satisfied with his life. Interestingly, he attributes a diagnosis of autism as only a partial explanation for his problems.

ATTITUDE TO CURE

Cure is not mentioned in this account.

PROGRAMMES USED

Mark's mother specifically refers to the following as helpful:
    The drug/enzyme *Deaner*
    Behaviour modification in a school environment
    Dietary adjustments: high protein and low sugar (ADDH)
    AIT

NARRATIVE 8   DONNA

The final narrative given here is that of Donna Williams, the author of many books. Four of these together form her autobiography: *Nobody Nowhere* (1992); *Somebody Somewhere* (1994); *Like Colour to the Blind* (1999) and *Everyday Heaven* (2004). This narrative is a 'potted' summary, with the dates of each given where cited.

SUMMARY

Donna's is unlike the other narratives featured in that she did not have a loving or supportive parental home. On the contrary, her background was one of violence and emotional abuse from her mother, and violence, weakness and absenteeism from her father. Born in Australia in 1963, Donna was brought up for three years by her grandparents, because her mother did not want her and was mentally unable to relate to a child. Donna believes, however, that her mother's reaction to her, although extreme, was largely the result of her autism rather than its cause. She also suggests her father had many similar symptoms to herself. What is most shocking, is that not a single person, medical, educational or household friend, did anything to help Donna or to curb her mother's violence towards her. Although an uncle had hoped to adopt Donna, this did not come about. Donna recovered herself. Indeed, she describes her first book as a story of two battles: "… a battle to keep out 'the world' and a battle to join it" (1992, p. xvii). As a small child Donna displayed many behaviours and difficulties, such as a dislike of being hugged, an inability to look at people, increased social anxiety and fears, obsessive sensory stimulations. An early photograph shows poor eye contact and divergent vision. Her father described how Donna 'screamed all the time' in a way which did not sound like a baby crying normally, but 'sounded frightening, like you were sick and in pain'. She had been tested for deafness, early on, as she did not seem to hear people, but this came back negative. She was labelled 'emotionally disturbed'. After one week of school Donna was placed in a small class with 4 children who stayed together with the same teacher, 'a hard woman', for three years. They received special treatment, attending psychological guidance from time to time. Other children would be attracted to Donna as she would swing from a tree 30 feet up, climb monkey bars and do other 'mad things'. Donna loved letters and learned them quickly. Her reading was good but she did not understand the content:

"Although words are symbols, it would be misleading to say that I did not understand symbols. I had a whole system of relating which I considered 'my language.' It was other people who did not understand the symbolism I used, and there was no way I could or was going to tell them what I meant. I developed a language of my own. Everything I did, from holding two fingers together to scrunching up my toes had a meaning, usually to do with reassuring myself that I was in control and no-one could reach me, wherever the hell I was. Sometimes it had to do with telling people how I felt, but it was so subtle it was often unnoticed or simply taken to be some new quirk that 'mad Donna' had thought up."

(1992, p26)

Numbers were easier than coloured rods in mathematics, and fractions impossible. Donna also talked to herself incessantly, which others found annoying:

"I participated too much, but never in the right way."

(1992, p23)

And:

"Unless the task was something which I chose, I would drift off, no matter how hard I tried to be alert."

(1992, p38)

Instead, she loved to copy, create and order things, and enjoyed the set of encyclopaedias at home.

FEELINGS

As she reached puberty and began to grow up Donna became more concerned at the differences between her nature and other people:

"I was sure that I had feelings, but they did not seem to make the jump in my communication with others. I began to become increasingly frustrated, violent and self-destructive. This was made worse by expectations for me to behave like a young lady....I would talk and talk regardless of whether any of my classmates were listening or not. The teacher would get louder and so would I. She would send me to stand outside the classroom. I would go for a walk. She would tell me to stand in the corner. I would spit and shout, 'No!' She would try to come near me. I would arm myself with a chair like some sort of wild animal. She would shout. I would bring the chair crashing down or throw it across the room. I was no young lady."

(1992, p41)

HELP

In her final primary school year, aged 12, a new teacher, Mr Reynolds, spent a lot of time trying to understand how she felt and why she did the things she did. He did not emphasise intellectual ability alone, but brought in a record player and asked the children what they felt about different pieces of music, or what the songs were saying:

"Even when he raised his voice, I could still sense his gentleness. He was the first teacher at school to whom I had made an effort to explain what was happening at home, though I still never discussed what was happening within myself. His mood never changed. He never seemed to betray my trust."

(1992, p43)

During this year, Donna, already considered a 'weirdo', stood up for other unpopular children and gained the name: 'Zombie.' The violence of the other children towards new ones also increased with no control from the school. At the end of her primary years, Donna, whose attendance was poor, achieved 94, the highest score of any girl in the school, and only two points less than the top mark. The top prize was a scholarship to 'an expensive, private Grammar School'. Donna became a 'High School drop-out' three years later.

DELAYED DEVELOPMENT

Donna writes:

> "I always loved the saying, 'Stop the world, I want to get off!' Perhaps I'd been caught up in the spots and the stars at a time when other children kept developing and so I had been left behind. The stress of trying to catch up and keep up often became too much, and I found myself trying to slow everything down and take some time out."
>
> (1992, pp39-40)

These 'spots and stars' refer to the perceptual habits Donna experienced. She would focus on lights and other sparkly things, almost as a way of phasing herself out of the present moment. As she got older it became obvious to herself that Donna had some form of communication difficulty. At home she spent hours in front of a mirror, trying to call herself 'back'. Her ability to close out her abusive home-life, physical attacks from her mother and tormenting bullying from her brother, kept her sane. Donna's motivation to interact came from a desire to prove to others she was sane.

MUSIC

Donna was clearly musically gifted and, at this time, her mother bought a piano. She herself loved classical music and tried to teach Donna to play, but Donna had an ability of a different sort which had been present from birth:

> "I was not interested in sheet music. I began to hang about the house, and when she was not around I would play the piano, though always playing 'up in the tinklies'. I had created a beautiful piece of music. It was a classical waltz with melody and accompaniment."
>
> (1992, p66)

During adolescence, Donna spent any time at home in her room, turning up the music loudly, playing it over and over again and singing. If her brother came in she would scream at him, and her mother would then scream at Donna. She writes:

"One day my father came up to try to talk to me. It was the first time in my life that he had come into my room to talk to me. My father tried to make conversation with me. He asked me about the records I was listening to. I played some of the songs that had special meaning for me. I never explained why; this was one of the only real efforts I made at trying to share how I felt with anyone in my family."

(1992, p67)

At aged 15 Donna got a job button-hole making at a fur coat factory. Unfortunately she made buttons randomly in the fur coats:

"I hadn't realised the buttons were meant to go anywhere in particular."

(1992, p73)

Donna was placed in an array of different jobs in the company, which she preferred to school, ending up working in the storeroom.

PSYCHIATRY

Donna describes herself at 16 as 'completely cut off' from herself and afraid of being alone. She attempted suicide and while in hospital met Mary, a psychiatrist who reached out to her. A little later, Donna sought out Mary and began psychiatric sessions with her saying 'I just want to be normal' when asked what she wanted from these. Donna had by this time developed agoraphobia and a variety of facial tics:

"I needed a mother desperately, but could not remember ever having had one…I felt homesick for the home I'd never had because, as myself, I'd never been able to reach out freely."

(1992, p88)

Mary was the next choice. Reassuring Donna that she was not mad and was not going to be locked up, Donna was able to express her grief. She began to see Mary twice a week. Her visits continued for several years overall. Drugs were tried, which were based on Mary's diagnosis of schizophrenia, but these did not suit Donna and made her feel paranoid. Mary concluded that most of Donna's problems stemmed from the way other people responded to her.

BACK TO SCHOOL

At aged 18 – one year after beginning her sessions with Mary – Donna decided she wanted to return to school. Mary helped Donna in getting around the gaps in her past schooling and she was offered a place at college where she studied music, English, biology, philosophy, sociology and psychology – which she 'lived for'. She passed the first year with reasonable marks. Donna began to have nightdress, something she had experienced as a child, and requested Mary help her examine her past in order to understand it better. She also moved to the country which was within an hour's drive of college and learning to drive:

> "I had cats and I had a vegetable garden and a special place to put my piano."
>
> > (1992, p118)

At 21, she was relatively at peace living in the country but:

> "I still hadn't found the mythical sense of home which seemed to evade me."
>
> > (1992, p119)

A LOST DIAGNOSIS

It was at this time that Donna contacted her father to find out why she had been sent to a 'special school' as a young child. After initially evading her, he told her:

> "…'you were a little bit funny when you were small, but that was your mother's fault. There's nothing wrong with you.' 'But what was I like?' I pleaded. 'Please, I don't blame anyone…I really need to know. What was I like?' 'They thought you were autistic', my father said. I asked him why. 'Well, you wouldn't let anyone come near you and you talked a bit

funny. You used to go round saying what everyone else said all the time. But it's no wonder. Your mother used to hit you and shout at you all the time. No-one listened to the things you said.' he explained defeatedly."

(1992, p124)

Donna had no idea what autistic meant, assuming it just meant being withdrawn. She scoured the psychology books which were part of her university course, but they 'made no reference to autism'. Donna passed college, but was afraid of further education. Through a series of jobs and relationships with men who were largely parasitical, Donna drifted and travelled for a while. Working in a theatrical shop, dressing up in all the costumes, doubled their takings:

"The boss thought I was completely mad, but I suited the nature of the shop and my eccentricity seemed to attract customers."

(p142)

NATUROPATHY

Donna had always had asthma, but not developed muscular pains. Her concentration was poor and she began to lose herself in the town. She had tremors and would faint frequently. She visited a naturopath who referred her to an allergy specialist where she was advised to eliminate a number of foods from her diet. She was also prescribed vitamins, minerals and other natural health remedies. Donna immediately stopped fainting and the tremors from her hypoglycaemia reduced. Both clinics were privately run by pioneers in allergy/diet connections. One of the clinics was operated along Western medical lines, and the other was Eastern in its approach, adopting some of the methods of acupuncture. The diet was difficult to stick to, Donna having become addicted to sugar:

"After the first few weeks, my boss was amazed. I had begun to talk calmly and patiently to the customers, even when they became impatient with me. My mood-swings had become less pronounced and my ability to get along with people improved with it. I became a lot quieter, becoming far more peaceful and shy than boisterous, manic and aggressive."

(1992, p144)

WRITING

At 26, Donna left Australia and went to England where she began writing comedy scripts and was paid for them. She found a job as a secretary where she again encountered the term 'autism' and decided to find out what it really meant. By the age of 29, Donna had written the first part of her autobiography, purely as a form of self expression, although she nearly lost the manuscript. When it was complete, she went to the nearest hospital and asked for the psychiatry department where she told a professional she had written a book:

> "The response which came back was overwhelmingly supportive. My book had, it seemed, portrayed what is typically seen in autistic children, though I had no doubt done better at overcoming my difficulties than many ever would. I was encouraged to send the book to a publisher."
>
> (1992, p169)

Donna wanted to meet other autistic children, and found she could work with them to help them express themselves and reduce their coping behaviours. She met more professionals who supported her, and became an advisor and consultant for autistic children. She writes:

> "The way out (of autism) in complete contradiction to normal interaction is *indirect* in nature. In this way it is less all-consuming, suffocating and invasive. The child can then reach out, not as a confirming role-playing robot, but as a feeling, albeit extremely evasive, human being. The best approach would be one which would not sell short individuality and freedom for the parent's, teacher's or counsellor's versions of respectability and impressiveness."
>
> (1992, p180)

In her subsequent three autobiographical volumes, Donna continues what she describes as 'picking up the pieces after a war'. Book two: *Somebody Somewhere* is:

"…a story of learning how to build a somewhere out of a nowhere and a somebody out of a nobody."

(1994, Author's Note)

Donna describes her journey through a gradual exposure to the 'enemy' of 'the real world'. She was driven by a realisation that her own world represented, 'a spiritual body' which, although 'uncontaminated', was 'a gilded straightjacket of knots within knots within knots':

> "For my first three years I had moved freely within 'my world', observed incomprehensibly by 'the world' which moved around me….In my teens the walls had cracked and I was back for a few silent 'my world' months. But the walls had been patched up, not with bandages but with steel doors and solid concrete. At twenty-two I had met someone else like myself for the first time in my life. Without tools, I began to smash my way out with my bare hands but gave up. At twenty-five I had met another 'my worlder' and I was handed the tools. I attacked…with everything I had…the walls I had built so well."

(1994, p12)

Donna continued to work teaching special needs children. This experience gave her the opportunity to express her own understanding of the real world of the children in an environment which did not have any expectations. It made her angry on their behalf – a great motivating force. At the same time she continued to make contact with anyone who could explain her autism to her. In this way she met Dr Theo Marek. He assessed Donna using a variety of 'intelligence' tests to show the strengths and weaknesses of her thinking style. Donna had some areas where she functioned highly and others where she functioned well below these levels. This understanding relieved her and explained why she sometimes seemed an 'idiot' and at other times a 'genius'.

PARENTS

Donna writes with empathy about her parents, even though neither was much help to her in her early life. Her younger brother Tom was also unable to cope with her problems: 'Why do you always have to make us feel?' he demanded one evening. Donna discovered from her father that she had a female cousin, similar to herself, on his side of the family. She too was subjected to physical violence at home, which was how Donna's father accounted for both their problems. Donna does not accept this explanation. Rather, she believes it was easier for men to blame women – who were responsible for the childcare – than to take half themselves, as with a genetic problem. In her narrative, Donna chooses to avoid contact with her mother and clearly does not like her. Nevertheless, she shows compassion for her and other mothers of autistic children, who were clearly misunderstood at that time:

> "There were victims of this syndrome. But I think most of them were mothers. Autistic children probably suffered indirectly from the effects of societal ignorance and lack of community support. Mothers who did seek help from these kind of professionals were often scrutinised and left to feel shame and guilt. The other way open to mothers to handle the problem was to try to deny it or get rid of the evidence and institutionalise the child."
>
> (1994, p50)

Donna was accepted on a university course for teaching junior children and rented a flat nearby. She continued to see Dr Marek every few weeks in the hope that she would find 'rules I could carry around' to make sense of the world and which would apply in all situations. This gave her someone with whom she could understand herself as her 'own' world 'crumbled'.

SELF DEVELOPMENT

As an explanation for some of her problems, Dr Marek explained the effects of poor information processing in the brain. He validated Donna's experiences, accepting her for herself, in what she calls her 'straighten out Donna' sessions. Each session was 'a lesson in disarmament'. She also sometimes had difficulty extracting the specific meaning of other people's speech and, despite improvements, found 'the foreignness of it' frightening. She explored all this with Dr Marek:

> "Speech is changing too and this is scary. Before, I used to say everything people said back to myself and therefore got no closeness

through language (and my feelings weren't so scared...because I was by my perspective answering myself). Now I am hearing people directly most of the time – I am learning to feel like a part of things...and can really understand people....Also language is not a weapon like before. It is not a tool to hide behind or attack with. It is also not just meant for information....It is to help people communicate like equals."

(1994, p98)

She also wanted to understand emotions and was able to ask him what his voice meant when it changed, and to understand from him what people's responses to Donna sometimes meant. She did the same with concepts, taking him a list of those she did not understand, and wanted the 'world definitions.' She came to understand what 'friends' were. For example, as a teenager she thought these were 'people who touched you and used you.' Donna found her inner world 'dead around her feet' but for a long time lived in a state of not really being a part of the 'real world' either, and no longer being able to protect herself with her old 'my world' ways. Curiously, as her physical health increased, she became less able to retreat into the old inner world:

"The distinction between 'my world' and 'the world' implied that I had a choice to be in 'the world' or not. The realisation that autism stole this choice from me became the linchpin for the final shattering truce that would bring my world under glass crumbling to the ground. I learned that there never was and never had been a 'my world.'"

(1994, p113)

Donna continued to explore and understand being 'real' and found there was a wider choice of emotions than 'fear or indifference'. Her own expression in the mirror began to reflect 'a fragile realness'. Although she felt she was getting close to others mentally and 'even beginning to try to have more respect and consideration for their emotions and to listen more and talk on their topics'. However, dealing with her own social or touch problems was:

"...the most frightening of the lot."

(1995, p134)

TOUCH

For Donna, clothes were 'like armour'. At 27, Donna voluntarily touched a friend, to say 'I trust you' and because she wanted to. She did the same thing with a kind aunt, who broke down in tears.

> "A whole world seemed to be opening up to me. My roots settled into this new soil and I named it 'belonging'. My branches grew out wildly to meet the light around me and I named it 'sharing'. I blossomed and named this 'the freed expression of my true self'."
>
> (1994, p137)

Donna successfully completed a teacher training course. She also embarked on publicity tours for her book. During these hectic schedules, Donna experienced problems with her breathing and eating, largely as a result of adrenaline over-stimulation. Although she explained her needs for adjusting to these demands without succumbing to sensory 'overload', hypoglycaemia returned if Donna didn't eat every two to four hours. Having a break for Christmas was also difficult:

> "The sudden fall into a total lack of structure after days and days of appointments and involvement with people left me swimming in space so free it was overwhelming. In my pre-diabetic state I forgot something else. I totally forgot to eat."
>
> (1994, p175)

Donna's schedule was interspersed with meeting other autistic people. They gave her further insight into how she was similar to or different from them. She settled into a cottage with her own garden of weeds and played the piano, composing and writing.

MIRRORS

While deciding to buy a piano of her own, she met Ian, a man with high-functioning Aspergers and they decided to write music together. They eventually married. Ian and Donna were able to discuss autism together, which gave Donna more insights into how she was similar to and yet different from Ian:

"There was absolutely no suggestion that this person could be me. Intimacy had had no place in my life. It had had no place in 'my world', where closeness to people and touch were against the law."

(1994, p215)

Ian showed Donna that her reflection – Donna's constant companion – was not real. That she was just light bouncing from Donna to the glass;

"I was angry because the mirror was my last bastion of escape."

(1994, p225)

Three years after writing her first book and five months after meeting Ian, Donna writes:

"With Ian my emotions were reaching five on a scale of one to five. Both of us were afraid yet both of us knew we would be safe with each other, despite the inner battles and compulsions to run that came with fear of losing control in the face of big emotions."

(1994, p229)

At the end of her second book, Donna states that the most important thing she has learned is that 'Autism is not me' and 'I will control it. It will not control me'. In trying to understand her autism, and her urge to recover from it, she could not understand why she no longer tried to leave 'the world' and disappear as she had once done. There seemed to be a part of her that 'wanted to stay in the world'. This was the part that 'strained for mental images within the intrusive words flooding from this someone's mouth into my ears' and 'searched someone's eyes for something to make it care enough to turn from oblivion and clutch awareness'. Her dependency on mirrors remained; the presence of her reflection helping her feel 'safe and understood.' She writes:

"Without an internal feeling of personal connection to my body, I had felt I had little idea where all the bits were without seeing their reflection. Reflection somehow framed them, made them less disembodied, a visual disqualification from what perception in 'the world' told me."

(1999, p17)

Donna and Ian consulted an organization called B.I.R.D (brain injury, rehabilitation and development) recommended by a reader of Donna's first book. B.I.R.D offers an infant reflex inhibition programme through movement. Their assessment of Donna found:

> "...my brain had strayed off its development tracks or different parts of my brain hadn't gotten to know their neighbours or weren't on speaking terms."
>
> (1999, p33)

Infant reflexes are usually inhibited during the normal steps of child development, and at the same time, the sensory system integrates itself. Sue, the practitioner, thought Donna had:

> "...learned to compensate for what didn't happen right and that this put everything else out of sync and things had snowballed from there....If she was right it was an indication of something I had always felt but never been sure of. It would indicate that things had gone wrong before anyone ever laid a hand on me, that nobody's behaviour had caused my difficulties."
>
> (1999, p33)

Some reflexes had remained which would usually have been turned off at about 10 months, and others at about twelve months. These automatic reflex reactions were still reacting while Donna was 29. It was as though Donna 'was only half born'. Under stress, Donna would still self-abuse, hitting her face and herself without appearing to feel it. With Ian's help – he working on his own difficulties – she gradually began to connect with her body:

> "Lifting a leg and putting it down in front of me, it connected with feeling. I had recently connected with the feeling of leg but I still couldn't both feel it and use it consistently and simultaneously."
>
> (1999, p87)

Interestingly, her unconscious could do it – but conscious thought would interfere. There followed a period of intensive re-learning of their bodies, until they gained a mastery over the actions and intentions that had been missing all of their lives and, with this body mind re-connection, a sense of 'self':

> "Though it took me forever to work out the physical mechanics of getting undressed, turning a tap, and stepping into a bath and took Ian almost as long to monitor his own moves, these were our baths that we took and we didn't see our bodies get into them. We were our bodies."
>
> (1999, p91)

At the same time, Donna began to be able to hear her own voice and to know that it was herself talking:

> "All day I exercised moving each limb with intention as myself: Even operating an eye was a major effort, since it didn't listen easily to intention and had to be willing to open. I exercised the making of shapes with my mouth and the making of noises in my throat. I exercised getting my lungs and throat working together and then both of them at once with my mouth. Finally I heard the most beautiful sound in the world: my own whole connected voice….'My voice', I said, crying uncontrollably, 'Donna's voice.'"
>
> (1999, p92)

IRLEN FILTERS

Donna constantly struggled with bouts of physical illness as her immune-system reacted to food and other stimulation. Again, Donna visited a naturopath who discovered a variety of food allergies. DMG and food adjustments were prescribed, which helped Donna mentally in reducing the 'Big Black Nothing' moods as well as boosting her immune-system and digestion. Donna's headaches, tension, inability to sit still and tendency to read in dim light, were all helped by Irlen filters, for which she and Ian were assessed. *Scotopic Sensitivity Syndrome* – an inability to process certain light wavelengths – was diagnosed and individually assessed filters fitted to help correct the difficult ones. The effect was striking:

> "Still holding the filters over my eyes, I looked at Ian. 'Your face' I

stuttered. 'It's joined together'. The face I had mapped out bit by bit to form a constructed mental impression was now perceived for the first time as a whole. Here lay the path to trust. In a perceptual world where my body-sense, my auditory comprehension, my personality, and my sense of surroundings were fragmented, I finally could do more than struggle to imagine an un-fragmented whole. If only on one channel…that of vision…I no longer had to imagine. I could experience."

(1999, p159)

With their filter glasses they found the same effect in everything they looked at.

MARRIAGE

At 30 Donna married Ian and cast aside 'helping others' understand autism:

"…because there were so many who wanted the limelight and had as much to say. Besides, I was more than a walking bundle of autism and believed that no one person was necessarily a spokesperson for others just because they shared a label."

(1999, p190)

Donna writes:

"With Ian I learned about letting down walls, letting in pain as well as love, and through that, I better found the key to sharing my soul with others. Ian met me in my own world and together we built an island and each, in different ways, outgrew it. For my part, it was inevitable that I would build a bridge to the mainland."

(1999, p237)

The fourth book in Donnas' autobiography, published five years later in 2004, charts her return to Australia for a reunion with her brother, father and other family members, although not her mother whom she avoids 'for safety reasons'. Donna still found it hard to assert her own existence in the presence of someone else, 'to whom I could relegate the responsibility for my inexistence' but was able to tell those around what she needed them to do. She coined the term 'exposure anxiety' for the mixture of agoraphobia and sensory over-sensitivity which caused her physical symptoms whenever her anxiety levels rose, describing it as a means by which a battle ensued with herself to lure her back into the 'trap of expressive non-existence'. Much of this anxiety and its concomitant physical illness occurred when she was once again swept up in the promotional activities and demands of her publishers' schedule and television appearances. Very few things didn't trigger:

> "...the fight or flight responses in me which were so highly programmed to sense the slightest social invasion."
>
> (2004, p30)

Eventually, after trying a number of approaches, Donna found 'the old enemy' anxiety was eased almost completely by the drug *Risperidone* which was formerly used in schizophrenia, but now used for self-injurious behaviour and panic disorder.

RESCUING

Donna describes herself as about aged three under her adult skin, and that she relates more easily to lost or young animals: for example, cats rescued from homes, or people who need rescuing. After breaking-up with Ian, she ultimately met Chris. He was also in a relationship from which he needed rescuing. Although affectionately describing him as 'a male doormat' Chris provided the nurturing and calm she needed. For example, when Donna required surgery:

> "He treated me like a princess, snuggled up with me and read stories to me, made me cups of herbal tea and cooked Donna-safe dinners. I looked at this man and his warmth. He was everything I would ever have needed in a parent. With a simultaneous sense of self and other, with body connectedness, with an absence of total shutdowns and Exposure Anxiety that was at least much less than it ever used to be, I was the child I wished I had been."
>
> (2004, p155)

Donna asked Chris to marry her. Together they moved back to Australia where she continues to write and record music, paint, sculpt and live a life in keeping with her artistic and sensitive nature. (Her work can be seen at her website donnawilliams.com.). Donna also offers a controlled consultancy via her website and has continued to write books about autism and related subjects. Throughout the autobiographical four books, Donna gradually recovers a sense of her bodily self, through dance, self-expression (the arts), her friendships and then sexual relationships, slowly re-forming (or forming for the first time) cohesive concepts to match her feelings with her thoughts and physical reactions, until she is able to recognise a 'self' from which to relate with others without terror. Because of her abusive early years, there are clearly aspects of Donna's narrative which may not apply to everyone. Despite this, her story raises many interesting and helpful points on recovery from autism.

ATEC OUTCOMES

Table 12, below, shows ATEC assessment for Donna, following her fourth autobiography (2004):

I. Speech/Language/Communication:	0
II. Sociability:	0
III. Sensory/Cognitive Awareness:	2
IV. Health/Physical/Behaviour:	6
Total ATEC Summary Score:	8

Table 12 ATEC Scores for Donna age c 40

This score shows some sensitivity to the environment and to certain foods, as well as a slightly heightened need for control in her environment. Despite this, Donna would not now be diagnosed as autistic with any standard assessment.

DIAGNOSIS OF AUTISM

A diagnosis of PDD/autism was made by Dr Marek, an Australian psychiatrist when Donna was 25. Donna was considered autistic as a young child, but the source for this diagnosis is never given and she herself was unaware of it until early adult life.

WHAT IS MEANT BY RECOVERY?

Donna never uses the word recovery. She uses words such as 'overcome' and 'walls' being removed or 'crumbling'. However, her narrative is about the recovery of herself, and what she describes as a war between two worlds: inner autistic and the 'real world'. She states clearly that she is not her autism and it is 'not me'. However, Donna clearly feels she is different in some way and on her website uses the word 'autie'. This seems to be as an explanation for her differences.

ATTITUDE TO CURE

Cure is not a word mentioned in Donnas' narrative: In the next chapter, I outline each of the programmes cited in the narratives together with any research support they may have, and sources for further information.

PROGRAMMES USED

> Psychiatry – once in her teens for two years and again aged 26-27
> Naturopathic – sugar free diet and allergy removal
> DMG supplementation
> Sensory Integration: B.I.R.D
> Irlen Glasses
> *Risperidone*

CHAPTER 5

PROGRAMMES ADOPTED IN THE NARRATIVES

The programmes and methods mentioned in Chapter 4 fall into the following categories:

Dietary interventions

Immune system detoxification

Primitive reflex inhibition

Sensory programmes

Social interaction programmes

Pharmaceutical treatments

Homoeopathic medicine

Touch programmes

Each programme is described below with research for the most established programmes. At the end of each section I have given website addresses for more research and details of the programme, together with books and further information.

1   DIETARY INTERVENTIONS

Dietary adjustments are one of the most established ways of helping an autistic child. Bernard Rimland, for example, has researched and recommended dietary changes for over 30 years. Jepson and Johnson (2007) suggest diet forms a part of a 'multi-tiered' approach, where the steps are: 1) to replace what the child is missing, 2) remove what is causing harm, and 3) break the cycle of inflammation (especially in the gut). Similarly, Professor Paul Shattock, of the Autism Research Unit, University of Sunderland, UK considers them complementary to other interventions. The narratives describe how a change of diet frequently enabled another intervention, such as applied behavioural analysis, (ABA) to be more effective.

A)   A GLUTEN FREE/CASEIN FREE (GFCF) DIET

This diet is based on the 'opioid-excess theory' in which undigested foods act as toxic opiates to the brain. The two main foods implicated are gluten: the protein in wheat, oats, rye and barley, and casein: the milk protein found in all dairy foods. The autistic child is often 'addicted' to these foods, because of the opiate-effect they create, and will experience 'withdrawal' for a short period after a GFCF diet is commenced. While the body can be free of casein after 3 days, it can take up to 8 months for gluten to be fully eliminated from the system. Following a period on the GFCF diet, the child will usually begin to widen their interest in other foods. Karyn Seroussi writes of how her child began to speak following this diet, which meant the interactive programme (ABA) could progress:

> "When we had removed dairy products, Miles' silence had changed to language that consisted of a constant stream of meaningless jargon. It sounded like real language, or like a foreign language. His voice rose and fell melodically, but the words were unintelligible. After Miles mastered some basic imitation, such as clapping his hands, patting his head, and touching the table, Jill (his ABA worker) decided that it was time to begin verbal imitation."
>
> (Seroussi, 2002, p58)

To ensure sufficient calcium, nutritional supplements are given in place of cow's milk. In fact, Frank Oski, of John Hopkins Medical School, Paediatric Department, concludes from accumulated research that cow's milk is not ideal food for human children and may even interfere with protein breakdown. Dietary guidance on a GFCF diet provides full information on nutritional alternatives for sources of all the necessary nutrients for the child, and often includes recipes too. This is largely because these proteins are used so freely in modern food products that eliminating them completely can be an arduous task. However, unless they are completely removed from the diet, the child is unlikely to show any improvement. Sometimes, following complete elimination, the child will reveal 'hidden allergies' to other foods, which can also then be removed. Allergy testing, or the removal of a food for a period of time, before re-introducing it and watching for a reaction, is recommended for any 'suspect' foods. This is a rigorous approach but, because dietary approaches to helping autistic children are well established, there are plenty of companies providing specially prepared nutritional supplements, dietary guidance and support to parents.

RESEARCH

More studies have been carried out into the GFCF diet than any other diet. From 2001-2008, there had been 11 group studies; 2 surveys; 3 case studies and multiple anecdotal reports. Shattock stresses, however, that dietary interventions remain 'under investigation'. A recent appraisal (Shattock, 2008) of peer-reviewed studies found general support for the effect of a combined GFCF diet and for separate casein-free and gluten-free diets. One Norwegian study by Knivesberg of a combined GFCF diet showed improvements in social interaction, language use, sensory motor skills and a corresponding increase in peptide-like urinary material. Improvements had continued four years later. A second study testing a casein-free diet against placebo, found positive findings after eight weeks of the diet, with deterioration when casein was reintroduced. A gluten-free diet given for five months gave improvements in motor control (p=0.04); eating disturbances (p=0.01) and attention (p=0.02) plus improvements on thee out of six cognitive tests. Although there are also studies which did not seem to uphold the positive results, generally improvements in attention, concentration, communication, language, social interaction, motor-control and self injury have been found from removal of either or both of these substances in the diet. A GFCF diet was also found to reduce the elevated levels of white blood cells (mucosal eosinophils) associated with allergy reaction (Shattock, 2008). These effects seem greater and more pronounced in younger children and those more severely affected. There is also often an initial 'withdrawal' stage with transitory increased symptoms of clingyness, whinging, staring, dizziness, reduced mobility, increased urination/defecation, and flu like symptoms. If the diet lapsed, increases in 'spaced out' behaviour, hyperactivity and aggression might occur until the diet was re-adopted. Donna Gates has designed an extension of the GFCF diet in the *Body Ecology Diet* to additionally introduce fermenting foods:

"These essential foods lay down a critical foundation for establishing a healthy inner ecosystem in the intestinal tract and follow Nature's way of building strong, healthy immune and digestive systems. Soon after incorporating fermented foods into their diets, our autistic children are able to digest high quality fats essential to becoming well."

(Gates, 2018)

B)   ANTI-YEAST DIET

Many children with autism have a yeast overgrowth (*Candida Albicans*). This is frequently connected to 'Leaky Gut' (where inflammation of the stomach has damaged the lining rendering it porous, and so allowing particles of undigested food t pass through). See the Resource section for detailed information on the anti-yeast diet. For more serious effects additional interventions have been used (such as *Prednisone* the pharmaceutical drug described later) in conjunction with the diet.

C)   SPECIFIC CARBOHYDRATE DIET (SCD)

The mother of Campbell, whose narrative was given in Chapter 4, is a neurologist, whose clinic now treats autistic children with dietary approaches, describes excluding carbohydrate entirely from her child's diet. This allowed his gut to heal fully, removing the 'toxic fog' from his brain. Her experience led to her developing her own probiotic formula, and a book outlining the diet (see below), suitable for a range of problems originating with gut dysbiosis.

D)   VITAMIN B & MAGNESIUM SUPPLEMENTATION

Autistic children frequently suffer a loss of vitamin B6 due to 'leaky gut' syndrome. Vitamin B6 aids in nervous system function and a deficiency can cause disruption in many biochemical pathways. A leaky gut diminishes the ability of B6 to be absorbed, so it is considered important to directly supplement this vitamin:

"B6 and its metabolite P5P (pyridoxal 5-phosphate) are vital nutrients in the body. P5P is a cofactor in 113 enzymes, including those which form serotonin, dopamine, norepinephrine and other neurotransmitters essential to the nervous system. It is involved in the convertion of glutamic acid, an excitatory neurotransmitter, to GABA, an inhibitory one. Children with autism have an elevated glutamate-to-GABA ratio that can result in excitotoxic damage to brain cells. B6 deficiency might be one explanation for this."

(Jepson & Johnson, 2007, p192)

Following vitamin B6 supplementation, improvement in social engagement, decreased tactile sensitivity, improved language, more appropriate facial expressions, decreased stereotyped behaviours and obsessions, and improved eating habits have been documented. (Jepson & Johnson 2007, p93)

MAGNESIUM

Magnesium acts as a coenzyme in over three hundred enzyme reactions. It influences energy transfer in cells and is important for the formation and regulation of many proteins, nucleic acids (DNA) and neurotransmitters (dopamine, norepinephrine, serotonin, etc.). Magnesium is also necessary for the utilisation of essential fatty acids, the building blocks of the brain. It acts as a cell membrane stabiliser, regulates ion channels in the membrane and inhibits the glutamate NMDA (N-methyl-D-aspartate) receptor on brain cells, which allows calcium into the cell. A deficiency decreases blood flow to areas of the brain, which can lead to oxygen deprivation (ischemia) and cell death (apoptosis) (Jepson & Johnson, 2007). Hypersensitivity to noise is 'a common sign of magnesium deficiency' (Edelson & Rimland, 2006, p395). In 1997 researchers assessed magnesium levels in 116 children with ADHD using serum, red blood cells and hair samples. Magnesium deficiency was found in 95 per cent of these children. Almost 59 percent had low magnesium levels in red blood cells. Magnesium supplementation has been found to improve neurological symptoms." (Stock, 2005)

RESEARCH

Vitamin B6 is always given with Magnesium. Rimland cites 18 separate studies which have evaluated this treatment combination with autistic children. All found positive results. Rimland remarks that this is a remarkable result, as in drug-trials if a drug shows positive results in half the studies it is considered a success. Research in the use of these supplements began in 1966, when Heeley and Roberts reported that 11 out of 19 autistic children excreted abnormal metabolites in their urine when given a tryptophan load test. A single 30 mg tablet of vitamin B6 normalised their urine. In 1968, a German study showed behavioural improvements in 12 out of 16 children following doses of 11 mg-600 mg per day of vitamin B6. Three of these children spoke for the first time after the vitamin B6 was administered. Rimland was at that time sceptical of the results being claimed, but after contacting 1,000 of the parents on the Autism Research Institute (ARI) mailing list, he found 57 had experimented with high doses of B6 to good effect. He then ran a study on over 200 autistic children, using megadoses of B6, niacinamide, pantothenic acid and vitamin C, plus multi-minerals. These were all children living with their parents in the USA and Canada and each was medically supervised by the family's own physician. (He writes that over 600 had volunteered for the study, but most could not overcome their doctor's scepticism so could not participate). At the end of the four-month trial, 30-50% of the children showed significant improvements. B6 was found to be the most effective supplement. Some had minor side effects such as irritability, bed wetting and sound sensitivity, which cleared up when additional magnesium was given. Another study with vitamin B6 and magnesium led to better eye contact, less self-stimulation, more interest in the surrounding world, fewer tantrums, and more speech.

E)   DIMETHYLGLYCINE (DMG)

DMG is a natural, simple compound present in calcium pangamic acid, sometimes known as vitamin B15. It has no known negative effects and has been found to enhance the function of the immune system.

RESEARCH

In 1965 a Russian study by Blumena and Belyakova found DMG given as vitamin B15 led to considerable improvement in the speech of 12 children, diagnosed at that time as 'mentally handicapped'. Following this a psychiatrist, Allan Cott, visiting Moscow gave the supplement to a number of autistic children in his own practice. Many of these children also showed rapid speech improvement. Rimland writes:

> "Although speech is the most notable positive change in those children helped by DMG, behavioural improvement is also often reported."
>
> (Edelson & Rimland, 2006, p339)

Of a group of 39 autistic children aged 3-7 years, who took DMG for 3 months, 80% showed improvements in speech, eating, excretion, and general willingness. Some experienced a more active phrase, or slept less well, before improving again.

F)   5-HYDROXYTRYPTAPHAN (5-HTP)

This is derived from tryptophan which is an essential amino acid found in turkey and other foods. It is a precursor to serotonin, the neurotransmitter which is most usually abnormal in ASD. 5-HTP is able to cross the blood-brain barrier and so enter the brain. It helps to reduce nightmares, regulate sleep, blood and bowel function, and is a powerful ant-oxidant. In low doses 5-HTP can also help with attention difficulty.

G)   SUPER NU-THERA

This is a nutritional supplement specifically designed for people with autism. It is a balance of vitamin B6, magnesium and other nutrients, taken in powder, liquid or pill form. Many parents mention Super Nu-Thera in their narratives.

H)   ESSENTIAL FATTY ACID SUPPLEMENTATION

Essential fatty acids (omega 3, 6 and 9) comprise over 60% of the fats in our brain, acting like 'bricks' to create the walls of the cell membrane. In a deficiency, different fats must be used, which create an insufficiently sealed wall in which 'bricks' are likely to fall out or leak. These bricks must be regularly replenished for brain function to be either possible or efficient. Due to the lack of omega 3 (found in oily fish and some plant oils) in the western diet, deficiencies in the general population are common. Supplementation has been found helpful in feeding the brain structure in a number of different developmental and learning areas, in particular in dyslexia and ADHD (Stordy & Nicholl, 2000).

RESEARCH

A recent study of 20 children with ASDs, by Gordon Bell (Bell, 2004) at the University of Stirling found that children with autism break down fatty acids more rapidly. A larger study is currently underway. He states:

> "We have already seen a connection between omega levels and schizophrenia and dyslexia...If cell function in the brain is changed, the behaviour of the brain will change as well. In exactly what way we do not know, but...it could be a first step to uncovering some of the mysteries of autism."
>
> (Harrell, 2005, p1)

Dr Sydney Baker has found between 10-50% of autistic children with seizures improve in comparison with 90% of hyperactive children. He believes ASD is:

> "...a tough population to deal with in terms of their behaviour, attention and aggression."
>
> (Stordy & Nicholl, 2000, p226)

Parents of eighteen children with autism given fish oil supplements for six months, described improvements in overall health, cognition, sleep patterns, social interactions and eye contact (Bell, 2004). Unfortunately, this was not a double-blind study. In a double-blind, randomised, placebo controlled pilot study, Amminger and colleagues gave 1.5 g/d of omega-3 fatty acids (.84 g/d eicosapentaenoic acid, .7 g/d docosahexaenoic acid) to 13 children (aged 5 to 17 years) with autistic disorders accompanied by severe tantrums, aggression, or self-injurious behaviour. The outcome measure was the Aberrant Behaviour Checklist (ABC) at 6 weeks. They report:

> "We observed an advantage of omega-3 fatty acids compared with placebo for hyperactivity and stereotypy, each with a large effect size. Repeated-measures ANOVA indicated a trend toward superiority of omega-3 fatty acids over placebo for hyperactivity. No clinically relevant adverse effects were elicited in either group....The results of this study provide preliminary evidence that omega-3 fatty acids may be an effective treatment for children with autism."
>
> (Amminger, et al., 2007)

These authors also found reduced hyperactivity and stereotypy (repeated movements like hand-flapping) in children who received 1.5 gm of fish oil per day, as compared to children who received placebo. In one case study, a child with autism given 540 mg of the omega-3 fatty acid EPA per day over a four week period experienced a complete elimination of anxiety about everyday events, as reported by his parents and clinician. They also described an improvement in his overall quality of life. The mother of a seven year-old boy with ASD provides another case example. The child had a severe language disorder as well as tantrums, anger and crying episodes. She reports:

> "The fish oil tablets seemed to wake him up and unlock something. His speech went from a two-word level to seven-word sentences and he's now even reading the Oxford school series. From scribbling in black he painted a rainbow with bright colours. I don't have wallpaper in my hall any more, just all of his pictures. I started to see a person coming out. He now wants to know what's going on and is making his own decisions. I'd waited four years for him to say 'mummy I love you' and put his arms around me. He used to be very inert at school, taking out his frustrations at home. But his behaviour changed dramatically: The first thing people say to me

now, is 'isn't he a happy boy?' He never had empathy, but now if he hits out he will turn around and say 'I didn't want to do that mummy, I'm sorry'. It's as if he was at last at peace with himself."

(Bates, 2006)

FURTHER INFORMATION ON DIET AND NUTRITIONAL SUPPLEMENTS

The Autism Network for Dietary Interventions has information, books and recipes for a range of diets for children with leaky gut at:
    www.autismndi.com and/or: www.dietarysupport.com
Advice and parent feedback on Donna Gate's diet can be found at:
    www.bodyecology.com/autism.php
For the Anti-Yeast Diet see:
    www.nutritioninstitute.com.
Details of Natasha Campbell-McBride's book and health products are available below and at
    www.medinform.co.uk

BOOKS

The following contain dietary advice for children with ASDs:
    Feast without Yeast by B. Semon and L. Kornblum (1999). Dr Semon is a child psychiatrist, nutritionalist and parent of a son with autism. It contains over 225 yeast and sugar-free recipes. Most are also gluten and casein free.
    Gut and Psychology Syndrome by N. Campbell-McBride (2004). It describes the gut as the source of many diseases, and the importance of the central gut-brain connection: contains strict carbohydrate recipes and resources.
    Facing Autism by L. Hamilton (2000). Written by a mother whose son, Ryan, fully recovered from a diagnosis of autism.
    Healing the New Childhood Epidemics: Autism, ADHD, Asthma and Allergies by K. Bock and C. Stauth (2007).
    Unravelling the Mystery of Autism and Pervasive Developmental Disorder: A Mother's Story of Research and Recovery by K. Seroussi (2002).

Climbing out of Autism One Bite at a Time by M. Cheney (2001). Written by a mother who recovered her son from a diagnosis of autism.

Research on nutritional supplementation, including parent ratings, is given in *Recovering Autistic Children* by Edelson and Rimland (2006) and at ARI:
www.autism.com
Additional sources for nutrients used in the narratives are:
www.kirkmanlabs.com
www.behealthy.org.uk
Fatty acid supplementation and research can be found at:
www.autism.healingthresholds.com/therapy/essential-fatty-acids

2   IMMUNE SYSTEM DETOXIFICATION

Substances that are initially harmless can become toxic during normal metabolism. Any imbalance between the oxidation process and the counter-process which renders free radicals harmless (redox) can create oxidative stress. This and/or a shortage of the anti-oxidants required can result in tissue damage. Anti-oxidants include vitamins A, C, E and B6 and the minerals zinc, selenium and sulphate. Like every system in the body, the immune system depends on adequate supplies of the right vitamins, minerals and fatty acids.

A)   METHYLCOBALAMIN (METHYL-B12)

Some independent researchers have found abnormalities in the methylation cycle in children with autism. Methylation is the critical metabolic pathway which produces the precursor molecules for detoxification and anti-oxidation. Methyl-B12 was an accidental discovery made by James Neubrander in 2002. By adding injectable methyl-B12 to the dietary schedule of children with autism for a period of 3-4 months the child's methylation capacity and anti-oxidant potential can be significantly increased. Jaquelyn McCandless, a medical practitioner and author, describes methylcobalamin (methyl-B12) as one of the:

"…most important treatment modalities to come out of the strong focus on biomedical and metabolic aspects in autism in recent years."

(McCandless, 2009)

RESEARCH

Methyl-B12 is estimated to be effective in 80-90% of children with ASDs. Using parent-feedback surveys, ARI found the primary response to be improved executive function, speech, language, socialisation and emotion expression. Methyl-B12 can be given orally or by injection. It is suitable for all ages with a suggested dose of: 25mg.ml at 64.5 mcg/kg every three days. Although some side-effects have been noted, McCandless states:

"…the children with the most side-effects who stay the course are the ones who make the most recovery."

(McCandless, 2009, p425)

Within two-six months the majority of side effects have disappeared while improvements continue. Dr Neubrander notes that one effect of this treatment can be the child mouthing objects, as previously inactivated peripheral nerves 'wake up'.

NUTRIGENOMICS

The methylation pathway is the central treatment aspect in a sophisticated programme designed by Dr Amy Yasko, initially to treat those with chronic fatigue but more latterly autism/ASD. Working as a pioneer in the field of DNA/RNA based diagnostics and therapeutics Yasko was a consultant to the medical and research community for over eighteen years. Her focus on RNA began more than thirty years ago when she isolated single copy RNA messages from transformed cells on RNA levels of the c-myc cancer oncogene, and she has been active in the field ever since. She designed *Nutrigenomics* as a personalised programme which takes into account the genetic inheritance of the individual, (including epigenetic mutations and tags) and then designs a programme to fit the multi-factorial pathway of that individual. It therefore embraces an allostatic load concept and an ecological awareness that different substances interact with particular genes to decrease health risk. And that these will vary between individuals. As such:

> "...it is possible to utilize combinations of nutrients, foods and natural nucleotides to bypass mutations and restore proper pathway functioning."
>
> (Yasko, 2014, p35)

In this way the 'genetic risk' is lowered. The focus of *Nutrigenomics* is on the methylation cycle as this is the way in which genes are 'turned on and off' by environmental factors, including nutrition. This cycle includes methionine, and foliate, and is dependent upon sufficient vitamin B12 and BH4 (tetrahydrobiopterin) which is essential for making serotonin and dopamine (both dysfunctional in autism/ASD). Although not specifically mentioned in any of the narratives cited earlier, this programme has developed a substantial application in autism/ASD. She writes:

> "This program began with adults, was adapted to help those with autism, and now has come full circle to be used by children through adults for a range of health conditions. This program is not just about autism; it is about health and well-being. I believe that autism, as with other chronic conditions such as chronic fatigue, fibromyalgia, ALS, MS, among others are multi-factorial conditions. Underlying genetic susceptibility, along with exposure to infectious agents, toxic chemical and the stress of lifestyle all contribute to complex health issues. Understanding the contributing factors gives you the information needed to pick the right tools to get back on a path to health and well-being. Every child with autism has a parent, a grandparent and siblings, and hopefully will have children of their own someday. The predisposing genetics come from somewhere. According to current statistics the rate of autism is one in fifty. In other words, with a rate of 1 in 50, every one of us has a relative, a child, an uncle a cousin or a brother that may be on the autism spectrum. Even if those same related genetics are not manifesting as autism they may be a factor in Parkinson's, CFS, MS, Lupus or

some other inflammatory condition. Recognizing that this is not just about autism, and realizing that the genetics are inherited in a familial pattern, means every single person in today's society needs to be thinking about charting their personal road map to health."

(Yasko, 2017a, Website)

PERSONAL NARRATIVES

There are many personal narratives of this programme on the Yasko websites. The following are a few examples in relation to autism/ASD:

"Dr. Amy Yasko is the hope, the small flickering light, and the quiet in all this chaos of mainstream thoughts on autism…I as a mother of a very special girl am blessed to have crossed paths on the internet and through groups to happen across her breakthrough work…and make other choices for our treatment protocol…the lights are on and I'm always home now! Thank you for loving all our children!"

"Dear Dr. Amy, All our thanks goes to you, your family, staff and of course cyber mums! Your tireless work and encouragement is moving us forward and gives us and our brave children a chance to enjoy life and be truly thankful for every single moment we share together, for every new word we hear, for every new achievement that would not be possible without you! We love you Dr. Amy!"

"Federico clinically completely recovered from the autism, we are so grateful to Dr. Amy and her team that they saved Federico's life."

"Never say Never to MY boy! This from my boy, the one they told me would probably never talk again, never walk properly again and never be able to hold a pen. Eight years later, I wish those doctors were here to listen to him and to read his stories and to watch him run."

"Dr. Amy's protocol saved my son Andrew, plain and simple. Her brilliant protocol has done absolute miracles for him. A few months before turning 2, Andrew was diagnosed with Autism, and today, the few people I tell about his prior diagnosis are completely shocked, stunned and usually say I didn't know you could fix Autism. Dr. Amy brought him back to me and the words thank you could never suffice. In March of 2007, my 19 month old son, who had previously been a completely normal child, regressed into Autism. We first tried a biomedical protocol that was not based on individual genetics, and thus it was not tailored to each child's specific needs. Theirs was a try everything on every child and see if it works approach. Not only was this not helpful, due to some specific mutations my son has, some of the amino acid supplements they gave him actually made him so much worse. I then found Dr. Amy's protocol and it made so much sense to test genetics first, and then see what has to be corrected biochemically, specific to Andrew. I didn't know for sure if it was going to work, but her approach seemed to make so much sense."

(Yasko, 2017b, Website)

RESOURCES

Amy Yasko gives away free books (as downloads) articles and information on this programme. She also analyses free of charge the self-test assessments for identifying which genetic elements are involved in the individual's methylation pathway, which are available on her websites. These can be found at:

http://www.dramyyasko.com/resources/

https://www.scribd.com/lists/4410144/Articles-by-Dr-Amy

Her previous research, on which this programme is based, can be found at:

http://www.dramyyasko.com/about-us/resume/

B)   HEAVY METAL DETOXIFICATION: CHELATION

Heavy metals include lead, mercury, antimony, arsenic, cadmium, aluminium, tin, chromium, mercury and platinum. All have known toxic effects. Autistic children have particular difficulty metabolising these. Mercury is known to be more neuro-toxic than lead, affecting the developing brain, and its presence in the environment is rising. A paper by Dr John

Green provides an overview of detoxification through chelation. Green has been treating autistic children since 1999. He writes:

> "Chelation works like the body's natural sulphur defence system, when sticky molecules bind toxic metals to sequester and eliminate them. The commonly used chelators in autism treatment are DMSA, DMPS, and EDTA. All these three are effective for removing lead and cadmium, while DMPS and DMSA are also effective for mercury, tin and arsenic. EDTA is also somewhat effective for aluminium. EDTA and DMSA are available over the counter in the US, as is DMPS in several western European countries."
>
> (In Edelson & Rimland, 2006, p433)

Toxic metal overload is tested by the 'chelation challenge' or through hair analysis. The chelator creates a non-toxic complex of the chelator and the metal, making them water soluble and enabling their excretion in urine and stools. DMSA was approved as a chelator by the FDA in 1991 for the treatment of lead toxicity in children. It is also effective against mercury, arsenic, copper, antimony and nickel. It has low toxicity and any side-effects are mild and transient. Some common adverse effects are gastro-intestinal cramps, diarrhoea, nausea and vomiting, a transient and reversible increase in liver function markers and sore skin symptoms such as rash, hives and itching (Jepson & Johnson, 2007). DMPS does not cross the blood-brain barrier. Chelators can be given orally or rectally, and DMPS and Calcium EDTA can also be given intravenously. A urine test timed to follow the administration of the chelator will indicate treatment outcomes. Choice of chelator is made to suit the individual, as tolerance of the chelator must be balanced against benefit. A gradual and slow process is therefore recommended.

SAFETY OF CHELATION

In 2005, Rimland responded to media reports of the death of a boy linked to chelation. The child had been prescribed the wrong drug by his doctor (*Disodium*) in place of Calcium Disodium (EDTA). Nevertheless, this provided:

"...a golden opportunity to crow about 'quackery', foolishness and impressionable parents 'grasping for straws' and the dangers of 'unproven alternative treatments for autism.'"

(Edelson & Rimland, 2006, p430)

Although a report was issued by Mary Jean Brown, of the Centres for Disease Control and Prevention, stating doctor-error had killed the boy, none of the doctors retracted their comments. There have been no deaths from chelation and no evidence that it is unsafe when practised competently – as with any other health practice. In contrast, Rimland notes the documented dangers of frequently prescribed drugs for autism including *Risperdal*, *Ritalin*, antidepressants and other psychotic medications (see a later section of this chapter for information on some of these).

RESEARCH

Because of its high rates of effectiveness in removing lead (its original medical history), chelation is frequently recommended for children with autism, although studies are quite rare and have proved controversial. However, since 1967 the ARI has been collecting 'Parent Ratings of Behavioural Effects of Biomedical Interventions' which has over 25,000 responses to date. Chelation is a recent addition to the interventions but of the 479 parents who had responded in 2006, 75% reported 'Good' results with chelation (Edelson & Rimland, 2006, p430). This is the highest 'Good' response reported for any of the 88% biomedical interventions, including 53 medical drugs, rated by the parents. Clearly, only those children with measurable high heavy metal levels should undergo chelation, but it does appear beneficial where appropriate. Jepson concludes:

"My experience and that of many other physicians treating autistic children is that children with autism improve with chelation therapy, and that it is generally safe and well tolerated if done under appropriate medical supervision with mineral supplementation and monitoring of potential side effects. Chelation is promising, but needs to be further explored with quality research."

(Jepson & Johnson, 2007, p233)

C)   HEALING 'LEAKY GUT'

70-80% of children with autism have gut inflammation problems ('leaky gut'). This results in a number of problems including opioids reaching the brain, and dysbiosis – an imbalance in the micro-flora of the gut tract. Injury to the bowel wall contributes to nutritional deficiencies and allows harmful inhabitants of the gut, normally kept under control by a healthy micro-flora, to run riot. These include candida and clostridium, for example. Treatment for rebalancing the gut using probiotics to replace lost essential gut flora is mentioned in many recovery narratives. Probiotics have been found to shorten the duration of acute diarrhoea in children, (Isolauri, et al., 1991) and eradicate *Clostridium difficile* infections that have withstood repeated antibiotic use (Biller, et al., 1995).

PROBIOTICS

Lactobacilli, Bifidobacteria and Enterococci are the most commonly used probiotic lactic acid bacteria. They are known to produce molecules that fight pathogenic bacteria, lower the pH of the stool and form oxidants which help prevent the colonisation of harmful bacteria. Probiotics are added to food, or taken as supplements. They are living, are therefore stored in a cold environment, and subsequently have a shelf life. Laboratories can test stools for the presence of bacteria and guide the selection of appropriate supplementation, and monitor progress. In the case of antibiotic use, Jenson and Johnson use probiotics as a matter of course to re-colonise the autistic child's gut.

FURTHER INFORMATION

ARI continue to gather parent feedback on this and other biomedical treatments. This is available on their website at:
    www.autism.com

Dr Neubrander's work can be found at:
    www.drneubrander.com

BOOKS

An explanation of immune system detoxification and 'leaky gut', including the mechanism in treatment, is given in the following:

> *Changing the Course of Autism: A Scientific Approach for Parents and Physicians* by B. Jepson and J. Johnson (2007)
> *Children with Starving Brains, 4th Edition,* by J. McCandless (2009)

Amy Yasko's approach is described in:
> *Feel good Nutrogenomics: Your roadmap to health.* A. Yasko. (2014)

3   PRIMITIVE REFLEX INHIBITION: THE ROLE OF PRIMITIVE REFLEXES

In the first few weeks of foetal development a number of reflexes emerge. These are genetically innate survival based movements, possessed by all animals in some form. In human infants they are known as the 'primitive reflexes'. During the first two years of life these primitive reflexes are gradually replaced (inhibited) by 'postural (adult) reflexes' through the developmental movements made by the infant and toddler. Whereas these adult postural reflexes are controlled by the cortex of the brain, infant primitive reflexes are orchestrated by the brain stem. In some cases primitive reflexes remain uninhibited. Neurologically speaking, this means a person can remain in a state of arrested or incomplete development. An uninhibited reflex can significantly impact on gross and fine motor skills, attention, concentration, communication, emotions and behaviour. Under pressure, consequence of this may be neurological overload, resulting in increased levels of frustration, anger or emotional sensitivity. If these reflex dysfunctions can be detected and treated, the person is released from this delayed and confused developmental state, able to cope better, develop further and to learn.

RESEARCH

Paul Teitlebaum and his colleagues have postulated that movement disturbances of infants can be interpreted as reflexes 'gone astray' and can be indicators for a later diagnosis of autism. This was based on earlier work (Teitelbaum, et al., 1998) which showed infants identified later as autistic showed a characteristic cluster of movement patterns at aged 4-5 months. In particular the asymmetric tonic neck reflex (ANTR) may persist too long with these infants, and/or the lack of a head-verticalisation reflex in response to body tilt, which does not appear in a sub-group of 'autistic–to-be' infants at the appropriate time. Further work connecting reflex disorders with ASD is described by Sally Blythe (Blythe, 2006).

A)   BRAIN INJURY REHABILITATION PROGRAMME (BIRD)

This was established by Barbara Pheloung in 1982. The BIRD centre in Chester offers a treatment programme for Organic Brain Dysfunction. This focuses on abnormal neurological reflexes, unresolved laterality, eye muscle dysfunction, abnormal motor developmental patterns and perceptual difficulties. BIRD uses a defined set of physical movements to inhibit primitive reflexes. These replicate the movements that would be made by a developing child. Such movements act as 'feedback' to the brain, providing the information it needs to inhibit the primitive reflex and enable the later postural reflex to take over. They provide a 'second chance' to pass through the natural developmental patterns. The movement patterns required are taught to the individual or carers. These take about 30-60 minutes each day to carry out. The length of treatment required varies from person to person: generally patients with learning difficulties are treated over the course of a year, whereas people with more severe types of brain injury can be treated for up to four years. Three review sessions ensure that the programme enables modifications to be made as progress occurs and provides feedback on the effectiveness of the programme. After one year, a second full assessment takes place. A report is provided and further recommendations made. These might be a discharge from the BIRD programme or a further year of treatment; a decision which is taken for each person with their families and the staff together. The BIRD programme is seen as entirely complementary to other approaches and often enables these to be more effective as it establishes a 'normal neurological basis' upon which other programmes can build. (B.I.R.D, 2017, *Website*)

FURTHER INFORMATION

The original work on primitive reflexes and developmental problems was carried out by Dr McGowan, who pioneered the 'Developmental Reflexive Rehabilitation' approach. Full details of the BIRD programme can be found at:

www.birdcharity.org.uk/work/neurological-reflexes/

BOOKS

Two books on this approach are:

An Organic Basis for Neurosis and Educational Difficulties: a new look at the old minimal brain dysfunction syndrome, by S. Blyth and D. McGowan (1979) and:

Developmental Reflexive Rehabilitation by David McGowan (1990.

B)   INSTITUTE OF NEURO-PHYSIOLOGICAL PSYCHOLOGY (INPP)

Sally Blyth's own work on primitive reflexes is extensive. She also works with a colleague of McGowan, Peter Blyth, at the Institute of Neuro-Physiological Psychology (INPP) also in Chester but independent of BIRD. The BIRD movement programme varies slightly from that of the INPP, although both focus on movement as feedback inhibitory methods. More information is available at:

www.inpp.org.uk

And:

www.primarymovement.org/research/index.html

BOOK

Movement-based advice for parents with young children can be found in:

What Babies Really Need, by Sally Goddard-Blythe. (2008) Hawthorne Press.

C)   HOLISTIC NEUROLOGICAL PROGRAMME (HANDLE)

Movement also forms the major part of HANDLE: (the Holistic Approach to NeuroDevelopment and Learning Efficiency):

> "The HANDLE Institute provides an effective, non-drug alternative for identifying and treating most neurodevelopmental disorders across the lifespan including Autism, ADD, ADHD, Dyslexia and Tourette's syndrome. HANDLE incorporates research and techniques from many disciplines. It includes principles and perspectives from medicine, rehabilitation, psychology, education and nutrition. It is founded on an interactive, developmental model of human functioning. The HANDLE Institute International, LLC offers clinical services, community information, and professional training programs."
>
> (Handle Institute, 2009, *Website*)

This programme was developed by Judith Bluestone, who herself recovered from autism. Her approach is based on providing the necessary ingredients of diet, lifestyle and stimulation to allow the brain to repair and heal the individual. Bluestone also combines this with homoeopathic medicine (see later section).

RESEARCH WITH HANDLE

A study by Lewis (2006) and colleagues at Harborview Medical Center, Washington, USA, by the American Society of Neuroimaging in partnership with the HANDLE Institute, with individuals with traumatic brain injury (TBI), found benefits on a range of tests and a possible role for the hindbrain (vermis and cerebellum). While this study was not specifically with ASD it showed that a movement-based programme may induce aspects of brain recovery and suggested a possible mechanism for this.

FURTHER INFORMATION

The website for the Handle Institute in Seattle provides full details of this approach at:

www.handle.org

BOOK

HANDLE is described fully in:

> *The Fabric of Autism: Weaving the Threads into a Cogent Theory*, by Judith Bluestone (Bluestone, 2005). In this book Judith Bluestone presents her own personal view of autism, as well as her HANDLE programme.

4   SENSORY PROGRAMMES

Sensory programmes are frequently mentioned in the narratives of individuals with ASDs. These range from focussing on single senses, to integrating sensory information. Three different programmes of this type and given below.

A)   AUDITORY INTEGRATION TRAINING (AIT)

AIT was developed by Guy Bérard, a French otolaryngologist, based on the work of Alfred Tomatis. It has been found beneficial in several conditions including autism, dyslexia, ADHD and hypersensitive hearing. Bérard thought that sound sensitivity and consequent behavioural disturbance could result from distortions in hearing. He believed his therapy could not be called a 'cure' for autism, but many could benefit greatly from the treatment. Because there are different sorts of autism, different means of helping the individual will probably be required. Bérard felt that an auditory intervention could be developed which would be similar to physical therapy for the hearing mechanisms. Over a 5-year period he developed the *AudioKinetron Earducator*. The device consists of a machine containing a number of electronic elements, including a variety of auditory filters. The child/adult wears earphones while specially selected music is played into the machine. The machine filters and amplifies the music as necessary and feeds the resulting modified music to each ear independently. Volume is set as loud as is possible without discomfort. The treatment comprises thirty-minute sessions twice a day for ten days. Bérard believed that AIT would bring about a re-education of the hearing process in those children whose autism was connected with a hearing dysfunction.

RESEARCH

In a recent review of twenty eight AIT studies, twenty three conclude this programme benefited various population subgroups (including children with other developmental problems). Three studies claim to show no benefit over that seen in a control group while two studies report rather ambiguous or contradictory results. The Autism Research Institute (ARI) concludes:

> "Considering the great difficulties in both providing a credible placebo treatment and assessing improvement in the subject populations, these results are quite encouraging. The balance of the evidence clearly favours AIT as a useful intervention, especially in autism."
>
> (Autism Research Institute, 2010, *Website*)

ARI has a summary of research studies from 1993-2001 on their website at: www.autism.com

Two more recent studies are:
> Simpson, R.L. et al. (2005) Physiological/biological/neurological interventions and treatments. In: *Autism spectrum disorders: interventions and treatments for children and youth.* Thousand Oaks, CA: Corwin Press, pp. 169-205.
>
> Sinha, Y. et al. (2004) *Auditory integration training and other sound therapies for autism spectrum disorders.* The Cochrane Library

WEBSITE

Guy Bérard's website is at:
> www.drguyberard.com

AIT, USA

Information on auditory training in the USA for special needs is at:
> www.auditoryintegrationtraining.co.uk

Availability of AIT practitioners by State is given at:
> www.aitinstitute.org/ait_usa.htm

AIT UK

The following all offer AIT in the UK:
National Light & Sound Therapy Centre, London:
 www.light-and-sound.co.uk
Tracy Alderman, Shropshire:
 www.TracyAldermanait.co.uk
The Sound Learning Centre, London:
 www.thesoundlearningcentre.co.uk

BOOKS

In 1982 Bérard published *Audition égale comportement.* The book was translated into English in 1992 as *Hearing Equals Behaviour.*

> *Sound of a Miracle* by A. Stehli (1992) is the narrative of Georgia, daughter of the author and written about her experience with AIT, which brought about a complete recovery from autism.
>
> *Sound of Falling Snow* (Stehli, 2004) is a compilation of personal narratives by others who have used AIT.

B)   IRLEN LENSES

Donna Williams and her first husband Ian both benefited from Irlen glasses. 70% of the information an individual receives is through the eyes and must be correctly interpreted by the brain. Any problem in the way the brain processes information can cause difficulties in the general ability to function. Irlen glasses aim to correct those of the perceptual sense, allowing the other senses to function better and avoiding overload. Irlen uses coloured filters worn as glasses to reduce or eliminate perceptual difficulties. The colour is assessed for the individual and will vary from one to another. The correct glasses appear to change the rate at which information is processed by the brain and allow the brain to integrate, identify and process information. Improvements in integration of senses; perception; ability to respond; body awareness; spatial awareness; eye contact; communication and self-control were noted.

RESEARCH

Brain scans of readers with ASDs taken with and without Irlen glasses have shown a difference in sensory profile, as shown in Figure 14, below:

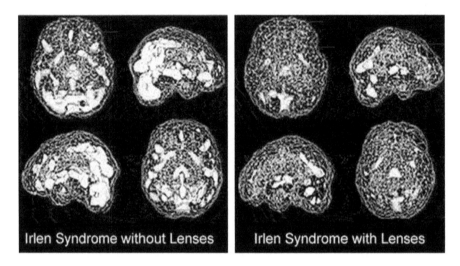

Figure 14 Differences in Sensory Activity with Irlen Glasses.
Irlen East, *Website* (2011)

This scan is taken from research by Daniel Amen at the Irvine Medical School, California. The illustration on the left shows areas of overload and the right, the same reader with glasses, and reduced overwhelm. A selection of research papers on Irlen glasses can be found at:

www.irlen.com/index.php?s=research

More information on Irlen and ASDs is available at:

www.irleneast.com/autism_aspergers.htm

IRLEN CENTRES

For the USA, Canada, South and Central America, Asia, Europe, Africa and Australasia:

www.irlen.com/index.php?s=findclinic

For the UK:

www.irlenuk.com

BOOK

Sensory Perceptual Issues in Autism and Asperger Syndrome by Olga Bogdashina (2003) contains a chapter on sensory approaches, including Irlen, AIT and sensory integration (below) plus a theoretical background.

C)   KAPLAN'S VISION THERAPY

This therapy was developed by Dr Melvyn Kaplan. It was not specifically mentioned in the narratives chosen for this book but has been found helpful with other children with autism. Dr Kaplan related the notion that vision is largely a learned perceptual facility, to the difficulties faced by children with autism. Ambient vision results from processing local motion cues into global motion. This is a complex perceptual task as real world scenes contain multiple overlapping objects which can be moving in different directions. Many individuals with ASDs suffer from visual perceptual dysfunction. They may demonstrate normal visual acuity on standard eye chart tests. But visual perception, as opposed to sight, is a process of receiving, integrating and interpreting visual stimuli. A lack of integration between the visual and vestibular (balance) systems, or an inability to orient oneself in space and adapt to changes in the visual environment, are examples of visual perceptual dysfunction. When the task becomes overwhelming for the brain to manage, one adaptation is 'tunnelled vision'. This is a survival-based response aimed at making the world controllable. Focusing only on what one sees in this 'tunnel' results in two-dimensions and blocking out that which cannot be controlled. Such a personality may be tenacious, highly organized and single-handed. In some cases this is the inherent perceptual style while in others it is an over-compensation.

DELAYED DEVELOPMENT

Developmental delays in our visual time/space interactions can trigger emotional reactions before the brain's perceptual systems have fully processed the stimulus, thus affecting the perceptual representation and the evaluation of the object. These delays in representational processing in turn affect the storing and retrieval of memories, creating a significant emotional response at all levels of visual processing of a stimulus. Visual development should follow a sequential maturation process from perception to cognition (awareness). The former is unconscious and the latter is conscious. When conflicting information (binocular rivalry) from each eye interferes with this process, a child will exhibit difficulties with coordination and learning abilities. Visual processing delays will create difficulties constructing and organizing a representation of the visual world and therefore affecting decision making and cognitive creativity. A visual management programme will first identify the level of visual processing dysfunction and then design a program to reorganize the neuro-physiology. The goal is to enable developmental maturation in visual processing.

TREATMENT

This entails measuring the patient's visual performance while sitting looking at a stationary object, while standing and moving and while the object is moving. Peripheral vision and depth perception are measured and also the individual's posture, mood and response to various visual tasks. This will reveal the individual perceptual style. Kaplan uses lenses in combination with visual exercises to enable the patient to process visual stimuli in an organized, integrated fashion. Such therapy can allow the patient to achieve harmony with their environment and reduce the panic responses to visual information which are symptomatic of autism.

FURTHER INFORMATION

Kaplan's website for the Center for Visual Management, USA, contains more details and research over several decades with individuals with ASD:
    www.autisticvision.com/Abstracts.html

BOOK

Seeing Through New Eyes by Melvyn Kaplan (2006) describes this approach with case studies of individuals treated at Dr Kaplan's clinic.

D)   SENSORY INTEGRATION THERAPY

Sensory integration is the process of simultaneous firing of multiple sensory neurons in the brain. In many learning and developmental disorders, this does not occur. It is possible to improve sensory integration by focusing on one sense, as described in earlier sections, or to work on multiple senses at once, as in sensory integration programmes. The resulting sensory stimuli will create new pathways of neurons in the brain and thus 'rewire' it. The concept of sensory integration therapy was first developed by Dr. Jean Ayres. Lorna Jean King is Founder and Director of the Centre for Neurodevelopmental Studies, Inc. in Phoenix, Arizona. She states:

> "The goal of sensory integrative therapy is to facilitate the development of the nervous system's ability to process sensory input in a more normal way. Sensory integration is a term for a process in the normal brain which pulls together all of the various sensory messages in order to form coherent information on which we can act. Basically everything we do requires sensory integration. This normal process can be missing or very badly organized in some people, notably autistic individuals."
>
> (Edelson, 1996)

The three major areas are the: vestibular, proprioceptive, and tactile sensory systems. The vestibular system, located in the inner ear, relates us to gravity and orientation in space. Proprioceptors are neuroreceptors in the tendons, muscles and joints which feed back information on activity there. The tactile or touch system has three different types of receptors. One responds to light touch and is a protective, alerting sense such as an insect crawling on the skin. The second receptor is for discriminative touch such as whether you are touching your house key or your car key. The third receives information on temperature and pain. The vestibular system and the visual system are very closely associated, and ability to use the eyes in a coordinated way will improve from better vestibular input. Lorna King suggests 85-90% of children with autism have sensory integration problems, although some are more obvious than others.

TREATMENT

Practitioners of sensory integration (SI) therapy are usually occupational therapists who focus on the tactile (touch) vestibular (balance) and proprioceptive (orientation) systems. SI therapists work on 'normalizing' the individual's reactions to touch, enabling better body awareness and thus improved daily life. SI therapists initially assess for sensory defensiveness, hypersensitivity and sensory cravings, using several different scoring techniques. These include:

> Sensory Integration and Praxis Tests (SIPT) for 4 to 9 year-olds
> The Test of Sensory Integration (TSI) for children of 3 to 5 years
> The Bruininks Osteretsky Test of Motor Proficiency for 5-15 year-olds
> The PEERAMID for ages 6-14 years

These use a variety of techniques, such as: swinging; deep pressure therapy (which may include squeezing and rolling); jumping on a mini or full-sized trampoline; playing with a toy that vibrates; gross motor play, such as wall climbing, balance beam, etc; brushing the skin and joint compression. Some of these activities are similar to those which children with autism display – such as swinging and spinning. These behaviours stimulate the vestibular system and so serve a purpose for the child.

RESEARCH

A double-blind study by Pfeiffer & Kinnealey (2008) at the Occupational Therapy Department in Temple University's College of Health Professions found children with ASDs exhibited fewer autistic mannerisms after SI compared with those receiving standard treatments. Such mannerisms, including repetitive hand movements or actions, making noises, jumping or having highly restricted interests, often interfere with paying attention and learning. The children assigned to the sensory integration intervention group also reached more goals in the areas of sensory processing /regulation, social-emotional and functional motor tasks. A second study also supported SI in ASDs.

FURTHER INFORMATION

USA, SI centres include:
    Towanda, PA: www.memorialhospital.org/sensoryintegration.htm
    Washington: www.neurolearning.com

UK:
    Devon: www.snowdrop.cc
    London, UK: www.thesensorysmartchild.com
    Wales, UK: www.theautismcentre.co.uk

BOOKS:

The Hopscotch Therapy Centre in London, UK has an extensive books page at:
    www.hopscotchtherapy.co.uk/reading.html

See also:
    The Out of Sync Child by Carol Stock-Kranowitz
    Sensual Perception Issues in Autism, by W. Lawson (2003)
    The Mislabeled Child by Brock & Fernette Eide (2006)

5   SOCIAL INTERACTION PROGRAMMES

So far the programmes described have been largely bio-medical or active
on the physiological level of the individual. Once improvements in these
areas have been brought about it is often necessary for the child to learn, or
re-learn if they have been lost, basic communication skills and language. As
described in Chapter 1, intersubjectivity describes the to-and-fro foundation
of communication prior to speech and is usually lacking in children with
ASDs. Social interaction programmes attempt in different ways to either
replicate or initiate this basic pattern and stimulate the desire for external
communication and relationship with others. In some cases the child is
pressed to respond, as with ABA. In others the parent/adult 'joins' the child's
world, as with Son-Rise.

A)   APPLIED BEHAVIOURAL ANALYSIS (ABA)

One of the most popular and frequently mentioned programmes for helping autistic children is applied behavioural analysis (ABA). ABA is:

> "...the science in which tactics derived from the principles of behaviour areapplied systematically to improve socially significant behavior."
>
> (Cooper et al., 2007, p20)

ABA teaches complex tasks using a reward system and an individually planned educational curriculum. It is based on the work of early psychologists in 'shaping' animal behaviour through positive reinforcement. It was Dr O. Ivar Lovaas who first applied ABA techniques with autistic children. Devising the curriculum involves:

> "...a functional assessment that begins by defining possible causes of the behaviour, predicting when the problem behaviour will occur and finally designing effective treatment programmes."
>
> (Keenan, 2004, p73-4)

ABA utilises trained professionals to work with the child usually in their home, although some schools for autistic children offer ABA as their first approach. Early intervention is recommended because the younger child is more likely to change existing behaviours, or develop new ones. A sample ABA curriculum is shown in Table 13, below. Parents become involved as/when they can act as one of the trained professionals. An adult will model the desired behaviour and require the child to replicate it. Rewards as 'reinforcers' are given when the child gives the desired response. This is now usually praise rather than sweets and food. Undesirable behaviour is ignored, corrected or re-directed. Precise data on each learning episode is recorded and adjustments in the programme are made based on these. Lovaas suggests about 80% of a programme should focus on helping children develop meaningful language. A mute child can also be helped to communicate in other ways.

Educational Curriculum For A Child on the Autistic Spectrum

Attending skills
Basic   Child sits in chair independently. Child makes eye contact in response to name
Intermediate   Child asks 'What?' when their name is called
Advanced   Child makes eye contact during conversation and group activities

Imitation skills
Basic   Child imitates gross motor, fine motor and oral motor skills and actions with objects
Intermediate   Child imitates a sequence of actions or sounds
Advanced   Child initiates peer play

Receptive language
Basic   Child follows one-step instructions and identifies objects and pictures
Intermediate   Child identifies and follows two-step instructions
Advanced   Child follows three-step instructions and discriminates concepts

Expressive language
Basic   Child imitates sounds and words, and labels, objects and pictures
Intermediate   Child labels gender and objects based on function
Advanced   Child labels categories and retells a story

Pre-academic skills
Basic   Child matches identical picture and objects. Child undresses
Intermediate   Child indicates for bathroom, washes hands and puts on some clothes
Advanced   Child brushes teeth and buttons clothes

Table 13 Sample ABA Curriculum. From: Keenan (2004) p43

Lynne Hamilton, mother of Ryan, an autistic child, writes:

"Over time Ryan has learned more complex language, first through drills at the table and then through our modelling it in natural settings."

(Hamilton, 2000, p84)

It is possible that ABA helps establish 'executive' functions (which are initially performed for the infant by the mother) through, which the child can then internalize for themselves.

RESEARCH

Lovaas found some children were able to 'overcome the effects of autism' using this approach. He suggests about 50% can become 'indistinguishable' from non autistic children (Lovaas, 1987; McEachin, Smith, & Lovaas, 1993). A replication of Lovaas's 1987 work by Sallows et al. (2005) found at aged seven years, 48% were succeeding in mainstream education, while Cohen et al. (2006) found those children in the ABA group scored significantly higher IQ and adaptive behaviour scores than the comparison group. Of these, 29% (6 of 21) were in regular education without assistance and another 52% (11 of 21) were included with support. This compares with only 5% (1 of 21) children in the control group who were placed in regular education. Follow-up research in early adolescence showed that children in the 1987 study maintained their skills and could succeed in life without costly special education and residential services (McEachin, et al., 1993). However, the Academy of Sciences USA found the Lovaas 1987 study limited by the lack of randomly assigned groups, citing only one study which had resolved these (Smith, Groen & Wynn, 2000). This showed modest educational and little or no social gains, however.

FURTHER INFORMATION

ABA is relatively popular in the US, although hard to access except privately in the UK. This is largely because of a perception of ABA as harsh or even bullying, based on sugary rewards, or too psychologically intense. However, from the narratives, such criticisms no longer seem applicable to modern ABA practice.

THE LOVAAS INSTITUTE

This website gives a history of Dr Lovaas's work over 40 years; information on ABA with questions and answers; availability and a research section:
   www.lovaas.com

AVAILABILITY OF ABA

UK
Peach is a parent-based registered charity offering practical advice on setting up a home-based ABA programme plus family support and communication with other parents:
   www.peach.org.uk

USA
The Cambridge Centre for Behavioral Studies, based in Massachusetts, USA, has many other ABA-based resources:
 www.behavior.org

UK Schools:
Highfield Centre, Cheshire:
 www.highfield-centre.org.uk
The Island Project, Solihull:
 www.theislandproject.co.uk
The Jigsaw CABAS School, Surrey:
 www.jigsawschool.co.uk
Rainbow School, London:
 www.rainbowschool.org.uk/schoolhomepage.html
Step by Step School, Sharpthorne, E Sussex:
 www.stepbystepschool.org.uk

USA and International Schools
A detailed list of schools and providers of ABA for autism and others with pervasive developmental disorders is available from:
 www.members.tripod.com/rsaffran/aba.html
This site also offers other resources for ABA.

BOOKS

Example narratives written by mothers adopting ABA are:
 Facing Autism by L. Hamilton, (2000)
 Let Me Hear Your Voice by C. Maurice, (1993)
 A Real Boy, by C. Adams, (2005)
 When Everybody Cares by B. Newman (2002) is a collection of ABA case studies.

B)   DIR/ FLOORTIME

The name DIR stands for 'development, individual-difference, relationship-based' and is a developmentally-based approach devised by Stanley Greenspan and Serena Wieder. DIR aims to build healthy foundations for relationships, communication and thinking. It has four goals: encouraging attention and intimacy; engaging in two-way communication, encouraging the expression and use of feelings and ideas, and developing logical thought. It is applicable to all forms of ASD from its earliest signs until adulthood. Unlike ABA, developmental programmes tend to use naturalistic learning through interaction and discovery to help the child gain skills such as engaging, relating to others and reading social signals. The DIR model involves creating those learning relationships that will help the child move forward in their development, enabling them to move up the developmental ladder as they master each functional emotional developmental capacity of which they are capable, (Greenspan, 2004). The DIR programme is built upon three primary insights:

1. Language and cognition including emotional and social skills are learned through relationships that involve emotionally meaningful exchanges. Multiple interactions that provide a fundamental sense of relatedness are essential to development and emotions are key to this process.
2. Children vary in their underlying motor and sensory processing capacities. Over the past two decades research has shown that children differ in how they respond to sound, touch, and other sensations, and in their auditory, visual and spatial processing, motor-planning and sequencing.
3. Historically, development has been studied with 'milestones' for each, but: "We now understand that the lines of early development are interrelated. Rather than assessing language skills, motor skills and social-emotional skills separately, we should look at how well these abilities are integrated in a child, how the components work together as a whole."

(Greenspan & Wieder, 2006, p39)

These three principles are illustrated in Figure 15, below:

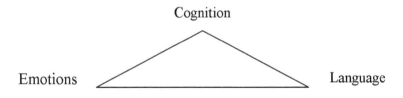

Figure 15 Elements of Communication and Language
Development in DIR/Floortime

Based on these principles, Greenspan and Wieder have formulated a 'functional roadmap' for DIR encompassing six levels:

1. Self-regulation and interest in the world; the dual ability to take an interest in the sights, sounds and sensations of the world and to calm oneself down. A typical infant learns to connect emotion and action with sensation. An infant at risk of ASD is unable to form these links. Movements may appear random, with no synchronicity between the infant and mother/care-givers.
2. Intimacy: the ability to engage in relationships with other people. Infants who cannot connect sensory to emotional and motor experiences cannot then engage with others as fully as infants without these problems.
3. Two-way communication: the 'back and forth' wordless dialogue between infant and mother/caregivers found in normally developing infants (known as intersubjectivity) involves rapid exchanges of facial expression and other gestures and means a baby is continually connecting sensation to emotion, and appropriate motor response. This flow of back-and forth communication between infants at risk of ASD and their mothers is usually lacking, with possibly fleeting responses and interactions but an inability for the infant to initiate them
4. Complex communication: Long chains of back-and-forth shared experience and communication known as 'joint attention', (begins at 10-18 months). Children at risk of ASD almost always show clear signs of difficulty in the area of joint attention and the chain of emotional and social communication. The lack of this ability will interfere with many core skills which develop at this stage, including recognising patterns, forming a sense of self and beginning to construct and use symbols.
5. Emotional ideas: Children at risk of ASDs rarely progress into the creative use of words and symbols; Stage 5.
6. Emotional thinking: the ability to build bridges between ideas to make them reality-based and logical.

In a non-ASD child these stages are usually mastered by about aged 4-5 years. With ASD children it can take much longer or may not occur at all. In DIR early intervention is thought to be important so as to enter at the foundational stages of the child's development, as this will support all later stages:

"When risk factors or problems are detected early, the intervention programme has two goals: to alleviate the identified risk of problems and to facilitate overall healthy emotional, social, and intellectual function."

(Greenspan & Wieder, 2006, p35)

These stages are addressed within the overall emotional and cognitive developmental context and integrate emotional, social, intellectual and educational goals for each child:

"The first step in helping any child with ASD is engagement... entering the child's world and helping her enter into a shared world with others."

(Greenspan & Wieder, 2006, p65)

FLOORTIME

Although the DIR programme is sometimes referred to as Floortime this is only one component. However it is at the heart of the DIR programme:

"This is a particular technique were we get down on the floor and we work with the child to master each of their developmental capacities."

(Greenspan, 2004, p1)

Floortime returns a child to the very first milestones which s/he may have missed and begins the developmental process – through the stages outlined – from the beginning. Although the work does not need to be done on the floor, the idea is that the adult care-giver 'joins' the child to share in their world and this is usually on the floor. It is recommended that specific periods of about 20-30 minutes be put aside through the day, although any activity can be utilised as 'Floortime'. Greenspan describes Floortime as:

"A general philosophy that characterises all the interaction with the child, because all interactions have to incorporate the features of Floortime as well as the particular goals of the interaction, be it speech therapy or occupational therapy or a special set of educational goals."

(Greenspan, 2004, p2)

There are two main emphases to this: Following the child's lead, which harnesses their natural interests, and by joining them:

> "…pulling them into a shared world in order to help them master each of their Functional Emotional Developmental Capacities."
>
> (Greenspan, 2004, p3)

Sometimes 'playful obstruction' may be utilised. This is a way of challenging the child to make a small step into a shared world, perhaps by coming between the child and the desired object. Greenspan describes one such example:

> "He didn't like that and made a sound like Rrrr!. So I pulled my hand away. But gradually I started getting behind the door. The child used sounds and gentle pushing to get me away from the door; he was now purposeful and started to interact.…I let the interaction evolve very gradually, always sensitive to the child's reaction. In this way he got, not over-loaded, but just a little annoyed, always stopping short of having a tantrum. Slowly it changed into a playful interaction in which eventually he said, 'No'. Later on, he learned to say 'away' with a great bit smile of satisfaction because he was the boss of the door. Just by getting involved with his apparently mindless door routine, I gradually helped this child engage, learn to gesture purposefully, and give meaning to words such as 'no', 'away' and 'leave alone.'"
>
> (Greenspan & Wieder, 2006, p73)

Greenspan and Wieder see the child with ASD not in isolation but as part of a family who also have special needs (an ecological perspective). They emphasise the primary role of parents in a child's development. DIR is usually part of a wider approach which may include, Floortime, speech, occupational and physical therapies, but also support/training for parents working on their own responses and styles of relating, so as to help create a family pattern supportive to emotional and intellectual growth in the whole family.

RESEARCH

This work has been described in Chapter 2, but is again summarised for completeness. Greenspan and Wieder undertook a review of 200 children with ASD over an 8-year period, following DIR. All had been diagnosed between 22 months and 4 years of age. More than two-thirds of the children had shown a clear developmental regression between 2-3 years (new phase autism). All the children evidenced auditory processing, motor planning and sensory modality dysfunction. After a minimum of 2 years of DIR, 58% evidenced 'Good to Outstanding' outcomes:

> "These children became trusting and intimately related to parents, showed joyful and pleasurable affect and, most impressively, had the capacity for learning abstract thinking and interactive, spontaneous communication at a preverbal and verbal level."
>
> (Greenspan & Weider, 1997)

This group no longer showed symptoms such as self-absorption, avoidance, self-stimulation or perseveration. On the Childhood Autism Rating Scale (CARS) they registered in the non-autistic range, although some still experienced auditory or visual-spatial difficulties (which were improving) and most had some degree of fine or gross motor planning difficulty. A second group of 25% (Medium Outcomes) made slower more gradual progress, but still gained significantly in their ability to relate and communicate with gestures, entering into long sequences of purposeful interaction but not necessarily a continuous flow. They could share attention and engage in problem-solving and improved speech. They were also warm and loving. The authors note that the ability to show affection was the first change noted in all these children. The third group (17%) had 'Ongoing Difficulties'. These were those with the most complicated neurological problems originally, including seizures. Although most eventually learned to communicate with gestures or simple words and phrases or both, they continued to have difficulties with attention and with sequences of gesturing, retaining episodes of self-absorption, avoidance, self-stimulation and perseveration. Many showed increased ability to relate warmly to others and their problematic behaviours had decreased. Eight children of this group were 'wavering or losing abilities'. Twenty of the children in the 'Good to Outstanding' group were found on standardised measures 'indistinguishable' from the non-autistic control group. The authors conclude:

> "The fact the intervention subgroup was comparable to a peer group without developmental disorders suggest, at a minimum, that as sub-group of children initially given an autistic spectrum diagnosis can develop sustainable patterns of healthy emotional, social and adaptive behaviour."
>
> (Greenspan and Wieder, 2006, p381)

LONG TERM FOLLOW-UP

A 10-15 year follow-up study of 16 children from the 'Good to Outstanding' group of the original 200 was also carried out. Using a battery of tests including parental and independent clinician ratings:

> "The study showed that the children had developed high levels of empathy and were often more empathetic than their peers....As a group, they showed the expected range of mental health problems often depending on family circumstances (a few were anxious or depressed as adolescents). Importantly, however, they coped with the stresses of puberty and family concerns while maintaining their core gains in relating, communication, and reflective thinking and making further progress as well. For this subgroup, the core deficits and symptoms of ASD were no longer observed ten to fifteen years after they initially presented."
>
> (Greenspan & Wieder, 2006, p385-6)

A more recent pilot study (the PLAY Project cited previously in Chapter 2) was conducted by Dr Richard Solomon, published in the May 2007 edition of *Autism* DIR-Floortime, with parents as the child's primary play partner. A trained team made monthly home visits, videotaped parents in play and recommended activities and techniques to increase reciprocal social interaction. Sixty eight children with ASD were evaluated after a period of one year. The results showed 52% had made 'very good clinical progress' with a further 14% making 'good progress'. Although there was no control group, Solomon writes:

"...as a model (DIR) has a very good track record in the US and promises to be very helpful for families in dire need of service right now."

(Solomon, 2007, p410)

FURTHER INFORMATION

The *Floortime Foundation* website offers an on-line course for parents; book shop, CDs and DVDs. There is also a forum and direct email to Greenspan. The website contains a web-based radio station with audio broadcasts, downloads and transcripts on every aspect of DIR-Floortime as well as up to date research:

    www.floortime.org

BOOKS

> *Engaging Autism* by Greenspan and Wieder (2006) provides a detailed account of DIR-Floortime including their research described above.
> *Interactive Play for Children with Autism* by D. Search (2007) is written to help establish shared play experiences with children with ASD in education, home or care settings, and so may be of help with either DIR/Floortime or Son-Rise (see next section) programmes
> *Reaching the Young Autistic Child* by S. Janert (2000) presents ideas, activities, strategies and games designed for even severely affected children.

C)   SON-RISE PROGRAMME (S-R)

The S-R programme was established in 1983 by Barry and Samahria Kaufman, whose child Raun was diagnosed as severely autistic. With an IQ of 30, they were told he would always be 'retarded'. By the three and a half years he had fully recovered going on to mainstream school and university. Barry Kaufman published a book on the method they devised to recover Raun and five other children with autism. This became a film following which other parents contacted the Kaufman's for advice.

PHILOSOPHY

S-R is based on the maxim: 'Children show us the way in (to their world) – we show them the way out'. And that it is imperative to accept the child 'where they are' and their behaviour as necessary to them. These behaviours have purpose, which is connected to a feeling of sensory overwhelm and on their world not being predictable. Children with autism experience high stress levels as a result, so that stress hormones circulate in their systems. The behaviours serve two purposes; a) they enable the child to exclude by focusing only on one or two ritualistic behaviours so the child can regulate their nervous system and, b) they provide themselves with predictability and control, and therefore security in the world. S-R argues that to attempt to alter these behaviours is to 'dysregulate' the child.

KEY ELEMENTS OF S-R ARE:

1. Joining in a child's repetitive and ritualistic behaviour.
2. Placing the parent as the child's most important and lasting resource.
3. Creating a safe, distraction-free work/play area. In this program the play area is defined as a specially created play room. The child is not allowed out of the room during the play period.

'JOINING'

The first step in the S-R treatment plan is to 'join' the child and show non-invasive acceptance, both of them and of the repetitive behaviours. By creating a relationship 'on their terms', the child is more likely to want to relate, which creates a bond. Provided the child's safety is not an issue, S-R facilitators do whatever the same activity as the child to show their acceptance and respect. If the child is spinning plates, for example, the adult will spin a plate alongside: Doing this for some time without attempting to alter the child's behaviour, or intruding on their activity has the effect of creating companionship. The child will ultimately make eye contact, begin to realise someone else is interested in what interests him and enter into social interaction on his own terms. Only when the first part of the maxim is fulfilled will there be any attempt to help the child engage in the adult's world. By this time, a relationship based on love, acceptance, trust and mutual respect has already formed.

PARENTAL ROLE

Although other helpers can work with the child, S-R sees the child's parents as their most important resource. For this reason parents are trained in the S-R approach prior to adopting it at home. It is recommended that parents/helpers work for at least 20 hours and, optimally, 40 hours per week with the child in a specially created and equipped play-room.

THE PLAYROOM

S-R utilises a designated room converted into a playroom for the child, parents and helpers. This is locked while the child and adult are inside. The toys are placed on high shelves so that they cannot be reached, so that the child will be encouraged to ask for what is wanted and encourage language. The windows frosted if necessary so that attention is paid only to what is taking place in the room. There is often a mirror on the wall to encourage eye contact when playing games; a child trampoline, gym balls; slide, and a small table and chairs to encourage drawing and creativity. Everything is done on the child's eye level so as to encourage eye contact.

BEHAVIOURAL TECHNIQUES

During the second stage of the maxim, when the child is being encouraged to play or expresses interests in a toy on a higher shelf, the adult will request eye contact, reward the child with praise and enthusiasm and then give the toy. These are behavioural techniques, aimed at shaping the desired behaviour as in ABA. However, unlike ABA, the child has chosen the activity and is still leading the way.

DIFFERENCES BETWEEN S-R AND DIR

There are two major differences between S-R and DIR. One is that in S-R the playroom is a separate, contained area, which the child cannot leave, and where most of the child's daily life will take place in the playroom. In DIR, 20-30 minute sessions are woven into the day on the regular 'floor' space. In S-R up to 8 hours a day may be spent in the designated playroom. The other main difference is in the nature and purpose of 'joining'.

JOINING & PLAYFUL OBSTRUCTION

Both S-R and DIR encourage parents to follow the lead of their child, discover their interests, elaborate and build on whatever the child is interested in, and assist them in their chosen play. However, in DIR the parent is also encouraged to do 'whatever it takes' to make play interactive. If a child begins to move away from a game, the parent is instructed to pursue the child and 'insist on a response' or 'playfully obstruct' to keep the child in the game. If the parent asks a question which the child does not answer, the parent is instructed to persist with this question until an answer is provided. In S-R, if a child turns away from interaction to engage in a solitary activity, the facilitator follows the child and joins him/her in that activity. The facilitator will perform the activity in a solitary way alongside the child. If the child makes eye contact, a sound, speaks or moves towards the facilitator, these cues will be responded to. But if the child pulls away again, the facilitator will again go back to solitary play until the child indicates his availability again. S-R suggests this allows the child to build the desire to interact with people and so initiate interaction themselves. Further, by fully absorbing him/herself in the activity, the facilitator gains an understanding of why this activity is motivating for the child. When the child later indicates his availability for interaction this information may then be employed.

RESEARCH

A joint study between Lancaster University, UK and Northwestern University, USA, examined the effects of the Son-Rise programme in six children with autism, aged between 47-78 months, matched with six control children. The six S-R children received 40 hours of intensive treatment, while the matched group received a novel passive interaction probe task. Results showed:

> "…an increase in the frequency of spontaneous social orienting and gestural communication for the experimental children (S-R group), compared to six age- and behaviourally-matched control children with autism. In addition, for the children who received treatment, the duration of social dyadic interventions and total time spent engaged in social interaction increased from pre-to post-treatment."

The authors conclude:

> "These findings suggest that intensive intervention (S-R) focussed on fostering child-initiated interaction increases social-communicative behaviours in children with autism."
>
> (Houghton, et al., 2013)

JOINING RESEARCH

The Son-Rise Center cite research by Gerard J. Nijhof and colleagues demonstrating that a child's repetitive behaviours are purposeful and, therefore, it is not in the child's best interest to stop these behaviours. These authors considered it 'doubtful whether a decrease of repetitive behaviours stimulates the appearance of desirable behaviours'. They also describe a study by Baker, Koegel and Koegel which found repetitive behaviours were not increased, but led to greater participation when play materials based on their 'obsessive' behaviours were created (ATC, *Website*, 2011).

NARRATIVES

There are also many parent testimonials on the Son-Rise website (below). For examples:

> "By the age of 2, our son, became increasingly withdrawn. It became difficult to take him out as he would throw tantrums for no

apparent reason and scream and scream. We could not effectively communicate to him what was safe or dangerous; he didn't seem to understand. Specialists then diagnosed our son with Autism, and gave us a hopeless prognosis. We discovered the Autism Treatment Center of America. The impact that their Son-Rise Program made on my family is profound. By the end of the first week, Liam had asked his first question, talked in his sleep for the first time and played purely for pleasure. Today, he has developed into such an enthusiastic communicator. He exhibits an imagination that often leaves us and strangers awed. He has progressed in all aspects to such an extent that he now attends his local mainstream primary school. The best indicator of his progress is that professionals visiting the school with the intention of examining Liam were unable to find the 'autistic child' and asked for assistance! William B."

And:

"My 16-year-old son and family were in a crisis when we first heard about the Son-Rise Program. He was having numerous seizures, becoming aggressive at school and was very unhappy. Fourteen months later, with the benefit of the parent-training program-Tyler is so happy. His conversation skills have developed incredibly his seizures have been reduced from every 5 days to as long as 6 weeks apart! He gives spontaneous hugs, talks about his feelings, has developed a great imagination and is more comfortable in groups and new situations. We are so thankful to have found a way to help Tyler." Gail P"

Son-Rise introductory seminars, including in London, Scotland and USA, plus resources are given at the website: Autismtreatmentcenter.org

BOOKS

The Miracle Continues, by Barry & Raun Kaufman (1995) describes how Son-Rise was used with more families, following recovery of their son, Raun (see Chapter 3).

D)   RELATIONSHIP DEVELOPMENT INTERVENTION (RDI

RDI was designed by Steven Gutstein, a psychologist initially trained in behavioural approaches to autism treatment. From this he felt that although children increased in skills, they remained unable to connect on an emotional level. He developed a family-based programme, supported by trained consultants and parent seminars.

ASD 'CORE DEFICITS'

Gustein proposed six 'core deficits' shared by every person with an ASD:

Emotional Referencing: The ability to use an emotional feedback system to learn from the subjective experiences of others

Social Coordination: The ability to observe and continually regulate one's behaviour in order to participate in spontaneous relationships involving collaboration and exchange of emotions

Declarative Language: Using language and non-verbal communication to express curiosity, invite others to interact, share perceptions and feelings and coordinate your actions with others

Flexible thinking: The ability to rapidly adapt, change strategies and alter plans based upon changing circumstances

Relational Information Processing: The ability to obtain meaning based upon the larger context. Solving problems that have no right-and-wrong solutions

Foresight and Hindsight: The ability to reflect on past experiences and anticipate potential future scenarios in a productive manner

According to Gutstein these share a common root. Rather than relying on the ability to know or memorise facts ('static intelligence') they rely upon 'dynamic intelligence'. This is the ability to flexibly and creatively respond to novel situations. The purpose of RDI is to build or remediate dynamic intelligence. Gutstein writes:

> "I said, let's look at the natural process and slow it down, make it more explicit. Let's see what happens if we take the same process and break it down, and then teach parents to do what they're already capable of intuitively and see them explicitly."
>
> (Gutstein, 2011, *Website*)

With the new understanding of the brain as 'plastic' and responding to environmental stimulation, new pathways can be formed between the limbic system (emotional learning centre) and the 'executive' (prefrontal cortex) to help those with ASDs overcome their difficulties. This can be done at any age as the brain is always capable of making new connections. RDI exercises are designed to stimulate these.

FURTHER INFORMATION

There is extensive information on RDI online at:
   www.rdiconnect.com
   www.about.autism.com (follow links)

The latter provide details on the approach, parent courses, books and video material.

BOOKS

Explanations of the RDI method include:
   The RDI Book: Forging new pathways for autism, Asperger's and PDDs. Gustein. (2010)
   Autism Asperger's: Solving the relationship puzzle. S. Gutstein. (2000)

E)   INTENSIVE INTERACTION (II)

This is a person-centred approach originally conceived in the 1980s by Dave Hewett and Melanie Nind for those with profound learning difficulties. This was in place of traditional approaches of exclusion and 'time out'. II is based in part on the 'augmented mothering' work of psychologist Geraint Ephram, which Hewett and Nind adapted into a more flexible, interactive programme. It focuses on the 'Fundamentals of Communication' which include learning to give attention to another, make eye contact, enjoy being with another, vocalise (where possible), engage in physical contact, use non-verbal communication and develop shared attention and turn-taking (as with joint attention and intersubjectivity). Using techniques developed from infant-caregiver interaction, II aims to join learners in 'their own world' by responding to what the individual were already doing, and developing interactions with a mixture of blended repetitions and imitations of their physical behaviour. In this II is similar to Son-Rise, Floortime and DIR.

FURTHER INFORMATION

Details of II courses, support networks and conferences are available at:
www.intensiveinteraction.co.uk/

BOOKS

A straight forward introductory text on II is:
A practical guide to Intensive Interaction. (2001) Nind, M. & Hewett, D
See also the II website at:
www.intensiveinteraction.co.uk/about/recommended-books/

6.   PHARMACEUTICAL TREATMENT

A variety of pharmaceutical drugs may be prescribed to help with behaviours and symptoms. The most frequently prescribed drugs are antidepressants (58%) antipsychotic drugs (29%) and anticonvulsants (8%) third (Bock & Stauth, 2007). Those mentioned in the narratives are listed below.

Risperidone (Risperdal)

In the USA, the only pharmaceutical treatment approved by the Federal Drugs Agency (FDA) is *Risperidone*. This is an anti-psychotic medicine (also known as a neuroleptic) approved in the USA for the treatment of older children with schizophrenia and bi-polar depression. It is also frequently prescribed 'off-label' (without approval) for anxiety, depression and obsessive compulsive disorder. *Risperidone* reduces the activity of the neurotransmitter dopamine, which is responsible for regulating levels of motor activity. *Risperidone* also acts at several 5-HT (serotonin) receptor sites, and can therefore help control the fear and anger that children with ASD may experience. It is not recommended over extended periods. Common known side effects of *Risperidone* include anxiety, insomnia, low blood pressure, muscle stiffness and pain, sedation, tremors, increased salivation, stuffy nose and weight gain. Antipsychotics inhibit dopamine and can cause non-cancerous tumours in the pituitary gland, trigger diabetes and other series conditions of glucose metabolism.

Imipramine (Tofranil)

This drug was prescribed to Temple and is one of the original benzodiazepam anti-depressants, although generally replaced now with newer products (below). In the late 1950s it was the first tricyclic antidepressant to be developed (by Ciba-Geigy) and was used for the treatment of psychotic disorders such as schizophrenia. However, it proved inadequate in these and can in fact induce and exacerbate psychosis. During clinical studies its antidepressant qualities were noted. In fact *Imipramine* is often considered the bench-mark antidepressant, especially for severe cases. It can also induce a high rate (up to 25%) of manic and hypomanic reactions, especially in patients with bipolar disease. *Imipramine* acts on norepinephrine, serotonin, epinephrine (adrenaline) dopamine and sigma receptors (whose exact nature is as yet unknown), enkephalinase, histamine, muscurane, and acetycholine neurotransmitters. *Imipramine* also antagonizes adreno-receptors (II) thus sometimes causing increased heart rate, orthostatic hypotension, and a general decrease in the responsiveness of the central nervous system, hence its potent anti-anxiety properties. With the more recent development of the serotonin specific re-uptake inhibitors (SSRIs) described below, *Imipramine* has become less commonly used except to treat major depression.

Sertraline (Zoloft) & *Prozac (Fluoxetine)* are serotonin specific re-uptake inhibitors (SSRIs). This means they allow increased serotonin into the brain. *Sertraline* is considered effective for the treatment of panic disorder and led to a modest improvement in social phobia. Cognitive behavioural treatment (CBT) was found more effective for obsessive-compulsive disorder. *Prozac* is sometimes prescribed to treat depression, anxiety, obsessive compulsive disorder and panic attacks. Side effects of SSRIs include a high rate of nausea, diarrhoea and insomnia. *Sertraline* has been associated with a higher rate of suicide attempts. The newer *Lexapro* has fewer side effects in low doses. A recent study found 25% of autistic patients did not tolerate doses over 10 mg per day (Bock & Stauth, 2007, p339).

Naloxone (Nacam)

This drug is a short acting opioid antagonist and blocks the action of the natural endorphin system as well as other opioid medicines. It can help interpersonal function, and reduce self-injurious behaviour and abnormal movements (Trevarthan et al., 1998). Side effects include damage to the heart. It is contra-indicated in people who have high levels of opioids in their system, (which suggests a counter-use in ASDs where there may be gut inflammation). *Naloxone* can also impair thinking and response, cause allergic reactions such as hives, difficulty breathing, swelling of the face, lips, tongue, or throat, chest pains, or fast or irregular heartbeat, light-headedness, fainting and seizure (convulsions). Less serious side effects include: dizziness, weakness, tiredness; nausea, vomiting, or diarrhoea, anxiety, restlessness, sweating, runny nose or trembling.

Deaner (Deanol)

In Europe this is available as *Deanol-Riker*. It has been used in cases of less severe depression and as a mental stimulant. It is closely related to the nutritional enzyme dimethylaminoethanol (DMAE) and as such can be considered as either a drug or a nutrient. It is generally thought to be mild in its effect without the negative side-effects of other stimulants. It is the tertiary nitrogen analogue of choline which stimulates and is the precursor of acetylcholine production – the main neurotransmitter for learning and memory. But, unlike choline, it is able to pass through the blood barrier. Effects can take several weeks to become apparent and dosage may vary for individuals. Some users experience mild headaches, weight loss and sleeplessness. It is contra-indicated in epilepsy. *Deaner* was withdrawn in 1983 by the manufacturer (Riker) in preference to others they make. However, DMAE itself is available as a nutritional supplement which is considered safer (Potter, Orfali, & Scott, 1993).

Prednisone

Prednisone is converted by the liver into prednisolone, which is a steroid and immunosuppressant. It is used to treat certain inflammatory diseases and (at higher doses) some types of cancer, but has significant adverse effects. Because it suppresses the immune system, it leaves patients more susceptible to infections. It is usually taken orally but can be delivered by intramuscular injection or intravenous injection.

Antibiotics

These include the Penicillin group (*Amoxicillin, Ampicillin, Flucloxacillin* etc) and cyclines (*Tetracycline, Doxycycline* etc) and are used to treat bacteria in the gut. Problems can arise from long-term use of antibiotics as they allow yeasts such as Candida Albicans and other, more dangerous and resistant bacteria, such as *Clostridium difficils* to proliferate. In addition, the Penicillin group generally have a damaging effect on the necessary 'good' bowel flora such as *Lactobacilli* and *Bifidobacteria*, while promoting the *Proteus* family (*Streptococci* and *Staphylococci*) allowing those bacteria normally found only in the bowel access to the lower intestines and so to the development of digestive disorders such as irritable bowel syndrome (IBS). 'Mycin' (*Gentamycin, Kanamycin, Erythromycin*) group drugs also devastate colonies of necessary beneficial bacteria in the gut. The faecal matter of children with ASD has been found to contain heightened levels of these, including *Clostridium histolyticum* (Clostridium clusters I and II) compared with that of healthy children (Parracho et al., 2005). However, this group creates toxins, which may contribute towards gut dysfunction, while their metabolic products also create reactive systemic effects as a response. In one study, symptoms of autism were eradicated when *Vancomycen* was given, but returned when it was halted (Bolte, 2000). Tetracycline family drugs are toxic to the gut wall as they alter the protein structure in the mucous membranes allowing invasion by pathogenic microbes and alerting the immune system to attack these proteins as 'foreign' (an auto-immune attack against the gut) (Campbell-McBride, 2004).

Antifungal Medications

Candida albicans and other yeasts are often present in the gut of individuals with ASD. This is often treated with a short course of an anti-fungal such as *Nystatin* or *Diflucan*. There appear to be few side effects as such connected with these drugs, but they can lead to stimulation of the growth of *Proteus* family and lactose-negative *E.coli* species, capable of creating serious disease. Of the medications used by parents with their children, anti-fungals achieve the highest feedback scores on the Autism Research Institute (ARI) website (given below)

FURTHER INFORMATION

Information on pharmaceutical use with autism is available at:
  www.autism.about.com/od/treatmentoptions/p/drugtreatments.
  htm
Parent ratings of the comparative effects of medications can be found at:
  www.neurotransmitter.net/autismclostridia.html (autism)
  www.autism.com/fam_ratingsbehaviorasperger.asp (Asperger)

BOOKS

Healing the new childhood epidemics by D. Bock and C.Stauth. (2007)
  Chapter 20 describes the most commonly prescribed drugs for
  children with ASD.
Recovering Autistic Children by S. Edelson and B. Rimland (Eds) (2006)
  containsinformation on the clinical use of *Nalatexone* and clinically
  prescribed *Marinol* (Marijuana) in comparison with *Risperidone* is
  described in:
Brain Boosters by B.Potter, S. Orfali and G. Scott (1993) gives both
  pharmaceutical and natural brain stimulants, including DMAE,
  together with a description for how these work in the brain.

7   HOMOEOPATHIC MEDICINE

Max's biography (Chapter 4, Narrative 5) describes how individualized
homoeopathy (also spelt *homeopathy*) formed the basis of his recovery.
Homoeopathy's central aim is to stimulate the individual's immune system
to self-healing and increased resilience. It is therefore a form of personalised
immunology. It is also 'holistic' in that treatment includes the mental,
emotional and physical symptoms of the individual.

PHILOSOPHY

The central principle of homoeopathic medicine was known to Hippocrates:
the Father of modern medicine. Its current form is founded on over 200

years of empirical, clinical practice. Because of its long history, much of what is written about homoeopathy is in somewhat antiquated language. For this reason, following a general description I have updated this to a more modern terminology. The sections below outline the essential tenet of homoeopathic practice – traditionally known as: *The law of similars,* followed by a description of 'potentisation' (the use of non material/ultra dilute doses of medicine).

A)   THE 'LAW OF SIMILARS'

The most recent discovery (or re-discovery) of homoeopathy was made by Samuel Hahnemann, a German doctor, in the early 1800s. However, homoeopathic medicine was initially established as a science by the Ancient Greeks around the central principle of 'treating like with like'. This is not unlike the modern practice of de-sensitisation (such as with nut allergies or phobias) except that it has a far wider application. Hippocrates referred to two forms of medicine as equally useful: by 'sympathies' (using similars) and by 'contraries' (to directly combat symptoms). Conventional medicine is now almost exclusively focussed on the latter of these, largely due to the commercialisation of medications. In contrast, the law of similars notes that: 'A substance which can produce a spectrum of symptoms in a healthy person will cure that same spectrum of symptoms in a sick person' (Gray, 2000, p9). Thus 'like cures like' (*similia similibus curentur*). The similar substance was called 'homoeopathic' by Hahnemann after the Greek words for 'similar' (homoeo) and 'suffering' (pathos).

PROVINGS

Over a period of about a decade, Hahnemann and his medical colleagues ran a series of 'provings' (the German word for 'trial') in which they (as healthy human participants) took small amounts of various substances until a symptom array specific to that substance was experienced. Interestingly, no two symptom arrays were exactly alike. They tabulated these findings, together with those of accidental poisonings from orthodox drugs of the day, such as *Arsenicum, Mercury* and *Sulphur* (all routinely used to treat syphilis) to form a *Materia Medica*. Provings have continued to be undertaken since that time, so that there are currently over 2000 homoeopathic medicines (known as 'remedies') each with a unique pattern of symptoms. When applied through the 'law of similars' (matching the patient's disease to a proved substance) the remedy will evoke a global immune system response. Peter Fisher (2018) Director of Research and Consultant Physician at *The Royal London Hospital for Integrated Medicine* (formerly *The Royal London Homoeopathic Hospital*) writes:

> "The body reacts to stimuli, which have physiological effects (drugs or toxins) by attempting to maintain homeostasis (a stable internal environment). Homeopathy makes therapeutic use of this effect."
>
> (Fisher, 2018)

That is, the immune system will bring about/re-gain homeostasis (equilibrium) through a healing response.

B)   ULTRA-DILUTE/NON-MATERIAL DOSES

Scientific scepticism about homeopathy arises largely from its use of highly dilute medicines. However, as Fisher explains:

> "...the methods used to prepare homeopathic medicines are remarkably similar to some used in cutting-edge nanotechnology and there is growing evidence that nanoparticles play a crucial role in the action of homeopathic medicines."
>
> (Fisher, 2018)

The use of ultra-dilute medications in homoeopathy came about through empirical practice. Originally, small doses of homoeopathic medicines were given to patients. These had the desired effect of stimulating the immune system, although this initial reaction could be somewhat lively and uncomfortable for the patient. The aim in homoeopathy, as in all medicine, is to be as gentle as possible. So, in an effort to avoid discomfort for the patient, Hahnemann and his medical colleagues prescribed smaller and smaller amounts. They did this by triturating and/or diluting the substance in water and preserving the dilute in pure alcohol. It was found that the more dilute (and smaller physical amount), the easier the patient's response, and the more effective a remedy became. This was especially so if the mixture was shaken vigorously each time (known as 'succussion'). Such dilutions often continued to the point where no molecule of the starting substance was likely to be present. Nevertheless, the remedies remained active. 'Potentising' is now a specific and exact mathematical science with a variety of different 'scales' of dilution and succussion made. However, a remedy which is potentised, but does not match the disease symptoms in the patient is not 'homoeopathic' but merely ultra-dilute, and will not therefore evoke the required immune system response. The remedy must be applied according to the principle of similarity to be 'homoeopathic'.

HOMOEOPATHY REDUCES ALLOSTATIC LOAD

It is likely that the overall beneficial reason for the success of homoeopathy, especially in chronic states, is that the immune system response through homeostasis it reduces the toxic load of the individual, allowing the immune system to re-establish a greater degree of health. As Fisher states:

> "…homeopathic medicines, like modern engineered nanoparticles, act by modulating the allostatic stress response network (… the process of restoring a stable internal environment), including cytokines, oxidative stress and heat shock proteins."

(Fisher, 2018)

In other words, homeopathy directly addresses the limbic/allostatic load of the individual to bring about improved coping and stabilisation (homeostasis). This may include a detoxification process as part of the 'lightening of the load'. The overall result is a higher level of resilience, and lower susceptibility, to disease.

ENERGY BASIS OF HEALING

Traditionally homoeopathy was part of a school of medicine based on 'vitalism': the concept that all organisms are animated by a non-material, organising 'life field'. In modern parlance this translates as an 'electro-magnetic field'. Medical systems based on this concept, seek to correct disease directly through the field. It is thought in energy based systems of medicine that disease will register on the electromagnetic field of an individual *before* physical symptoms manifest, and therefore that interventions can be aimed at restoring the balanced functioning of the energy field rather than by addressing each individual symptom. This is in contrast with biomedical approaches which intervene at the physiological and/or chemical level of the organism, typically through pharmaceuticals.

RESONANCE

The exact mechanism by which the similar remedy evokes a healing response from the immune system is not yet fully understood. However, several explanations have been proposed. One suggestion is that the 'sympathetic' energy, and/or electromagnetic vibration of the homoeopathic substance, *resonates* with the individual pattern of the patient's symptoms. In the same way that a single note of a sympathetic pitch can break a wine glass, the remedies seem able to break or alter the vibrational field of the disease pattern itself. This may be because coupled coherence phenomena (global perturbation across electromagnetic fields) depend on resonance. As Gray observes:

> "Cells, tissues and organisms function in a milieu of electromagnetic coherence. The old biophysics viewed interaction on purely molecular levels. New trends focus on interactions between molecules and electromagnetic fields, as well as between fields themselves."
>
> (Gray, 2000, p82)

The 'law of similars' can therefore be translated as: 'the action of healing through resonance, by directly influencing the immune response via the electromagnetic field of a living organism' (which latter term replaces the older concept of 'vitalism'). Given this, it appears likely that resonance phenomena and increased understanding of the electromagnetic nature of organisms provide the key to understanding the action of homoeopathic medicine. And that this can be better understood in terms of systems theory and the homoeostasis literature which perceives mind and body as one, self-regulating, whole. As such, homoeopathy can be said to represents a shift of medical science from a biochemical basis to a branch of applied physics. The main obstacle to this evolutionary shift has been the implication that medicine can become largely drug-free (and therefore non-profit making). Consequently, funding for research in homoeopathy is severely limited. Despite this, some good research exists.

RESEARCH

In addition to a 200 year old empirical research base of clinical practice there have been many placebo-controlled RCT and patient-outcome studies of effectiveness undertaken with homoeopathy. Up to the end of 2014, a total of 104 papers reporting good-quality placebo-controlled RCTs (on 61 different medical conditions) had been published in peer-reviewed journals. 41% of these reported a balance of positive evidence, 5% a balance of negative evidence, and 54% have not been conclusively positive or negative.

HIGHER QUALITY

Homoeopathic research is generally found to be of a higher quality than typical clinical research. In a review of the current research evidence for homeopathic medicine, Fisher states:

"By August 2017 1,138 clinical trials of homeopathy had been published [including] four systematic review/meta-analyses of homeopathy for all conditions…Of these, three reached a positive conclusion: that there is evidence that homeopathy is clinically effective. The exception is the review by Shang *et al.* This meta-analysis was controversial, particularly because its conclusions were based on only eight clinical trials whose identity was concealed until several months after the publication, precluding informed examination of its results. The only undisputed conclusion of this paper is that clinical trials of homeopathy are of higher quality than matched trials of conventional medicine: of 110 clinical trials each of homeopathy and conventional medicine, 21 trials of homeopathy but only 9 trials of conventional medicine were of 'higher quality'.

Higher quality equates to less risk of bias. A leading Swedish medical researcher remarked: *'To conclude that homeopathy lacks clinical effect, more than 90% of the available clinical trials had to be disregarded. Alternatively, flawed statistical methods had to be applied'*. Mathie et al. analysed randomized clinical trials of individualized homeopathy, showing that the highest quality trials yielded positive results. Systematic reviews of randomized controlled trials of homeopathy in specific clinical situations have also yielded positive results, including: allergies and upper respiratory tract infections (2 systematic reviews), Arnica in knee surgery, Childhood diarrhoea, Post-operative ileus, Rheumatic diseases, Seasonal allergic rhinitis (hay fever) (2 systematic reviews) and vertigo."

He concludes:

"Although, according to current scientific understanding, it is implausible that the very high dilutions used in homeopathy have effects which are not placebo, there is abundant evidence that they do… Clinical research and syntheses of such research show it to be safe and effective for a range of conditions. Integrating homeopathy in health care systems is associated with benefits including improved outcomes, less use of drugs including antibiotics, and economic benefits."

(Fisher, 2018)

HOMOEOPATHIC PHYSICS RESEARCH

Regarding the underlying physics of homeopathy, Luc Montagnier, the Nobel Prize-winning scientist who first identified the HIV virus, and his colleagues, have demonstrated a novel property of some bacterial DNA sequences to induce electromagnetic waves at high dilutions in water (Montagnier, et al., 2009). There is also increasing, reproducible evidence from biology that *in vivo* effects can occur at dilutions greater than 10^{22}mol/L. In a systematic review, 68% of high-quality and 73% of total experiments showed such an effect (Fisher, 2010). A recent review of basic research on highly dilute homeopathic medicines found 98 replicated experiments, over 70% of which were positive. Twelve independent research laboratories in the U.S., France, Italy, Russia, and India have found that the homeopathic medicines studied contained various nanostructures, including source material, silica nanoparticles and gas nanobubbles heterogeneously dispersed in colloidal solution (Fisher, 2018)

INDIVIDUALIZED HOMOEOPATHIC RESEARCH WITH AUTISM

A study with 60 ASD children of both sexes was undertaken in 2014 by the *Spandan Holistic Institute of Applied Homoeopathy* in Mumbai. This study used individualized homoeopathy based on presenting symptoms (physical and mental) in each case. The study was non-randomised and used a pre- and post intervention design, where the children had an initial 6 month period of observation as a control. The same children were then given one year of homoeopathic treatment with changes measured on the ATEC and the CARS. Results showed a decrease of ATEC scores by 34% in the first quarter. A significant improvement in behaviour was also found on the *Autistic Hyperactivity Scale* (AHS, 36 to AHS, 14.30: p=0.0001). Overall, 88.34% of children improved, with 8.33% unchanged and 3.33% worsened following treatment. On the CARS, nine out of 60 children (5.4%) were no longer in the autistic range of scores (Barvalia, et al., 2014).

BOOKS

A general text on homoeopathy can be found at:
> *Homeopathy: Science or myth?* by Bill Gray (2000) presents an exploration of the scientific basis of homoeopathy.
> *Human energy fields* by Colin Ross (2009) is a study of the electro-magnetic energy- fields of humans and their potential in healing.

Texts specifically addressing homoeopathy and autism include:
> *Impossible Cure* by Amy Lansky (2003) which contains a complete description of classical homoeopathy, Max's recovery and contact information.
> *A Drug-Free Approach to Asperger Syndrome and Autism* by Judyth Reichenberg-Ullman, Robert Ullman and Ian Luepker (2005) contains 17 case-stories of children treated for behavioural and developmental issues, including ASD.

WEBSITES

A two-page evidence summary of current research is available at:

> https://www.britishhomeopathic.org/wp-content/uploads/2018/04/2-page-evidence-summary-for-homeopathy-HRI.pdf

The general homoeopathic database is continually updated. This can be accessed at:

> https://www.hri-research.org/resources/research-databases/

A summary of types and numbers of studies is available at:

> https://www.britishhomeopathic.org/evidence/the-evidence-for-homeopathy/

HOMOEOPATHY AND AUTISM

Fran Sheffield a practitioner in Australia who specialises in classical homoeopathy and autism describes her work at:

> http://homeopathyplus.com/reversing-autism-part-1/

Amy Lansky's website can be found at:

> www.impossiblecure.com

The Reichenberg's website is at:

> www.drugsfreeasperger.com

AVAILABILITY

Homoeopathy is the third most used system of medicine in the world and is practiced in 80 countries including Germany, Norway, Greece, India, Switzerland, Israel, Tuscany, Cuba, Brazil, the UK, USA, Australia and Austria. It is available on the National Health Service in the UK (although currently under threat by cost-cutting). In India there are more than 100,000 practitioners who routinely treat diseases such as tuberculosis, typhoid, malaria, leprosy, hepatitis and HIV (Reichenberg-Ullman, et al., 2005). Following a review of current evidence, homeopathy is now fully integrated into the Swiss health-care system and is also a mainstream element of health care in Brazil. In France every pharmacist stocks homeopathic medicines. In the UK homoeopathy is also available through medical homoeopaths and professional practitioners in private practice. The latter have undergone extensive (four-year) training, including in anatomy and physiology, and are licensed and registered, with a *Code of Conduct and Ethics* and professional insurance. In the US regulations vary between states.

UK
Homoeopathic Societies for Registered professional practitioners, including nurses, psychologists and others can be found at a number of professional organisations including:
Alliance of Registered Homoeopaths:
    www.a-r-h.org/FindMembers/find.php
Society of Homoeopaths:
    www.homeopathy-soh.org/about-homeopathy/find-a-homeopath.aspx
For medical doctors, nurses, midwives, dentists, vets, pharmacists, podiatrists, osteopaths and other healthcare professionals trained in homeopathy:
Faculty of Homoeopathy:
    www.britishhomeopathic.org/getting_treatment/find_practitioner/

USA
The following site for the American Institute of Homeopathy provides reach and registered medical homeopaths:
    https://www.homeopathyusa.org/
The North American Society of Homeopaths provides a list of registered practitioners
    https://homeopathy.org/registered-homeopaths-directory/
A database of searchable directories can be found at:
    http://www.homeopathyhome.com/directory/usa/organisations.
    shtml

8.   TOUCH PROGRAMMES

A number of different touch programmes are referred to in the recovery narratives. Some, such as osteopathy, are concerned with ameliorating the effects of birth trauma, while others aim to reduce sensory problems or correct relationship difficulties.

BRAIN TRAUMA AT BIRTH

More than half of autistic children show focal neurological defects and EEG abnormalities. Many have damage to the temporal lobe causing memory problems. Problems during birth tend to be 'significantly more common than average among children with autistic disorders' (Wing, 1996, p79). A 2004 study of perinatal factors suggested:

> "Compared with control subjects, cases had significantly older parents and were more likely to be firstborn. Case mothers had greater frequencies of threatened abortion, epidural caudal anaesthesia use, labour induction, and a labour duration of less than 1 hour. Cases were more likely to have experienced fatal distress, been delivered by an elective or emergency caesarean section, and had an Apgar score of less than 6 at 1 minute. Cases with a diagnosis of autism had more complications than those with pervasive developmental disorder not otherwise specified or Asperger syndrome. Non-affected siblings of cases were more similar to cases than control subjects in their profile of complications."
>
> (Glasson, et al., 2004, *Abstract*)

These authors, as do most, attribute such complications to underlying 'genetic factors'. However, a newborn baby's cranium is soft in order to allow it to more easily pass through the vagina at birth and can therefore be damaged in many different ways. In a Danish Study (Larrson, et al., 2005) a breech position at delivery, low Apgar scores (<5) and a history of schizophrenia in the family, each showed increased risk of later autism. A study in Utah by Bilder, et al. (2009) found a combination of breeched position at birth and mothers over 35 when the child was their first, was twice as likely to result in a child who later developed ASD. At one London hospital babies had a 12% increased likelihood of being diagnosed with autism/ASD. This was accounted for by the policy of the hospital to schedule all mothers for Caesarean section one week prior to their due dates. Birth interventions utilising suction and forceps can also change blood flow patterns to the brain itself. These changes have been correlated with increased risk of neurological dysfunction such as autism and cerebral palsy (Centers, 2011).

A)   OSTEOPATHY

Osteopathy is practised by those trained to MD standard. It manipulates soft connective tissue in order to balance the tendons, muscles and ligaments attached to bones. These place tension on joints by manipulating limbs and body areas. Cranial osteopathy is not simply a focus on the cranium, but includes the whole body as with osteopathy generally. In ASD cranial osteopaths often work on areas which may have become pressured or damaged during labour and birth. Viola Frymann, a pioneer in the use of osteopathy with developmentally delayed children, showed that prolonged and/or difficult labour is the most common cause of development delays in children. 80% of children with learning difficulties, attention deficits and autism, suffered traumatic birth during which the cranium was compressed as it passed down the birth canal. This limited physiological motion disturbs the development of the nerve pathways, impairing coordination and confusing sensory input, so that the behaviours, psychological 'symptoms' and sensory disorder of ASDs are most likely effects rather than causes (Frymann, 1998). An infant's skull is only partially formed at birth allowing it to change shape or mould during the birth process, while protecting the brain inside. During normal labour, the infant's head is severely compressed, causing the soft bones of the skull to overlap, bend and warp. This reduces the size of the head and helps ease the baby's passage through the narrow birth canal. Elizabeth Hayden, a practising cranial osteopath writes:

> "The birth of a baby is one of the most stressful events of its life. As it squeezes, twists and turns along the short but stressful journey into the outside world, the baby's head normally absorbs these strains, which are then released naturally after birth. But if the baby has problems coping with the labour and recovery, many of these stresses can remain unresolved....Every structure of the body will then need to cope with this distortion, becoming the root of many different problems both in childhood and right into adult life."
>
> (Hayden, 2000, p34)

That is: the whole body, and not just the head and brain will be affected. After delivery, the skull normally de-compresses, re-expanding to its normal shape with the help of the baby crying, sucking and yawning. During the first 10 days of its life, the baby's head gradually loses most of the moulding pattern as the bones of the skull shift back into position. Breast feeding is one of the key ways the head releases this birth-moulding. Problems can arise if these distortions fail to release in the stiffer bones of the base of the brain and cervical region. These body parts become cartilage and are harder than the membranous tissue nearer the vertex. Any unresolved hardening here will become ossified as bone replaces cartilage into adult life.

CRANIALSACRAL THERAPY (CST)

CST is a slightly different version of this. Research by Pardo et al. (2005) showed a localised immune-response of the brain with increased levels of pro-inflammatory cytokines, neuroglial activation and inflammatory changes in the cerebrospinal fluid of the autistic patients studied. Consequently, CST practitioners suggest:

> "...ASD is partially caused by a loss of flexibility and probable inflammation of the membrane layers surrounding the brain. This compromise can create restrictive forces on the brain tissue leading to adverse strain on the internal body-regulating components of the hypothalamus, the reticular activating system and the autonomic nervous system; irritation and hypersensitivity of neurons, glial cells and neurological pathways; abnormal pressure change within the brain tissue; adverse affect on the limbic (emotional) system; over-heightened central nervous system immune response; brain tissue congestion and toxicity; and endocrine system compromise."
>
> (Wanveer, 2007)

Such effects would be very likely to impact both physically and emotionally on later development. CST practitioners believe that if the inner restrictive pressures can be relieved many of the ASD behaviours and symptoms can be removed.

RESEARCH

Osteopathy can significantly improve symptoms in children with developmental problems. A 3 year study of Frymann with 186 children in 1972 paper showed osteopathic treatment improved sensory, intellectual and motor performance in children with neurological problems. Dr John Upledger, who established cranial sacral therapy states his studies:

> "…consistently revealed that the intracranial membranes were very tight. Our findings suggested that for some reason the meningeal intracranial membranes, especially the dura mater that is very tough and waterproof, were not expanding along with the normal growth of the skull bones and the brain. I tested this concept by examining sixty three children who had been rated as either autistic or childhood schizophrenic…I was able to pick out the autistic children from the sample with over 90% accuracy simply by manually evaluating each child's craniosacral system."
>
> (Upledger, 2011)

However, favourable responses to CST were often lost when there was no treatment for three or four months, suggesting lack of growth of the *dura mater* while the skull and brain grow as a contributing cause for autism. For this reason weekly sessions of CST are recommended throughout the child's growth.

FURTHER INFORMATION

UK

More information on osteopathy for children (paediatric) generally is found at:
    www.fpo.org.uk/osteopathic-centre-for-children
    www.osteopathy.org.uk
Paediatric osteopaths can refer to cranial specialists registered with them. Their practitioners can be located at:
    www.fpo.org.uk/about/paediatric-osteopath-search
    www.osteopath-help.co.uk/osteopaths/cranial-osteopathy/major_uk_ towns
Sources for cranial osteopathy and practitioners can be found at:

http://www.cranial.org.uk/

http://www.cranial.org.uk/find.php

CranialSacral Therapy practitioners can be found at:

www.craniosacral.co.uk/

USA

Based in California, but providing contacts for cranial osteopaths in all States:

www.osteopathiccenter.org/autism.html

BOOKS/READING

Osteopathy for Children by Elizabeth Hayden (1999) provides an overview of osteopathy in birth, infancy and childhood.

B)   TOUCH THERAPY/MASSAGE

Language and thought (cognition) develop in response to talk, gaze and touch, (Sutton, Utting & Farrington, 2006). However, many children with ASD are highly sensitive to touch. Temple, for example, describes an intense desire for, but simultaneous fear of being hugged. Touch deprivation can therefore feed into the cycle of problems in ASD. Tiffany Field, a leading researcher and practitioner in the area of touch therapy, describes touch as 'our most social sense':

> "Touch, affecting both tactile and pressure receptors, stimulates the central nervous system (CNS) into a state of relaxation. Anxiety and stress levels, both behavioural and bio-chemical, are then reduced and the general effect is a relaxed, more attentive, state."
>
> (Field, 2003, p17)

TOUCH WITH AUTISTIC CHILDREN

Children with autism frequently display aversion to touch. At least some of this aversion appears to be learned, or conditional upon early experiences.

For example, Field found that many pre-term babies who received invasive medical procedures to the chest and abdomen remained permanently averse to being touched in that region, refusing massage in that area (Field, 2003). And, although some children with autism may be averse to cuddling, they can respond positively to touch with pressure and so enjoy massage. For example, when a group of children with Down's syndrome were encouraged to hug similar aged and sized children with autism, the latter were very responsive (Older, 1982, p79). Work by Waal also found that children with autism will accept certain kinds of massage and hugging (Waal, 1955). Interestingly, Temple described her aversion to being 'swallowed up' by her kindly relative, rather than to touch itself. Field suggests:

> "Children with autism are often described as extremely sensitive to touch; they often dislike being touched. In spite of this, however, we have noted that they love being massaged, maybe because, unlike random touching in social situations, massaging is predictable."
>
> (Field, 2003, p134)

Massage has been found to effect blood composition with increases of oxygen and decreases in stress-hormones (Harris & Lewis, 1994).

RESEARCH

There are a number of studies in support of massage/touch therapy with children with autism. In a study by Field and colleagues (1996) with pre-school children, ten days of massage therapy led to a decrease in disruptive behaviour in the classroom and an increase in relating with the teacher. In a similar study in which parents massaged their children every night, the children's sleep also improved (Escalona, et al., 2001). In a study by Cullen and Barlow parents of five children with autism were given a Touch Therapy Training Programme (TTTP) with semi-structured interviews before and after the programme. The results showed that, despite their low expectations of TTTP, these parents found their children were "cuddlier". They reported their children asked for the therapy and both parents and children found it relaxing. These parents also 'valued the opportunity to learn a practical skill they could do with their children' (Cullen & Barlow, 2001).

FURTHER INFORMATION

Details of the Touch Therapy Training Programme used in that study can be found at the Touch Research Institute website:

www6.miami.edu/touch-research.com

Massage with children with ASDs is described at:

www.massagetoday.com/mpacms/mt/article.php?id=13157

AVAILABILITY

Massage therapists can be found by location at:

USA

www.massagetoday.com/locator/

UK

www.gcmt.org.uk/

BOOKS

Touch, by Tiffany Field (2003) published by MIT Press, gives details of TTTP.

Therapeutic Massage and Bodywork for Autism Spectrum Disorders: A Guide for Parents and Caregivers by Virginia Cowen (2011), is a practical manual.

Baby Massage, by Amelia Auckett, (1989) describes how to assist an infant with massage therapy following a traumatic birth and in their general development.

C)   HOLDING THERAPY/PROLONGED PARENT-CHILD EMBRACE (PPCE)

This programme is based on the supposition that attachment (or maternal bonding) is the key element in autism. In the 1970s, while working with autistic patients in New York, Dr Martha Welch devised a family treatment aimed at repairing the regulatory maternal attachment necessary for child development. During the 1980s she developed what became known as 'Holding Therapy' now called *Welsh Prolonged Parent-Child Embrace Therapy* (PPCE). This involves the mother physically restraining the child by holding while requiring them to make eye contact. The aim is to break down the child's avoidance of personal interaction and establish a relationship through which development can progress. In the programme, the child is held in embrace by the mother with the father, or sometimes the mother's own mother, acting in support. Trevarthan et al. write:

> "It is likely that children can gain a calming effect from firm restrain, in addition to any benefits from enforced contact with a person. Holding is not likely to be more beneficial than less coercive techniques or overcoming avoidance, such as those employed in the Option approach...but may aid development of communication with some children."
>
> (Trevarthan et al., 1998, p149)

Welch believes no child is too old to benefit from PPCE and, although the child is held against their will, this is also the case in many normal daily situations for children with autism due to the problematic nature of their behaviour. Children with ASD frequently experience hours of distress, inconsolable rage or unhappiness and necessary limitations on their freedom. In ABA there is also a level of coercion with the child having no choice about performing the tasks demanded of them by the practitioners. Holding Therapy was one of the first forms of therapeutic treatment for children with autism which offered hope of a 'cure' (Tinbergen & Tinbergen, 1983/93) and so has suffered from institutional disfavour for this reason and because it is assumed that in doing so, blame is being apportioned to the mother. Ironically, however, 'Holding' itself has since been integrated fully into treatments for ASD and is often part of standard advice to parents and established ASD schools programmes. Nevertheless, both Temple Grandin and Donna Williams have suggested there are probably less traumatic ways to bring about the same results as PPCE. For example, Temple writes:

> "During my travels to many autism conferences several parents have reported to me that holding therapy was beneficial. It is not the 'cure'

that some of its proponents tout, but it had a beneficial effect on some children. In my opinion, the benefits of holding therapy could be obtained by less stressful methods....Fisher (1988) describes a gentler approach to holding that worked with her daughter. One mother told me that she gently encouraged her child to tolerate more and more holding and he responded with increased affection and improved eye contact. Owers and Thorworth (1985) found that eye contact and interest in people improved after a gentler behavioral method was used. In one case a young boy was held in a light hug until crying lessened. As soon as crying was reduced the boy was released. Gradually the amount of holding time was increased. In its less coercive form, holding can be initiated by the child and is often part of other programmes in this way."

(Grandin & Scariano, 1987/96)

It does seem that there are preferable methods to re-establishing the mother/child relationship than forcing the child into it, and holding in its original form is now not used in the UK.

LEA USE OF HOLDING

As part of a comparative *Report* of interventions for children with autism/ASD from 1989-1993, Jones and colleagues describe holding therapy being used by some local education authority (LEA) schools and units. Some variations in the method were adopted by LEA staff, and some from that proposed originally by Welsh. Some of the children experienced 20-60 minutes of holding, and were encouraged to look at their mothers and respond to what she was saying and gained 'an improvement in their ability to relate to an interact with her and other people'. Some but not all of the children talked about their own feelings (Jones et al., 1994, p28). The therapist's role was to help the mother and child tolerate the feelings that arose and continue the holding during them. It is important to bear in mind that Welch attributed the break in mother/child relationship (attachment) to conscious choice on behalf of the child, frequently adopting a Freudian stance (as a psychiatrist) critical of the mother's attitude to the child. However, in the ecological theory, this is not the case. The break in entrainment is not elected, or voluntary, but the result of a trauma which has psychologically isolated the child from its mother. The result is a survival response to a frequently physically-instigated trauma, which may also include a degree of toxicity. Some children may therefore not be able to respond to forced holding in this way, and it may not in fact be advisable for them. As Temple suggests, it may also not be the best way of achieving the required end. However, optional holding – once a child is able to request it – appears entirely beneficial.

RESEARCH SUPPORT

The re-establishment of attachment through PPCE has been found to lead to recovery from autism in some cases. For example, Zappella et al. (1991) identified 10 children as autistic using DSM III criteria. Following PPCE, 2 of the children improved rapidly with the complete disappearance of any signs of ASD. Six children improved to various degrees, while two remained unchanged. In a session with two children, witnessed by this author in 1983, a 4 year old boy remained largely unchanged (although he did became able to accept holding by his mother without objection at home) while the second, a girl of 3, altered significantly after 90 minutes of PPCE. She began playing peek-a-boo with her parents from under a blanket in the room, smiling and making full eye-contact.

FURTHER INFORMATION

The Martha Welch Center in the USA can be accessed at:
    www.marthawelch.com
A full description of holding as therapy by Gregory Keck, a practitioner at the Attachment and Bonding Centre of Ohio:
    www.abcofohio.net

BOOKS

Holding Time by Martha Welch (1989). Gives the Welch Method philosophy, details on her theory of the pivotal role of attachment and outlines the practice of PPCE.

Autistic Children: New Hope for a Cure by N and E Tinbergen,(1983/93) contains several case studies of children who experienced this therapy.

CHAPTER 6

THE STRUCTURE OF RECOVERY

As was shown in Chapter 1, individuals have varied pathways to autism so may require different types of support, and at various times, as part of their process of recovery. Generally, these programmes have been used 'ad hoc' by parents and individuals as and when they hear of them. This is largely because the underlying mechanism in ASD has not until now been fully explored. However, realising that autism results from traumatic overload of the limbic system (AL/MC) enables a greater understanding of both its real nature and the internal process by which (under the right circumstances) an individual may 'grow out of' autism or 'recover', physically and psychologically. In this chapter, I attempt to draw together a structure within which this process can be viewed, with the aim of making it simpler for an individual to find which type of programme/s may best help them. By identifying the elements of the trauma in autism/ASD, and relating these to both the recovery process and the type of programmes required, it becomes possible to construct an individual recovery plan (IRP) to optimise outcomes and to map progress along this path.

THE ELEMENTS OF THE TRAUMA: THREE DOMAINS

In Chapter 1 a number of pathways illustrating the impact of various physical traumas were described. Figure 16, below, shows the effect of hypoxia (as in Ann's pathway) on the limbic system:

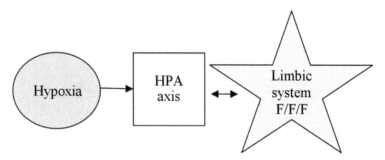

Figure 16 Traumatic Impact of Hypoxia

In autism/ASD each pathway results in an allostatic (limbic) overload, throwing the immune system into fight/flight and the associated difficulties described in the personal narratives. Some pathways will include toxicity from damage to the gut, with subsequent chronic gut/brain poisoning and/ or inflammation. All entail developmental derailment or dysregulation exhibited through the cognitive (mental) difficulties characteristic of autism/ ASD, such as with executive control, theory of mind (TOM) and *weak central coherence* (WCC). A closer study of these effects reveals that there are three distinct aspects, or domains, to the AL/MC trauma in autism/ ASD:1) physiological toxicity/damage; 2) de-railed/disrupted physical development and, 3) disrupted/delayed cognitive/social development. These three domains are interconnected, with the cognitive/social elements (3) resting upon sound physical health and development (1+2) as shown in Figure 17, below:

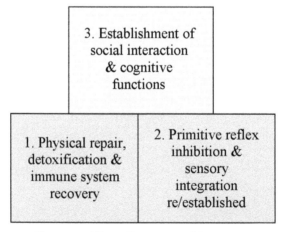

Figure 17 Three Domains of Recovery

For optimum recovery all three domains must be addressed. I examine each in more detail below.

1   TOXICITY & PHYSIOLOGICAL DAMAGE

Physiological damage includes inflammation of the gut, 'leaky gut', inflammation of the brain and dysregulation of the immune system. This may include neurotoxicity from errant food particles crossing the brain barrier; hypoglycaemia; the varied allergic states experienced by individuals with autism/ASD, and hormonal dysfunction impacting on sleep. While the immune system is in a state of chronic disarray these (and other health issues) will persist. Cytokines from chronic inflammation will continue to bombard the brain, triggering the limbic system's flight/flight/freeze response. Demyelination may occur, in which the covering (myeline) of the nerves breaks down, destroying effective brain-processing. As a result, skills previously gained (such as language) may be lost. However, if detoxification and repair of the immune system are possible, methylation (the 'turning on and off' of genes) and other essential bodily processes can re-establish, and healthy immune and nervous system function may be restored. This will clearly be subject to the amount of permanent damage that has occurred as a result of the original trauma.

PRIMITIVE REFLEXES AND SENSORY INTEGRATION

Sensory integration (described in Chapter 5) is usually disrupted in autism/ASD. In typical development multisensory processing occurs as tactile, visual and auditory sensory input becomes associated with its meaning. However, damage/disruption to physically-based functions, such as primitive and infant reflexes, will interfere with this. Poor sensory nerve connections (including from demyelination) will lead to difficulty in processing and interpreting, with the result that problems such as hypersensitivity (such as to touch and noise) may occur. Poor sensory integration may also result in weak central cohesion (WCH) which is a tendency to perceive fragmented details and not the 'whole picture'. An example of which was given by Donna Williams (Chapter 4, Narrative 8) who describes how vestiges of retained primary reflexes prevented her from integrating perceptual information from her own and her partner's faces, and how Irlen glasses corrected this. If these reflexes are not inhibited at the right time and in the right sequence their effects will also hinder developmental milestones and impede later cognitive development.

EMOTIONAL EXPERIENCE & EMPATHY

As with all sensory processing, emotional recognition and expression depend on how sensory stimuli are processed; of differentiation of body sensations, and on the associated 'meanings' and 'names' learned for each different feeling as it is 'felt'. Once we have repeatedly experienced a particular combination, and have learned to identify its emotional meaning, we create the brain connections necessary to recognise the same constellation (empathise) in others. If a physically traumatic disruption occurs early in life, this will prevent the necessary integration for this process to occur, resulting in sensory confusion. It has been suggested (e.g. Baron-Cohen, 2003) that individuals with autism/ASD cannot empathise. However, we know from the biographical narratives that this is not exactly so. Wendy Lawson gives an 'insider' view:

> "Recently, I have been able to talk to my family about why I appear so 'distant', 'scatty', forgetful and 'unemotional'. I explained that it is not that I do not have emotions, but rather that I connect with them differently and for different reasons than they do."
>
> (Lawson, 2000, p15)

And, in a study of *alexithymia* (a term referring to abnormalities in emotional expression) it was found that participants with autism/ASD were able to appreciate emotions in music, although not necessarily to talk about those emotions (Berthoz & Hill, 2005). These are examples of poor sensory integration, rather than lack of emotion. For emotional processing to occur both brain hemispheres of the higher cortex are required to work together, with nerve connections forged between the higher cortex (language) and the sub-cortical (limbic/emotional) brain. Without sufficient of these, states such as that described by Wendy Lawson can result:

"I was often confused and my sense of 'self' was very muddled and frightening. I could go to the shops and then forget why I was there. I got lost easily and even forgot my own name. Some days it was difficult to make even the smallest of decisions such as whether to eat one or two sandwiches."

(Lawson, 2000, p51)

However, as Wendy explains, emotional processing can be developed:

"I have learnt to recognise the subtle differences between anger, frustration and disappointment, and understand why I feel these things. By studying an individual's posture, actions, voice tone and facial expression, I can now usually work out what they are feeling."

(Lawson, 2000, p9)

Another example of poor sensory association is found in Florica Stone's description (Chapter 4, Narrative 1) of how her son, Alex, believed he changed his identity to 'Frightened' when he was afraid, and was no longer 'Alex'. Such a state is more akin to that of a very young infant who has yet to establish discreet sensory processing brain areas than to a permanent impairment (this suggestion is supported by his ATEC scores, which are all on the sensory sub-scale). This facet of his development altered as Alex recovered and was able to learn the necessary sensory associations.

3   COGNITIVE & SOCIAL DEVELOPMENTAL DISRUPTION

Repairing physical damage/toxicity (Domain 1) and correcting disruption to reflexes and poor sensory integration (Domain 2) together form the physical foundation of recovery. And it may be that, once these bodily aspects are ameliorated, cognitive/social development will re-establish unaided (as in some of the narratives described earlier). This is because the brain chemicals required (GABA/DHEA/Serotonin pathway) will now replace those of flight/fight (HPA/fear pathway), with dopamine channelled into exploring the wider world rather than fixed on possible threats. Additional measures to aid cognitive and social development (Domain 3) may then be required.

SURVIVAL VERSUS DEVELOPMENT

In autism/ASD the absence of the 'mother' in her role as regulator of fear leaves the child 'stuck' in motivational conflict (MC) until such time as the trauma state is resolved. Reducing the underlying limbic/allostatic load (AL) enables the necessary shift out of survival-driven functioning (MC) altering the biochemistry from fear- to exploration-based. This is illustrated in Figure 18, below:

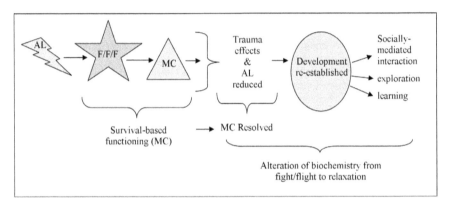

Figure 18 As AL/MC Resolves Development Re-Establishes

The concept of motivational conflict (described in Chapter 1) is therefore crucial in understanding how and why recovery is possible. In motivational conflict, chronic cortisol levels exhaust supplies of DHEA (the relaxation hormone) creating a fall in available serotonin and melatonin, encouraging social withdrawal and disrupting sleep. In contrast to the biochemical state in a secure, typically developing child, in ASD dopamine is utilised to target threats to survival or obsessive interests, rather than stimulating new experiences in the wider, social world. However, as Figure 18 shows, when MC ends, this state alters to enable social exploration to emerge.

PROGRAMMES WITHIN RECOVERY DOMAINS

Looking again at the programmes in Chapter 5, we can see how they address different aspects of the trauma and (where these apply) its toxic elements. And that all but two fit into the three domains of recovery, as shown in Figure 19, below:

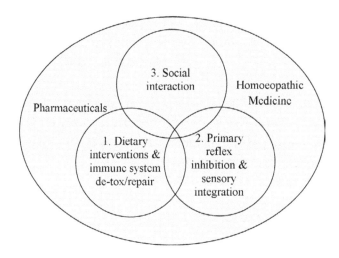

Figure 19 Programmes Within the Three Recovery Domains

Dietary interventions (such as the casein/gluten free diet; anti-yeast diet; specific carbohydrate diet; and nutritional supplementation), are all aimed at reducing chronic inflammation and brain toxicity by healing the gut, repairing demyelination and detoxifying the immune system (Domain 1). The BIRD and INPP programmes are both methods of inhibiting primary reflexes (Domain 2) with AIT, Kaplan's Vision Therapy and the touch programmes also designed to improve sensory re-integration (Domain 2). Social interaction programmes (Domain 3) include ABA, DIR/Floortime, Son-Rise, RDI and II. The remaining two programmes are generic medical approaches, represented by the pharmaceutical and homoeopathy options, and so embrace all three domains.

OPTIMUM ORDER

In recovery it would appear logical to address the three domains in numerical order as, while the child is suffering from toxic neurochemicals (due to leaky gut, for example) working to re-instate lost cognitive/social function may be less likely to succeed. James's mother (Chapter 4, Narrative 2) noted this when adopting ABA only after a gut healing diet:

"I think if we had not embarked on the diet and vitamin and mineral supplementation, we would have made little progress with ABA."

(Edelson & Rimland, 2006, p83)

However, in most of the personal narratives in Chapter 4 no particular sequence was followed. This is probably because recovery is currently a 'hit and miss' affair, with parents and others trying any programme that may be able to help, rather than a more individualised 'plan'.

INDIVIDUAL RECOVERY PLANS

It could be helpful to illustrate how an individual recovery plan (IRP) might be utilised to develop a more structured, personalised approach and optimise recovery potential. The following examples of hypothetical IRPs have been constructed from the eight narratives presented in Chapter 4. Although drawn up in hindsight, they are indicative of how an IRP can identify the particular needs of any individual, and so assist in programme choices. There are three steps to an IRP; a) assessment of what is needed, b) drawing up the plan and, c) choosing programmes that may help.

STEP A   ASSESSING WHAT IS NEEDED

It is not essential to understand what has contributed to/triggered the AL/trauma experienced by an individual in order to address its effects. However, it is important that each affected domain is indentified. This will save discomfort, time and money. There are tests that can be requested of any GP that will establish the presence of gut dysbiosis, allergies or chronic inflammation (for example). It is also possible to easily indentify retained primitive and primary reflexes by using a guide such as that of Goddard (2003). And, assessment of the cognitive difficulties experienced by the individual can be obtained as part of any typical, diagnostic ASD interview. (A GP or educational psychologist can help with a referral). All of this information is assembled into the IRP. The key point is that an IRP will reflect the nature of the trauma for that individual, and not the label or diagnosis of 'autism/ASD'.

STEP B   DRAWING UP THE PLAN

Figure 20, below, illustrates a sample layout for an ASD, IRP. The information gathered in Step A is entered as 'Symptoms'. Beside this the domain in which help is needed is identified. A matching programme can then be chosen according to preference. (Appendix III provides a blank IRP plan form).

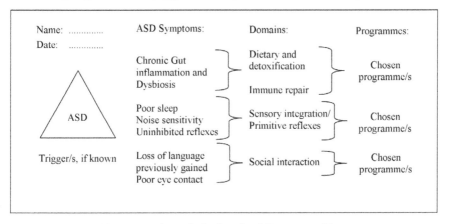

Figure 20 Sample Individual Recovery Plan

STEP C   CHOOSING THE PROGRAMMES

Programmes are chosen to meet the specific needs identified for that individual. Chapter 5 contains a varied resource directory reflecting the examples found in this study. However, there may be similar alternatives which are more convenient, affordable or appealing to the user than those described in that chapter. Unfortunately, until such time as established service providers recognise that autism/ASD is not 'genetic' but represents a traumatic state, requiring physical as well as developmental assistance, the general accessibility of recovery programmes is likely to remain limited. This study offers a first step in trying to address this difficulty by simplifying all but the cost element.

EXAMPLE IRPs

In this section the format shown above has been applied to each of the Narratives in Chapter 4 to give an idea of how an IRP might be used in practice.

NARRATIVE 1   ALEX

The illustration below shows an IRP for Alex:

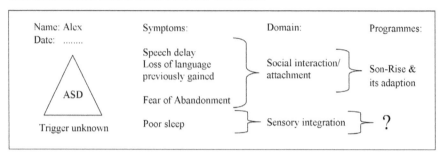

Alex was late speaking (18 months) and then lost what speech he initially had. He also showed poor social integration. His mother's adapted Son-Rise programme was highly successful with regaining and then increasing speech and language areas and, ultimately, with Alex's underlying insecurity. From his final ATEC (see page 71) it can be seen that his remaining scores are almost all on the Health and Physical Behaviour scale (9 points). This scale includes aspects related to poor sleep, sensory sensitivity and obsessive activities. So, while Alex has made excellent progress, from drawing up an IRP it can be seen that these sensory aspects may not have been directly addressed. Additional help with sensory integration programmes could therefore prove beneficial to Alex.

NARRATIVE 2   JAMES

James's chosen programmes are shown in the IRP below. As can be seen from the triangle section of the IRP, James experienced multiple triggers in the presence of a family BAE and, consequently, his autism is quite severe. His lack of speech contributes a total of 20 points on his final ATEC (see page 92). The majority (11 points) fall into the Health and Physical Behaviour scale. This suggests that, despite great gains, further help with James's developmental delay might prove helpful. Programmes other than those already utilised, such as individualised homeopathy (as with Max: Chapter 5, Narrative 5) might therefore prove useful.

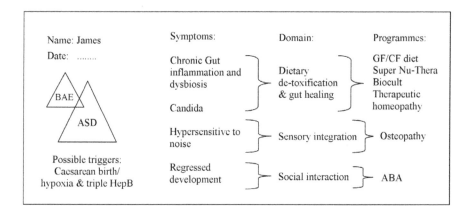

NARRATIVE 3   CAMPBELL

Campbell's treatment combined dietary and social interactive programmes successfully. His final ATEC (see page 98) is one of the few which scored 0 in each of the subscales. As a result of her experience, his mother (a doctor) developed her own gut dysbiosis treatment clinic in Cambridge, UK (see Chapter 5, Narrative 3). Interestingly, she comments that using ABA helped her to change her son's diet, so that ABA was used alongside dietary changes, rather than following it. However, it is possible that social interaction programmes will be more effective once the toxic elements from chronic inflammation are resolved. Campbell's IRP is shown below:

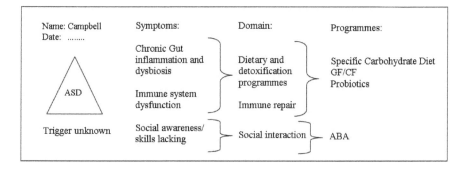

NARRATIVE 4   TEMPLE

At the time of Temple's recovery very little in the way of specific social interaction programmes existed, so that older individuals, such as Temple, Donna and Mark, depended upon self-help and/or parents and/or helpful others to assist them in understanding the world. At school Temple benefited from the social feedback and support of her teacher. Having experienced an early physical trauma (see page 267-8) Temple's infant brain has 're-wired' itself as part of her recovery, leaving her with unusual perceptive abilities. Her ATEC (see page 114) indicates that most of her remaining issues are physical health related (11 points on this scale). Her extreme sensitivity to touch is highly characteristic of the sensory integration problems common in autism/ASD. Consequently, further physically-based /sensory integration programmes could be of use to Temple. An IRP for Temple is given below:

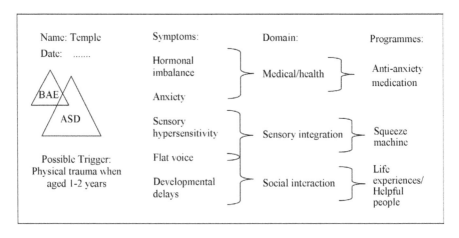

NARRATIVE 5   MAX

Max's IRP is shown below:

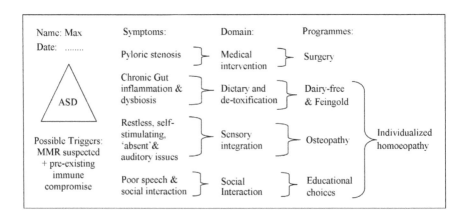

Max received a range of treatments including the Feingold Diet, osteopathy and individualised homoeopathy. He also changed schools freely as his needs altered. Max's social difficulties largely cleared without the need for a specific social interaction programme, suggesting it can be beneficial to begin with dietary and sensory issues as resolution of these may lead to a developmental 'reboot'. His ATEC score of 2 points (page 132) shows only slight Sociability and Sensory/Cognitive Awareness scores (1 point each) which are likely to improve as he continues with his chosen programmes.

NARRATIVE 6   WILLIAM

William's IRP, below, contains the range of programmes which together achieved the good progress he had made at the time of his narrative account. William's ATEC score (see page 140) showed a dominance of points (9) on the Sensory/Cognitive Awareness scale as a reflection of his developmental delay. Additional programmes which assist with this type of delay, such as individualised homeopathy, could therefore be beneficial.

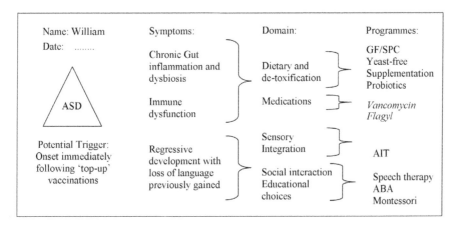

NARRATIVE 7   MARK

The importance of assistance with sensory integration, even at a later stage (adulthood) can be seen in the narratives of both Mark and Donna (below). Mark was 30 years of age when his narrative was written. Although Pat, his mother, adopted a sugar-free diet, she found it difficult, initially, to gain any help for him other than medications and educational settings.

Various changes in the latter were made until one suitable for Mark was found. Mark's ATEC score is 15 (see page 154) of which 6 points fall in the Sensory/Cognitive Awareness scale and 4 points in the Sociability scale. This latter may reflect Mark's difficulties establishing his niche and/or feeling equivalent to his peers, so that counselling/support through helpful people, such as that found by Donna and Temple, might prove useful to his self-esteem. I have therefore included this in his IRP below:

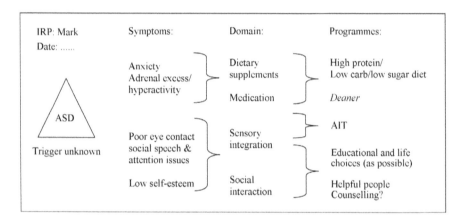

NARRATIVE 8   DONNA

An IRP is shown below for Donna:

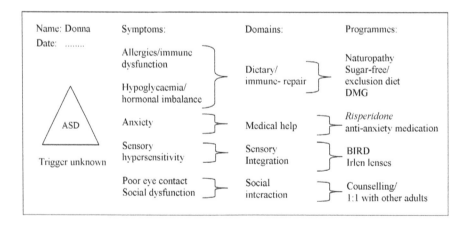

Donna experienced a high degree of physical immune dysfunction in the form of blood sugar/ hormone imbalances and food allergies. These reduced following naturopathic treatment, while her sensory and social skills improved following reflex inhibition and with Irlen sensory integration glasses. Anxiety medication appears also to have been prescribed. At times Donna found it helpful to find one trusted person with whom she could gain insight into her own and the 'other' world. Her final ATEC score (following the fourth part of her autobiography) is 8 points (see page 173). Of these, 6 points fall into the Health/Physical Behaviour scale, suggesting continued physical health and/or sensory support could be of assistance to her.

THREE Rs OF RECOVERY

The example IRPs above have been drawn up following interventions, rather than before these were selected, as would usually be the case. However, I hope they help demonstrate that there is likely to be an 'optimum order' to the recovery process, which reflects the impact of the original trauma in autism/ASD. This 'order' can be seen as the three Rs of recovery: *repair*, *reinstate* and *relate*, as shown in Figure 21, below:

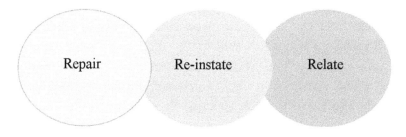

Figure 21 Three Rs of Recovery

The three Rs of recovery therefore parallel the three domains of recovery described earlier (see Figure 17). As noted earlier, in the narratives explored in this book, individuals used a variety of programmes. What is perhaps most noteworthy is that, although those for re-instating sensory integration and primitive reflexes (Domain 2/re-instate) are available, they appear to be the least utilised in autism/ASD recovery. One value of an IRP is that it highlights where this vital developmental step may have been overlooked in the need for attention to the more obvious physical health (Domain 1/ repair) and/or social (Domain 3/relate) problems.

'AUTISTIC' BRAIN ACTIVITY

Adopting an ASD behavioural social intervention programme without first addressing the underlying developmental and physiological foundation ASD may provide a positive outcome, but research using functional magnetic brain resonance (scanning) has found it leaves evidence of atypical language processing. For example, the study run at the University of Connecticut by Eigsti and her team (see Chapter 2) found the intervention used sparked compensatory brain changes, rather than promoting 'neurotypical' development:

> "The complete normalisation of language skills that we observed in children with optimal outcome [no longer diagnosed] from autism seems to reflect a rather atypical organisation at the level of the brain."
>
> (In: Griswold, 2016)

The children showed 'a unique signature' which reflected a tendency to compensate for difficulty with language. They additionally relied on right brain hemisphere regions as well as the more typical left hemisphere language areas. Those who lost their diagnoses of autism/ASD showed the highest level of activation in all of the relevant language areas of the brain. The study also noted that the younger the child when the intervention began, the more likely this positive outcome was, as Eigsti states:

> "One common characteristic of our kids with optimal outcomes is that they've begun receiving behavioural interventions really quite early, even as early as 18 to 24 months."
>
> (In: Griswold, 2016)

While it is possible that recruiting additional right-hemisphere areas is indicative of an individual's GI/ 'thinking style' (i.e. these children may be innately more right- or whole-brain dominant for language processing) it could, as Eigsti notes, represent a compensatory process. This is reminiscent of Temple's situation (see p267-8 below). Although she did not undergo a 'programme', her developmental recovery was nevertheless in tune with her innate GI.

REMNANTS OF AUTISM/ASD

As described in Chapter 2, Shulman and colleagues (2015) reviewed data on 38 ASD children, from racially and socioeconomically varied backgrounds, who were diagnosed between 2003-2013. Four years following diagnosis, ASD symptoms (on standard measures) in 7% (3) of the children were no longer present. Although the 'social impairment' of autism resolved and their IQ had improved, 92% (35 children) showed some residual signs of ASD. For example, language/learning difficulty was found in 68% and nearly half had externalizing problems such as attention-deficit/hyperactivity (ADHD). In addition, 24% experienced anxiety, obsessive compulsive disorder (OCD) or selective mutism (refusal to speak with no physical cause). Nearly three quarters required academic support such as a small class setting or extra resources. Shulman writes:

> "When an early diagnosis resolves, there are often other learning and emotional/behavioural diagnoses that remain. Understanding the full range of possible positive outcomes in this scenario is important information for parents, clinicians and the educational system."
>
> (Shulman et al., 2015)

The ecological theory of autism described in Chapter 1 (and in Poole, 2017) makes it clear why this partial resolution can occur. And, if we apply this new limbic trauma-based understanding of autism to Shulman's findings, we see that some of the psychological 'residual' aspects of autism/ASD are indeed outcomes of a chronic fight/flight response, as shown in the illustration below from Chapter 2:

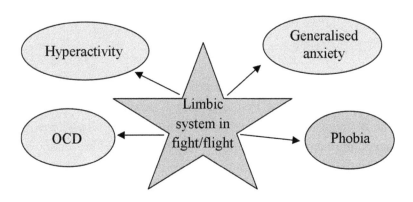

This suggests that with the children in Shulman's study social/cognitive factors of ASD have been effectively addressed. However, the underlying limbic-mediated trauma may not yet have been. The presence of such vestigial/residual 'symptoms' indicates that further work may be required with those children who exhibit them. This may possibly be of a biomedical focus, as *Treating Autism* note:

> "Many of our members have found that treating…biomedical conditions can lead to an improvement in a wide range of symptoms, including sleep, irritability, aggression, self-injurious, self-stimulatory and repetitive and obsessive behaviours. Some have seen improvements in the core symptoms of autism, speech and communication, sociability and imagination. A few parents have reported that treatment of co-morbid or underlying medical conditions, on its own, or alongside behavioural interventions and therapies, has brought about in their children a complete recovery from autism."
>
> (TA, *Website* 2017)

That this is so is understandable given what we now know about autism/ASD as being, not just a cognitive/social state, but a whole-person, developmental one, with limbic trauma, physical damage and developmental derailment. Given this, it is no longer helpful to view autism as a set of mentally-based 'impairments'. These 'residual' elements are not 'separate' but indicative of the initial trauma in autism/ASD. And, if they are not addressed as part of the recovery process, the limbic over-arousal underlying OCD, ADHD and other anxiety-based difficulties are likely to remain.

BRAIN RECOVERY

The degree to which recovery of speech and other functions (which may have developed initially but then been lost) is possible will depend largely on repair of demyelination and lost brain connections. Sadly, where there is permanent brain damage, full recovery may not occur. However, more may be achieved than historically thought possible. This is because it is now clear that the brain is receptive to environmental stimuli at any age, and grows in response to this. As such, it can 'rewire' itself to compensate for skills lost in another area of the cortex, as noted by Zimmerman:

> "A lot of the kids are improving, and we don't really know why, except we know there is a lot of moldability of the developing brain"
>
> (In: Goodman, 2012)

This potential comes from the fact that the brain – especially of the younger child – is essentially plastic. It is not a piece of 'hardware' as has so frequently been suggested in the past. On the contrary, it is a living, inter-relational system which does not initially have pre-defined areas designated for specific functions, but develops these in response to environmental signals and sensory information. This receptive nature of the brain means that the type and frequency of sensory input, the quality of nutrition (in building neuronal connections/myeline) and the subsequent emotional and cognitive meanings placed on them, will all influence brain development and function. It also means that findings from imaging research must be viewed as correlational rather than causative. That is, the differences found in the brain development of those with ASD are probably a reflection of the child's experience (or lack of it) rather than its 'cause' (Schulz, 2005). In early trauma to the brain physical compensation may even lead to some positive gains. Temple Grandin provides an interesting example of this and of the ability of the infant brain to recover from traumatic damage. In 2010 she underwent a series of MRI scans with Professor Schneider at the University of Utah. As she describes:

> "Afterwards, Schneider explained to me that he had been looking for areas in my brain that showed at least a 50 percent difference from the corresponding areas in a control [non-ASD]subject. Two findings 'really jumped out.'"
>
> (Grandin, 2014, p44)

One was that she had acquired a particularly large head. In addition, the left ventricle of her brain was found to be 57% longer than the right. It extended into the parietal cortex, associated with working memory and spatial orientation (hence mathematics and structural skills) and, through this, to the visual cortex. Another important finding was that the 'say what you see' sensory pathways: (sensory integration between what is seen and what is associated with it in speech sounds) was disrupted. Temple notes:

> "I asked Schneider to interpret these findings for me….Between birth and the age of one – infants engage in two activities that developmental researchers call verbal babbling and motor babbling. Verbal babbling refers to the familiar act of babies making noises to hear what they sound like. Similarly, motor babbling refers to actions such as waving a hand just to watch it move…during verbal babbling, fibres are growing to make the connection between the 'what you're seeing' and 'what you're doing' parts of the brain."
>
> (Grandin, 2014, p45)

The multisensory integration which links our physical bodies and cognitive functioning depends upon such 'babbling' activity throughout infancy. This generates brain connections, the most utilized of which become myelinated. Schneider hypothesised that Temple had experienced a disruption to her development between the age of 1-2 years, leaving her with a particular perceptive ability:

> "…some engineers use spatial visual thinking, but I use object visual thinking, so I am able to see a catastrophe before it happens…. During the Japanese tsunami catastrophe of 2011, the Fukushima nuclear power plants melted down because the tidal wave that came over the seawall flooded not only the main generator but its backup. And where was the backup located? In the basement – the basement of a nuclear power plant that is located next to the sea. As I read many descriptions of the accident, I could see the water flowing into the plant, and I could see the emergency generators disappearing under the water. (This is partly what I do as a consultant: I see accidents before they happen)."
>
> (Grandin, 2014, p169)

Although none of her three siblings did so, Temple's father demonstrated some of the traits associated with autism, so that she may have been susceptible to ASD through the BAE in a way that they were not. This may be because she and her father shared a similar GI/'thinking style'. However, it is important to note that Temple's special perceptions are not 'genetically determined'. Nor did they occur in the womb (in utero) which is the usual and favoured view of aetiology in ASD. Rather, they are due to an interaction between her innate thinking style and environmental factors during infancy. Temple's brain compensated of its own accord, as part of the innate healing ability which we all possess, resulting in a life-long physical compensation of brain development with resulting idiosyncratic perceptual skills. Between 10-30% of those with a diagnosis of autism/ASD appear to possess a 'special talent' such as Temple's (Howlin et al., 2009). And, like Temple, many talk about their special skills and the fact that they are happy to possess them. Some of these 'special talents' may result from a developmental adaption made in response to the initiating trauma, while others may be the result of constraint into limited areas of interest and brain function (See Poole, 2017, Chapter 13) for a discussion.

MEASURING PROGRESS

Using the ATEC at timed intervals during the recovery process could provide one way of assessing: a) what progress has been made and, b) what remains to be addressed. Similarly, constructing an IRP will help highlight the areas required for addressing remaining needs. It may also be helpful to update the 'diagnosis' triangle of the IRP (e.g. to ADHD/OCD) if the child becomes no longer diagnosable on a standard autism scale but retains remnants or vestiges, as found by Shulman. The new 'symptoms' will then become the focus rather than the previous diagnosis. The IRP can be dated at each review so that a record is kept. Overall, by these means recovery work may become more structured and less of a 'scatter-gun' affair.

THE AIM OF RECOVERY

As can be seen from Temple's example the brain is capable of recovery from gross trauma, especially under the age of eight years. In many cases, it can re-organise itself to compensate for physical trauma. The immune system is also capable of re-establishing optimum functioning when the physiological result of the trauma (chronic inflammation, gut damage, loss of nutrients) is repaired. The drive to communicate, learn and grow in human infants is innate. This means that enabling the individual to move out of survival-based function will open the door for developmental repair and 'catch-up'. There may be steps required to re-instigate this, such as re-establishing entrainment and intersubjectivity through increased social interaction, but once the allostatic load is reduced and motivational conflict resolved the system will automatically swing into psychological and emotional growth. Given what we know of brain plasticity, it is plain that we can always grow and change (this being easier, the younger we are). For this reason it is impossible for anyone to say what can or cannot be 'recovered' in autism. This study suggests it is only the degree of physical damage experienced that may constrain recovery but that, until the individual embarks on the recovery path for themselves, it simply cannot be known what is achievable. As Greenspan and Wieder found, some will do well and others will make minimal progress. It is up to the individual/s concerned what they wish to attempt. The aim therefore, in relation to recovery from autism/ASD, is to bring about the optimum physical health and happiness possible; reduce the chronic anxiety experienced by so many, and enable a more comfortable sense in social settings. For the latter, helpful others are required to compensate for the original break in the mother/infant dyad. (This vital relationship is explored in the next chapter)

ECOLOGICAL PARADIGM VERSUS MEDICAL MODEL

It can be seen from all of this that the conflict over whether autism is 'curable' or not rests inside a paradigm clash. That is: the dominant medical/genetic perception of autism/ASD is that the brain is fixed and 'impaired' (and therefore cannot be 'cured' or altered). In contrast, those who adopt an ecological perspective (environment/individual interaction), while finding the word 'cure' irrelevant, gain the perception that nothing is fixed in relation to human potential, as part of a more open-ended process, including towards recovery. This position may be more insecure in terms of certainty but it has the beneficial quality of being full of hope.

CHAPTER 7

THE MOTHER/INFANT
DYAD IN RECOVERY

From the personal narratives presented in Chapter 4 it is clear that, once toxicity, physical damage and immune-dysregulation are resolved (recovery Domains 1 + 2), social interaction (Domain 3) can be stimulated. The foundation for all social relationships is the mother/infant dyad: initially through entrainment, and then intersubjectivity. Consequently, in recovery from autism/ASD, aspects of this may need to be emulated or replicated in order to re/establish what has been lost. In this chapter I examine the social interaction programmes in Chapter 5 in the light of this suggestion. As a preliminary to this, the major functions of the mothering role are summarised.

THE MOTHERING ROLE

In this and previous writing (Poole, 2017) I refer to the 'mother' throughout. The reason is that mothering is a 'role': an important 'job' that is essential to the child's entire development. Mothering has evolved to ensure the survival of the infant and, provided she is able to undertake it, the biological mother is the optimum person in the dyad. This is because the mother and child are in a pre-existing relationship at birth (as described in Chapter 1) and so already 'know' each other. This may explain why individuals who were separated early on from their biological mothers frequently want to find her. Part of her will feel embedded in the child's memory simply because it is. Adaption to a new 'terrain' (mother) can occur, due to the plasticity of the infant brain. But this will take careful adjustment as, to the newborn, this will be rather like having a 'map' for a different country.

If the father has been sufficiently present in the environment during the mother's pregnancy, he will also be 'recognised' by the child: as will other close family members such as grandparents and/or other children, voices, and even music (Partanen, et al., 2013). Thus, although research suggests that the father's input is usually more related to the older child's peer-relationships and behavioural problems (Steele & Steele, 2001) he is well placed to provide mothering. A study using functional magnetic imaging (scanning) of the brains of first-time parents, who had been caring for their infants for less than a week, showed activation of what the researchers called a 'parenting network' of linked brain areas in both mothers and fathers (Norton, 2014). From this it seems that, although mothers' brains are more generally geared to understanding infant communication, fathers can also learn. And, of course, 'mothering' can also be given by others in the child's environment. The social interaction programmes for autism/ASD described in Chapter 5 tend to replicate aspects of the mother/child dyad (explored further in this chapter). Their practitioners – many of whom are male – are adept at assisting parents in recovering their children. Pat describes Mark's grandmother's actions (Chapter 4, Narrative 7):

> "With endless patience, my mother rolled a rubber ball back and forth with him and never quit when he wanted to wander off…Had I known this was the thing to do to help him, we would have stayed in his face every waking moment."
>
>   (Stehli, 2004, p4)

Also the support she received from the one helpful social worker who:

> "…offered practical mothering suggestions when I was 'at my wit's end', and personally counselled me when life was confusing….She and her husband became 'adopted grandparents' inviting my son to their home for weekends with them and their teenagers…"
>
>   (Stehli, 2004, p8)

And of course, in pre-nuclear families, or where there remains an extended family network, the mother would have the support of other, more experienced, mothers in her immediate community.

In recovery from autism/ASD there are three main areas in relation to mothering: A) the functions of mothering in the typical dyad; B) comparison of these with the range of actions of the social interaction programmes described in Chapter 5 and, C) how 'replicated mothering/parenting' in real life, such as described in the narratives of Temple and Donna (Chapter 4) may contribute to recovery.

A) MOTHER/INFANT INTERACTION IN TYPICAL DEVELOPMENT

Figure 22, below, illustrates the various functions performed by the mother in a typical dyad:

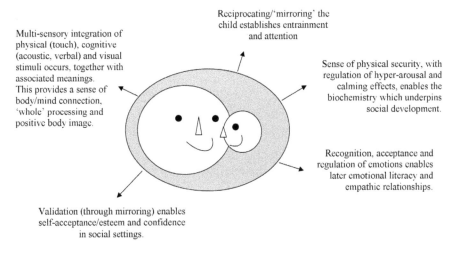

Reciprocating/'mirroring' the child establishes entrainment and attention

Multi-sensory integration of physical (touch), cognitive (acoustic, verbal) and visual stimuli occurs, together with associated meanings. This provides a sense of body/mind connection, 'whole' processing and positive body image.

Sense of physical security, with regulation of hyper-arousal and calming effects, enables the biochemistry which underpins social development.

Recognition, acceptance and regulation of emotions enables later emotional literacy and empathic relationships.

Validation (through mirroring) enables self-acceptance/esteem and confidence in social settings.

Figure 22 The Mother/Infant Dyad As Developmental Foundation

As can be seen, a functional mother/child dyad establishes a foundation for the survival, security, wellbeing and physical development of the child. Through entrainment and intersubjectivity she enables the social interaction necessary to provide a 'bridge' from the newborn state to the wider world of social relationships. This is summed up by Sirgar Sanger (Director of the *Early Infant Care Center* in New York) and John Kelley in their book: *The Magic Square* (their term for the dyad):

"Yes, they [mothers] are the source of emotional support….But they also help an infant shape his social, learning, and stress-management."

(Sanger & Kelley, 1986, p13)

Writing in the 1980s these authors outline the (then new) research into infant development which showed a much greater degree of inter-relatedness between mother and child than previously realised by professionals:

"Developmental experts call this new view of growth '*the fit*'. And what makes that an especially apt metaphor is that it sums up in a single, economical image our realisation that when parental looks, gestures, and sounds are tailored to the infant's needs, they not only hasten the emergence of his/her skills and talents, they also help ensure s/he realises these abilities to the fullest."

(Sanger & Kelley, 1986, p14)

These authors then highlight three aspects to 'the fit':

1.   Development is a two-sided process to which the infant and parents actively contribute.
2.   Mothers and fathers are primed with their own growth-promoting behaviours.
3.   A good fit enhances not only cognitive and social development but also emotional development.

All of this tells the infant, in a non-verbal fashion, that s/he is loved and understood. Even if there are a few 'blips', the overall sense given by a 'good fit' is that of security and trust in others; that people can be relied upon, and that personal confidence and competency can grow. Furthermore, as Sanger and Kelley conclude:

"One of the most satisfying and reassuring things about this new picture of development as a process of mutually fitting together is that it restores mothers and fathers to their rightful and central place in the child's growth cycle….*The Magic Square* [the dyad] represents an example of a natural process called ontogenetic adaption, which is how biologists describe the burst of development that occurs when an environment attains the perfect pitch of harmony with the needs of the organism it is supporting."

(Sanger & Kelley, 1986, p16-7)

As the infant brain reflects and responds to incoming environmental stimuli it is shaped and formed by these experiences, including how the mother/carer herself responds. Consequently, a child will refer to their mother to see how s/he should react to any new situation or possible threat (Sorce et al., 1985). Rothschild (2000) cites the work of Schore (1994) and Perry and colleagues (1995) who have proposed neurological models for understanding this crucial role. She states:

"A healthy attachment between infant and caretaker enables the infant to eventually develop the [brain] capacity to self-regulate both positive and negative stimuli."

(Rothschild, 2000, pp22-3)

The infant also develops self-worth and self-esteem through the validation enabled by a 'good fit'. Interestingly, research with students found lower self-esteem levels linked to greater efforts at validation (in their case on *Facebook*), indicating a general need to feel good about oneself (Graff, BPS, 2017). Like Sanger and Kelly, Daniel Stern, author of *The First Relationship* has studied the minute details of mother/infant interaction (Stern, 2002). He describes 'packages of behaviour' which consist of tiny movements and gestures forming 'the interactive dance of mothers and babies' (p3) which become the intersubjective relationship:

"For instance, a game of peek-a-boo does not consist of one single appearance of the mother's head accompanied by one surprise-face, but of a series of varied repetitions, in which the timing and the exact surprise-face differ slightly at each re-appearance. The sequence builds, in a pattern characteristic of each mother-infant dyad (for example, explosively or surreptitiously), to some equally characteristic end point. The end point may be sustained and shared hilarity....These packages of behaviour or 'episodes of engagement' or 'themes and variations' captured our attention because they are the material from which the baby learns what it is like to be with his mother."

(Stern, 2002, p5)

The mother adjusts her response to that of the infant so that this is a mutual process. She mirrors, validates and (for the most part) demonstrates her understanding of what the infant is 'saying' in the two-way behaviour:

> "These dyad-specific interactive packages are the experiences upon which the infant constructs a representational world of his caregivers."

(Stern, 2002, p5)

Initially this relationship develops with the mother/main carers and sets the scene for future relationships. From this follows the developmental milestone of pointing (usually by 12 months) which becomes sharing ('joint attention') in the second year, with the child pointing out things of interest to another person. The latter leads to the awareness that others may have a different point of view from us: a mental state known as *Theory of Mind* (TOM). TOM is one of the cognitive abilities considered to be lacking in autism/ASD (Hobson, 2002). In autism 'the fit' identified by Sanger and Kelley is largely absent due to the original traumatic break in entrainment between the mother/child dyad before intersubjectivity can fully establish. This is the case even if the mother is physically present. And, although she may then offer some degree of physical security, it is just as likely that some object dear to the child, or the arrangement of the room, will perform this role instead (see later section).

'OUT OF SYNC'

Daniel Stern has developed broader categories of 'regulatory failure' in which the characteristic patterns of mutual regulation by the mother and infant at the micro-level were observed. These occurred when the mother/child dyad were not in synchronicity (or entrained). Stern notes that perfect regulation within the mother/child dyad was unlikely, but that there was room for misalignments and misunderstandings between the mother and child pairs he studied. These often occurred with subsequent 'repair', which enabled the development of coping styles. However, a persistent lack of repair and insufficient attunement, such as over or under stimulation; the mother not understanding the infant's crying: or contradictory stimulation of the basic states that the infant required to be regulated; such as sleep, hunger, activity joy/pleasure, arousal etc, could all result in difficulties between mother and child (and later psychological problems).

A SENSE OF SECURITY

In autism/ASD a critical loss from disruption to the mother/infant dyad is of a sense of security. As we have seen, the mother regulates the infant's emotions, including fear, which enables the child to relax. She also interprets their world and, through repeated and repetitive routines (including 'games'), creates predictability and structure for the infant. All of this engenders a sense of safety and a desire to engage in the wider world. The child would typically internalise this sense, and the ability to calm themselves, as they grow up. 'Being together' becomes rewarding in itself, laying the foundation for a desire for social engagement as enjoyable. In autism/ASD, because of the early break with the mother, these functions have been disrupted. 'Being together' is also rewarding to the mother and she will usually wish to re-establish the typical dyadic relationship. This has been illustrated through a video interactive guidance (VIG) intervention with autistic infants and their mothers. Two mother/infant dyads were filmed interacting during play. The mother then observed the video with the practitioner. Following this, both mothers reported feeling more 'in tune' (in sync) with their child and they valued the opportunity to see their own interactions and improve effectiveness (McMillan, 2005). It is noticeable from this that entrainment can therefore be re-instated.

SECURITY OBJECTS

Typically developing children frequently provide substitutes for their mother by carrying a favourite toy or object around with them when she is no longer in direct contact or range. This tendency for favourite objects can also be seen in autism/ASD. For example, research by Geraldine Dawson found that 3-4 year old children with autism did not react to photographs of their mothers as do typically developing children and those with a learning disability. Instead, the autistic children reacted to pictures of their favourite toys (In: ScienceDaily, 2010). Interestingly, a report by the *National Autistic Society* found a possible explanation for the popularity of one such character:

> "The calm, slow, narration of the *Thomas the Tank Engine* TV programme helps children with autism and Asperger's syndrome to develop…the exaggerated fixed facial expressions of the characters make it easy for them to understand what emotion is being felt… simple scenery and bold colours also help children who are distracted by details and changes in sound or movement. The study of 81 parents found that children with autism identified with Thomas more than any other character. Around a third of parents said that they thought their child was obsessed with the character. A quarter said that the programme was a 'gateway' to leaning, helping their children with colours, numbers and language. Some children mimicked the language. One mother said, 'He speaks in Thomas language constantly'. He says, 'Bust my buffers!' as an expression of surprise."
>
> (Peek, 2002)

The calm and predictable presentation of this programme, coupled with its clear emotional, expression, replicates the initial experience of a secure child with their mother. Through such repetitive (predictable) interactions the child recognises what is typical and/or routine; what will usually happen and, therefore, what to expect. Wendy Lawson, a writer diagnosed with ASD writes:

> "For some people comfort can be found in a bottle of wine, good music, a good book, a good friend and a long walk, but for me soft materials, rocking to and fro, sucking the roof of my mouth, bright colours, routine and reassurance are able to calm and comfort me. Robbed of these things I am like a wild lion or a bat without its radar, and I crash miserably."
>
> (Lawson, 2000, p5)

And:

"I once had a special hat. It was purple on the outside and had a red lining. I wore it on the aeroplane when we travelled to England and even though it was a summer hat I wore it in the snow. I was very upset when it got left behind at my sister's place and felt really scared without it. It was as if that hat was part of me- without it I felt a sense of separation and fear."

(Lawson, 2000, p52)

One can interpret these emotions as those of a much younger person. In terms of the 'magic square' described earlier by Sanger and Kelley, Wendy had not yet internalised the sense of security she would typically have gained from the mother/infant dyad if she had been able to experience it. A similar feeling to Wendy's is described by Jamie about his lion soft toy. Jamie is a 27 year old developer for the BBC. The lion is 4 feet long and accompanies him everywhere. Jamie says:

"He is a toy. I'm not deluded into thinking he is alive.…Most people know me as Jamie + Lion. It's really not a big deal. I am autistic, which is a posh way of saying I have a different way of thinking and perceiving the world. For me the typical environment is pretty chaotic. A sudden loud announcement in a supermarket is pretty similar in effect to a flash-bang grenade used to confuse people during wars. My brain needs more structure than most. The more predictable the world is, the better chance I have of being able to process it."

(In: Rose, 2016)

As with Wendy's hat, Jamie's lion has 'become part of him': a function of the internalised 'magic square'. And Jamie is not alone in liking the company of a soft toy. In fact, one study found 51% of 1,000 male participants still owned their childhood cuddly toy, while 28% of these slept with their teddy and/or took it with them when they went away from home. The most common explanations given were: 'I just can't bring myself to get rid of it'; 'it reminds me of my childhood' and 'it helps me sleep' (DT, 2017). Similarly, a survey of 6,000 users of a UK hotel chain found more than half still had a teddy bear (average age of bear was 27 years), with guests reporting that they found sleeping with their teddy a 'comforting and calming' way to end the day (DT, 2010). These studies suggest that the soft toy acts as an extension of the dyad by either a link to home and loved ones left behind and/or through a sense of security. These men did not carry their bears around with them in the day (as far as they stated). But, unlike them, Jamie is hypersensitive to noise and finds stress 'overwhelming'. He is traumatised by sudden sensory input and cannot reduce the confusion and alarm he feels as a result. Carrying a security object (Lion) provides him with structure and consistency to his environment and serves the same purpose of calming him as that described by these more typical men. Professor Bruce Hood of the University of Bristol comments:

> "The reason [children] develop these relationships is still uncertain, but could arise from self-soothing habitual formation with familiar objects. For example, they have been shown to be useful to reduce stress of attending the dentist."
>
> (Rose, 2016)

In this they replicate a key function of the mother (and others) which is to provide the constant, secure centre to a confusing world, described by Donna as: 'the mythical sense of home which seemed to evade me' (Williams, 1992, p119). Donna's 'Travel Dog' performed the same function for her as the teddies did for the UK men. For Wendy, Jamie and Donna, their need for a security object indicates that this aspect of the original dyadic relationship is missing rather than unwanted or unnecessary.

SENSORY INTEGRATION

Early interactions between the mother and child establish a multi-sensory developmental base. Through repetition, the nerve pathways from visual, auditory and verbal stimuli become 'fired' as multimodal/multisensory wholes. And as a study of three-month old infants and their mother's play by Fantasia and colleagues suggests:

> "…structured, multimodal play routines may constitute interactional contexts that work as integrated units of auditory and motor resources, representing early communicative contexts which prepare the ground for later, more complex multimodal interactions, such as verbal exchanges."
>
> (Fantasia et al., 2014)

This also includes non-verbal behaviours. From this is can now be better understood why sensory integration difficulties are so prevalent in autism/ASD: disruptions at the very early stage of the dyad will prevent the necessary foundation, not only for social communication, but for body/mind sensory connections and their associated meanings to establish. Without these early sensory interactions future physical co-ordination, bodily awareness, (connectedness to one's skin) physical security in a gravitational context (i.e. when walking upright), non-verbal gesturing, as well as the emotional comprehension of the meanings of communication, are all likely to be affected.

PHYSICAL CONTACT

Tiffany Field, a leading researcher and practitioner in the area of touch therapy, describes touch as our 'most social' sense. She states:

> "Touch, affecting both tactile and pressure receptors, stimulates the central nervous system (CNS) into a state of relaxation. Anxiety and stress levels, both behavioural and biochemical, are then reduced and the general effect is a relaxed, more attentive, state."
>
> (Field, 2003, p17)

Physical contact is often extremely difficult for those with autism/ASD. Several narratives expressed a desire for touch or a hug, but also fear of the unmanageable sensory overwhelm that this would create. Temple (Chapter 4, Narrative 4), for example, describes this well, and also her ingenious way of providing this for herself through the cattle-shute, without the overwhelming nature of a human hug. The desire for touch appears to be innate, and it is likely that infants and children are motivated for physical contact as part of their security needs. For example, the famous experiments by Harlow with infant rhesus monkeys showed they preferred to cling to a soft wire 'mother' covered in cloth than to the hard, uncovered, wire 'mother' who had the food. Physical contact was therefore at least equally as important to these infant primates as food (BPS, 2016). Touch by the mother appears to be correlated with a part of the brain (*superior temporal sulcus*) which mediates both empathy and theory of mind (TOM) so is connected to both emotional and mental functioning. A study by Brauer and colleagues with typically developing children found that this part of the brain, in those children whose mothers touched them more during a 10 minute play session, showed greater 'resting activity' (when the child was inactive). There was also more resting connectivity between this part of the brain and other aspects of the 'social brain' (such as the *inferior frontal gyrus*). These authors write:

> "...one may speculate that children with more touch more readily engage the mentalizing component of the 'social brain' and that, perhaps, their interest in other's mental states is greater than that of children with less touch."
>
> (In: BPS, 2016, p752)

Poor sensory integration may also be connected to difficulties with 'body image', such as those described by Donna (Chapter 4, Narrative 8). And, in a study with anorexic women, Gupta and colleagues found it 'highly likely' that touch deprivation may play a role in body image pathologies (Gupta et al., 1995). Touch issues in autism/ASD have been addressed through a number of interventions (see Chapter 5). For example, research by Cullen and Barlow (2001) supports the use of parent-mediated touch as a therapeutic measure. In their study, ten parents were trained using the *Touch Therapy Training Programme* (TTTP). These authors found that TTTP helped both the parents and the child to relax, and that 'parents valued the opportunity to learn a practical skill they could do with their children'. Parent-mediated therapeutic holding (described in Chapter 5) has been used in a variety of forms for several decades. And, in reviewing brain research and maternal contact, Salzen concludes that 'contact comfort established before graded visual, facial interactions may be an effective treatment in autism' (Salzen, 2016).

THE STRUCTURE OF THE EARLY DYAD

As we have seen, the mother mediates the infant's experiences within a secure relationship. As with food, the child is gradually 'weaned' into life. The mother, father and other adults continue to help structure development, explaining the meaning of events and emotions, and shaping the child's behaviour and self-knowledge. All of this forms the foundation for later social relationships. Brazelton and Greenspan write:

"When there are secure, empathic, nurturing relationships, children learn to be intimate, and empathic and eventually to communicate about their feelings, reflect on their own wishes, and develop their own relationships with peers and adults….Pretend or imaginative play involving emotional human dramas…helps the child to learn to connect an image or picture to a wish and then use this image to think….The ability to create mental pictures of relationships, and, later, other things leads to more advanced thinking. For instance, a key element essential for future learning and coping is the child's ability for self-observation….Self observation also helps a person label rather than act out feelings. It helps him to empathise with others and meet expectations. The ability for self-observation comes from the ability to observe oneself and another in a relationship. We have thus come to understand that emotional interactions are the foundation not only of cognition but of most a of a child's intellectual abilities, including his creativity and abstract thinking skills."

(Brazelton & Greenspan, 2000, p3-4)

These authors have summarised the first four months of a typical, healthy infant's life: From 0-3 weeks the mother will have learnt how to help the newborn infant maintain an alert state; from 3-8 weeks, the infant will produce smiles and vocalizations which are responded to by the adult. (This 0-8 week period relates to establishing security and entrainment between mother and child.) From 8-11 weeks these signals, smiles and vocalizations are reproduced in bursts of four or more and imitated by the adult in a series of reciprocal 'games' (to use Stern's term). Through these, rhythm and reciprocity are established which form the basis of intersubjectivity: the give-and-take vital for successful, social communication and relationships. By about four months of age the baby will have taken some control of the 'game' and thereby gained a sense of self-agency, value and initiative in the relationship.

WHY EARLY INTERVENTION?

From this, the crucial role of the early weeks and months of a child's life can be seen and, also, why there is now an emphasis on early identification and intervention in autism/ASD. The younger the child when a programme commences the better. Also, the infant brain is particularly 'plastic': that is it is particularly capable of compensating through forming new neural pathways. Whatever occurs in the way of support at this time can therefore affect development long term (Jones & Johnson, 2016).

B)   REPLICATED PARENTING IN SOCIAL INTERACTION PROGRAMMES

Given all of the above, successful social integration programmes are likely to be those which enable the re/establishment of entrainment and intersubjectivity and, thus, 'turn off' the chronic fight/flight mechanism which underlies autism/ASD. The result of this is to allow the neurochemistry and motivation of the ASD individual to switch from fear and caution to security, and a desire for exploration of the wider, social world. The programmes outlined in Chapter 5 attempt in different ways to either replicate or initiate what typically takes place in the mother/infant dyad. However, their individual philosophies are not all as explicit as this and their approach and outcomes vary. In this section, I examine each of these programmes in relation to Brazelton and Greenspan's dyadic developmental structure from 0-11 weeks as described above.

a)   APPLIED BEHAVIOURAL ANALYSIS (ABA)

As we learned in Chapter 5, ABA is a behaviour-based programme which utilises a reward system, with increasingly complex tasks, in order to 'shape' the child into social interaction. It adopts a team of trained professionals to work with the child – usually in their home, but also in some school settings. Parental involvement is as part of this team. The professional will initially assess the child before constructing an ABA programme (an example is shown in Table 13, in Chapter 5). This is initially a largely one-directional process with the child required to comply. ABA and similar behavioural programmes tend to be the dominant intervention in ASD, especially in the US. As described in the previous chapter they can be successful in reducing difficulties and increasing social functionality in the child, to the point where they may no longer retain a diagnosis of autism/ASD. For example, Shulman's research team (2015) found 35 children lost their 'social impairment', although some of these continued to demonstrate learning, emotional and/or behavioural problems. Similar studies are cited by Goodman (2012) while Griswold found there was a tendency for the brain to compensate following 'normalisation of language skills' with this type of programme (Griswold, 2016). ABA is the least 'real-world'- like of the social interaction programmes described in Chapter 5, with the parent role akin to that of a teacher. It does not attempt to replicate the early newborn/infant elements of the dyad directly, but to simply change behaviour and so engender social interaction. Some foundational aspects of the dyadic relationship such as entrainment (which establishes from 0-8 weeks may therefore be inadvertently missed.

b)   DIR/FLOORTIME

In contrast to ABA, DIR/Floortime is a developmental programme. Its goals of encouraging attention and intimacy; engaging in two-way communication, and the expression of feelings parallel the early developmental structure given by Brazelton and Greenspan of: 0-3 weeks establishing attention, 3-8 weeks encouraging intimacy, and 8-11 weeks enabling the intersubjective activities ('games') which allow for the emergence of higher-order/cortical development. In DIR/Floortime the adult/carer joins the child in 'their world' (which is usually on the floor) in periods of 20-30 minutes. The adult follows the child's lead to harness their natural interests, and also utilises 'playful obstruction'. This is a way of gently challenging the child to step into a shared world, perhaps by coming between the child and a desired object. As Greenspan explains:

> "Just by getting involve with his apparently mindless door routine, I gradually helped this child engage, to learn to gesture purposefully, and give meaning to words such as 'no', 'away' and 'leave alone.'"
>
> (Greenspan & Wieder, 2006, p73)

This teasing (and even annoying) of the child is unique to DIR/Floortime. However, built within a 'game' it appears to emulate aspects of the mother/child dyadic interaction (from around 3-8 weeks of typical development) and to have positive outcomes in many cases. The role of parents in this programme is central, with the professionals emulating their typical role.

However, because of its 'challenging' practice, DIR/Floortime may 'skip' through the initial entrainment period somewhat prematurely.

c)   SON-RISE (OPTION) PROGRAMME

There are similarities between DIR/Floortime and the Son-Rise (S-R) programme. The S-R philosophy echoes the need to parent the child, rather than impose behaviours which the family or society might wish for. Their view is that 'children show us the way [into their world] – we show them the way out.' An integral part of this approach is to fully accept the child where they are, and with the behaviours they are using. S-R places the parent as the child's most important resource and begins by establishing a safe context (the playroom) within a secure environment tailored to the reduced sensory requirements of the child. In the playroom, with the exception of anything dangerous, the adult 'joins' in whatever activity the child has chosen. This passage from Kaufman's book illustrates the importance of 'joining':

> "Reggie's father had never tried joining before…but he had agreed to totally commit to joining his son for a few weeks and see what happened. The next morning Reggie pulled a box of LEGOs out first thing, not acknowledging his father….Reggie built his L-shaped figures. As he always had, he began walking around the room, holding the two figures up to the light, moving them closer together and farther apart. This time, however, his dad was different. He made his own L-shaped structures and began strolling around the room, moving the structures closer together and farther apart. Every so often, he'd look at his son and really study what he was doing so that he could understand it and get it right."

> "As he did this, he realized something. He had always thought that his son had been simply looking through the square shape he had created with the two L-shaped figures. He was wrong. In fact, Reggie was looking sideways at the surface of each structure. And, when his dad did the same thing he noticed that, when he held the figures up to the light, he could see a reflection of his own face on the LEGOs themselves. And when he moved the two figures farther apart and

then close together, the reflection of his face would get fatter and skinnier, as if he was looking at himself in a carnival mirror."

"Yes! He was ecstatic! He finally understood what his son was doing, and it was actually pretty cool. Whoo-hoo! He glanced back over at his son, and Reggie had dropped his LEGOs and was staring in abject amazement at his father. His dad, looking back at him, couldn't believe it. He smiled at his son, enjoying the moment. Reggie smiled back. Then, on an inspiration, he waved to his son. Reggie waved back!"

(Kaufman, 2014, p45)

Joining therefore imitates mirroring in early social development, where security and companionship are united. Once this is established and a relationship based on love, acceptance, trust and mutual respect has formed (emulating the 0-8 week period of typical development), the child may begin to engage with the adult in play (paralleling the 8-11 week period). As with DIR/Floortime, in S-R everything is done on the child's eye level in the playroom. However, there are two major differences between that programme and S-R: 1) the nature and purpose of 'joining' and, 2) the nature of the playroom, which in S-R is kept locked. While both programmes encourage the parent to follow the lead of the child, and use whatever the child is interested in to initiate joint play, DIR/Floortime advises them to do 'whatever it takes' to make play interactive, even to the point of disturbing and annoying the child. In S-R if the child does not wish to interact and returns to solitary activities, the adult simply follows the child and starts to do whatever the child does (joins them once more). This suggests that S-R intrinsically, then, treats the child as very young (rather than an older child, as in DIR/ Floortime) by moving 'backwards' to the 'earlier stage' if the child requires it. In addition, the locked playroom (as opposed to the open system of DIR/Floortime) more closely emulates the 'closed' dyadic security a very young infant would find with their mother. Son-Rise appears to recognise this aspect of the dyad, without necessarily making this explicit in their philosophy. In fact, Raul Kaufman's mother (and founder of Son-Rise) simply adopted this approach with her son in order to be 'with' him, only later finding that it also helped him (and others) to recover. This programme differs from ABA in that in Son-Rise the child chooses the activity whereas, in ABA, the programme is much more prescribed. Having said this, there is an element of behavioural shaping in S-R: something Florica Stone objected to and which caused her to establish her own version of S-R for Alex (Chapter 5, Narrative 1). However, this occurance seemed to be more to do with the length of time spent in the play-room than integral to the programme itself, and appears an isolated event.

d)   RELATIONSHIP DEVELOPMENT INTERVENTION (RDI)

RDI was designed by Steven Gutstein with the aim of directly addressing developmental difficulties in autism/ASD. Gutstein was disappointed in the results he was obtaining using behavioural approaches (such as ABA) even though his colleagues considered his results to be good. However, Gutstein felt the children still lacked an emotional understanding of their social interactions, and so were missing out on the enjoyment (and motivation) of relationships. To address this he attempted to replicate what 'typical' parents do, to slow it down and make it more explicit, and then 'teach' parents these skills with their ASD children. RDI therefore places parents at the centre of their child's programme by acknowledging the pivotal role they play in development. As with Son-Rise, RDI adopts a 'purposely artificial' context in order to control all of the incoming stimuli and focus on the emotional and social information. This then assists in the ability of the child to gain security and to give attention. Gutstein notes that most children with Autism/ASD do not have a desire (motivation) for the 'rigorous practice needed to master *experience sharing relationships*' (Gutstein, 2000, pxxi). These are the equivalent of the 'games' and routines that the typical mother/child dyad engage in over and over again from around 8 weeks of age. In RDI parents are trained to take the lead in 'guided participation' and to set limits and minimize distractions in order to establish an 'emotionally attuned' relationship emulating the 0-11 week period of the dyad. After this, they are encouraged to prepare the child to move 'beyond their sole reliance on parents' by introducing them to a carefully matched peer: a step unique to RDI. The programme continues into adolescence, with designated exercises and games designed for this age group (Gutstein and Sheely, 2002). Gutstein states:

"Treatment is long term and progress can be slow. Our average child will be with us for many years. But we are seeing the results. Last year we sent five of our children off to college. All are doing well. In fact, we've had three parents tell us their concerns are that their child is spending too much time socializing…"

(Gutstein, 2000, pxxi)

This programme appears to replicate each of the stages of the dyad outlined by Brazelton and Greenspan. It adopts a more parent-guided approach than ABA, DIR/Floortime and/or Son-Rise: the latter, initially at least, utilising a team of trained practitioners with each child. However, it is possible that RDI is less child-led in time-scale. For example, the shift from dependency on the parent to a peer is not necessarily naturalistic. In human development, retaining the central role of the mother/parent figure is important for relationship-building up to at least puberty, particularly for boys, although it has been argued that in some societies, including Western cultures, there is a tendency to push boys away from their mothers somewhat early (Silverstein & Rashbaum, 1994). In contrast, RDI seeks to move the child forward at the soonest opportunity. For this reason, unless the peer is able to emulate fully the mother/parent role, a break in the developmental trajectory occurs at the developmental point where the 8-week period of a typical dyad might be. It is therefore possible that RDI inadvertently omits some of the early foundation that would typically occur in a more child-led programme, and/or with a longer infancy stage (before the introduction of peers). This may explain the relatively long and slow progress made by these children in comparison with S-R, ABA and DIR/Floortime, for example.

e)   INTENSIVE INTERACTION (II)

As described in Chapter 5, Intensive Interaction (II) was developed from Ephram's 'augmented mothering' in order to emulate the role of the mother within the mother/infant dyad. It was initially adopted as a way of increasing intimacy for those with limited mobility, with an emphasis on physical behaviour. Through its *Fundamentals of Communication* II is designed to help people at 'early levels of development', including those with autism, and who may be without speech. These *Fundamentals* include sharing attention and turn-taking, to enjoy and play with another, to increase attention and concentration, and engage in non-verbal and physical contact. An II 'communication partner' will reflect back at the individual their movements and sounds 'following their lead' in a non-intrusive way and in a quiet, relaxed environment:

> "If they make a movement, respond by copying the movement; if they vocalise copy the vocalisation. These sessions may be very brief to start with."
>
> (II Institute, *Website*, 2017)

As such, II adopts techniques observed from interactions within the mother and child dyad from the very earliest stage (0-3 weeks). This entails accepting the nature of the individual 'in their own world' and incorporating repetitions (mirroring and joining) in physical behaviour. David Hewett, an originator and Director of the II Institute, states:

> "As we developed the approach and its effectiveness, we found that students who previously preferred a solitary lifestyle would start to take an interest in us, 'light up', share face-to-face times and become more vocal; students who already had some ability to interact would become more adept and focussed, more vocally noisy and conversational, some making further and greater progress with speech interaction."
>
> (II Institute, *Website*, 2017)

Intensive Interaction therefore places the mothering role (as the 'communication partner') at the centre of the approach, and appears to emulate the dyad from 0 and into the 8-11 week period. The entrainment this establishes enables the beginnings of intersubjectivity and social interaction between the partner and the individual, but was not designed to extend beyond this.

PROGRAMME COMPARISON WITH TYPICAL DYADIC RELATIONSHIP

The programmes described in this section appear to replicate aspects of the mother/infant dyad and this may be related to their outcomes. Figure 23, below, illustrates where each one may 'fall' along the time-scale of typical social development suggested earlier by Brazelton and Greenspan, from 0-11 weeks, and beyond:

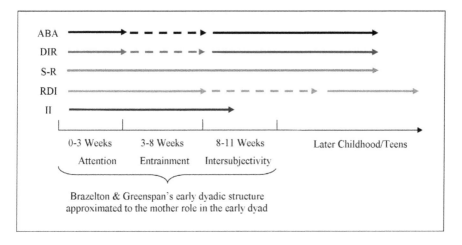

Figure 23 Social Interaction Programmes and Typical Development

This analysis suggests that some programmes might not entirely replicate the typical dyad pathway. For example, we can now see how an ABA programme might lead to the outcomes found by Shulman and colleagues (described in Chapter 6). This group made positive gains in social interaction but vestigial difficulties remained, which are all associated with limbic hyper-arousal (see Figure 11, p27). The early stage of gaining the infant's attention (0-3 weeks) is strongly present in ABA, although not within an equable relationship. But, as can be seen in Figure 23, there is a 'gap' (illustrated by a dotted line) in the programme paralleling the period from about 3-8 weeks. This would typically be filled by establishing entrainment between the mother and child, in which the child might sometimes take the lead, with the mother joining and mirroring. The 'optimum outcomes' of children using ABA, or other behavioural programmes, might therefore be further improved by addressing these aspects of the dyadic relationship (particularly the 0-8 week period). Similarly, DIR/Floortime omits some of the early 3-8 week platform of typical development by reducing the time spent in allowing the child their own 'space' and autonomy and, instead, introduces 'challenging'. And in RDI, it can be seen that there is a 'gap' where a peer takes over the role of the mother/parent. This break in the dyadic relationship may account for why progress is perhaps slower than it might otherwise be for that programme. RDI might therefore continue with a longer parent- rather than peer-mediated step in its programme? Both DIR/Floortime and RDI appear to 'rush through' the early stages of the original dyad. II is focussed almost entirely on the very early 0-8 week period of gaining attention and establishing entrainment and intersubjectivity. As this is the developmental point where the traumatic break in autism/ASD occurs, II may therefore be under-utilised in ASD, and could be combined with other programmes that do not yet emphasise this element as strongly, such as DIR/Floortime and ABA. Interestingly S-R is the only programme that appears to 'begin at the beginning' of the dyadic relationship and run right through to later development. It gives the child autonomy and the 'psychological space' in which to take their time, and the opportunity to lead the relationship. It also incorporates natural regression: allowing the child to return to a previous developmental point, which is an important security element in typical infant development (Poole, 2017). It is worth noting too that some programmes may be more effective with a particular genetic identity (GI) and thinking style. For example, ABA is heavily verbal and could possibly best suit the verbally-strong (Asperger) child. This is in contrast to the dyad, which is wholly multi-sensory and therefore suits any GI. These are my personal perceptions of how these programmes may emulate aspects of the mother/child dyad. Others may have their own interpretations. In any case, my hope is that highlighting these differences may prove of benefit to programme providers in further improving the already good outcomes being obtained.

A NOTE ABOUT BOYS

It has been estimated that a typical newborn girl is 4-6 weeks more developmentally advanced than a typical newborn boy (Kraemer, 2000). Any disturbance during the early months of a boy's life may therefore be more disruptive to the vital foundation of development, including social, than for a girl. The implications for this are clear. They are that a newborn boy is likely to require a longer attention-gaining period of entrainment (typically 0-8 weeks of age) before commencing on the later games. Worryingly, Baron-Cohen and his team found it easy to disrupt the newborn, mother/male child dyad (Baron-Cohen, 2003). And Trevarthan observed that mothers' behaviour does seem to reflect this difference, finding that in early interactions she makes more effort to synchronise (entrain) and match boys' behaviour than girls'. 'Chat' was also usually more easily achieved with girls than with boys (Trevarthan et al., 1998). Boys are generally more 'emotionally reactive' in temperament than girls, displaying more negative and positive emotions and a greater focus on the mother. Marcus summarises current research in this area:

> "As children, [boys] are more easily stressed, which means they cry more when they are upset and have a harder time calming down. And they are more emotionally vulnerable to the ill effects of extreme lack of affection."
>
> (Marcus, 2017)

I have argued elsewhere (Poole, 2017) how all of these differences might explain the increased numbers of boys diagnosed with autism/ASD. Overall, they indicate that maintaining the very early phase of the mother/infant dyad relationship is particularly important to the life-time development of boys and their future relationship success. And, in recovery, programmes may need to ensure that they do not 'rush' through important aspect of the early dyadic relationship, with boys in particular.

C)   REPLICATED PARENTING IN THE REAL WORLD

Three narratives (Temple, Mark and Donna) show specific examples of replicated parenting by individuals in their surrounding environment. Mark's mother Pat has described how her own mother spent hours rolling a ball back and forth with him as a baby (Chapter 5, Narrative 7). Temple (Chapter 5, Narrative 4) had desperately wished she could hug and be hugged, and dreamed of a 'magical machine' that would soothe her overwhelmed sensory system. Her aunt encouraged her interest in the cattle-shute on her farm, which led to Temple designing her own, controllable, 'squeeze machine'. The 'Crow's Nest' became a proxy small, 'safe' and private space in which she could feel calm and enriched through 'self-discovery' (interestingly akin to the 'special room' of Son-Rise and DIR/Floortime). In addition to her self-discovered aids, Temple found her head teacher, Mr Carlock, extremely supportive:

> "Mr Carlock didn't see any labels just the underlying talent....He

didn't try to draw me into his world but came instead into my world."
(Grandin & Scariano, 1987, p92)

As we can now see, this is exactly how the mother initially reacts with her infant, and is the core feature of those social interaction programmes that 'join' the child. Social feedback from Mr Carlock enabled Temple's voice to gradually alter to reflect her lessened need for 'defence against the world'. When he heard of the 'flack' Temple had received over her cattle shute he encouraged her to build a better one, using scientific research to test her theory of how it might help calm calves:

"He aroused my interest in science and directed my fixation into a worthy project. I spent hours in the library looking up everything I could find on the effect of sensory input on sensory perception."
(Grandin & Scariano, 1987, p99)

By his acceptance and validation Temple was able to develop both her self and her talents. This was in contrast to the Freudian psychiatrist who appeared only interested in the sexual connotations of the cattle-shute, none of which existed. Of the standard help on offer Temple writes:

"Practising with a tape recording and playing back would have done more for my social life than trying to ferret out the dark secrets of my psyche. I wish one of the psychologists would have told me about my speech problem instead of worrying about my Id."
(Grandin & Scariano, 1987, p83)

Again, this is the sort of 'mirroring' the mother (and others) would typically provide. Such mirroring is also brain-based. For example, it was found that particular 'mirror neurones' in the brains of primates became more active when the monkeys saw the experimenter copy what they were doing. Chris Frith, a neurologist at University College London, describes how this 'social mirroring' has important functions:

"...it makes us less selfish and more cooperative. It also increases alignment between people, which enhances communication."
(Frith, 2009)

'Alignment' is the equivalent of entrainment or rapport, in which mirroring occurs without conscious awareness. The existence of 'mirror neurones' in the brain indicates this is a 'hard wired' (innate) activity in primates, which may help explain the success of those programmes which adopt it. Deliberate mirroring, such as in Son-Rise and II, enables entrainment and then intersubjectivity to establish just as in the initial mother/child dyad: the root of all social development. Parent mediated social communication therapy (PACT) also works this way. As described in Chapter 3, this therapy was offered to a group of randomly chosen parents of 152 children aged 2-4 years, diagnosed with autism. Parents visited a clinic with their child twice a week where they were videoed with a box of toys. On viewing the videos they were encouraged to notice when their child offered a reaction to the toys and to respond to it. If the child spoke the parent repeated (mirrored) it and also added something. They were encouraged to continue this behaviour at home (Pickles, et al., 2016). Simply mirroring the child was therefore highly effective. In the same way, Temple's mother, aunt and Mr Carlock were able to accept and validate her. As a result, she gradually became able to speak and touch more typically, as Mr Carlock noted:

> "You seemed quite at ease…with the audience…rubbed shoulders with the crowd during break, shook hands without hesitation and generally seemed calm and assured….You used to have a lot of trouble dropping one subject and going on to another….Now that seems a thing of the past."
>
> (Grandin & Scariano, 1987, p139)

Some of this improvement may be attributable to the medication Temple found helpful for her anxiety, but it is interesting that she progressed so well with the parenting (of her mother) and 'proxy parenting' of surprisingly few others. In contrast, Donna describes in her narrative (Chapter 4, Narrative 8) how she:

> "…needed a mother desperately, but could not remember ever having had one….I felt homesick for the home I'd never had…"
>
> (Williams, 1992, p88)

Fortunately, a number of people gave Donna the replicated mothering that she needed. These included Mr Reynolds her primary school teacher, and psychiatrists Mary and Dr Marek. Dr Marek helped Donna to understand emotions; provided feedback on what her voice meant when it changed, and what other people's responses meant. Donna also gave him lists of concepts that she didn't understand. In addition, her husbands (first Ian and then Colin) provided valuable aspects of replicated parenting. Ian, himself diagnosed with high functional Aspergers (and a fellow 'my worlder'), provided someone similar enough in his experience with which to share the more frightening 'ordeal' of coming to understand emotion:

> "Both of us were afraid yet both of us knew we would be safe with each other, despite the inner battles and compulsions to run that came with fear of losing control in the face of big emotions."
>
> (Williams, 1994, p229)

With Ian's help Donna gradually became able to connect with her own body. Together they learnt how to integrate processes such as turning on a tap, stepping into the bath or getting dressed. These actions initially took a very long time because they were slowed right down. Donna repeated them over and over again moving each limb, opening an eye voluntarily, making shapes of sounds with her mouth and noises in her throat:

> "I exercised getting my lungs and throat to work together and then both at once with my mouth. Finally, I heard the most beautiful sound in the world: my whole connected voice…'My voice', I said, crying uncontrollably: 'Donna's voice.'"
>
> (Williams, 1999, p92)

This rehabilitative replication of activities in which an infant would typically engage with her mother/others, enabled the sensory integration that had become so delayed and disrupted to re/establish. But, as Donna explains, in autism this 'way out' has to be indirect rather than direct. This is due to the overwhelming nature of the traumatised state and consequent sensory confusion, as sometimes in the dyadic relationship, the individual must lead the way. After two years, Ian and Donna parted. Donna describes how:

> "With Ian I learned about letting down walls, letting in pain as well as love, and through that, I better found the key to sharing my world with others. Ian met me in my own world and together we built an

island and each, in different ways outgrew it. For my part it was inevitable that I would build a bridge to the mainland."

(Williams, 1999, p237)

This is a perfect description of dyadic mothering. Florica Stone too describes the 'mother' role she ultimately adopted with Alex, which was:

"...to shelter my son from doing harmful things to himself; teach him language so that he may talk to me about his problems; provide him with comfort..."

(Stone, 2004, p233)

In short:

"He is looking to you for love, acceptance, understanding, help and protection."

(Stone, 2004, p221-2)

For Donna, while the 'flight/flight' mechanism (the traumatic basis of autism/ASD) remained, she felt she had progressed to 'about three years of age' under her adult skin. This is still a vulnerable child, who would just about begin to look to a wider (than family) social world. At this time, Donna met Chris. She writes:

"He was everything I would ever have needed in a parent. With a simultaneous sense of self and other, with body connectedness, with an absence of total shutdowns and Exposure Anxiety that was at least much less than it ever used to be, I was the child I wished I had been."

(Williams, 2004, p155)

These insights and examples of replicated parenting highlight the vital role of 'mothering' in laying a foundation for social development. Social interaction interventions and 'replicated parenting' can help re-establish this platform where it is lost. And although these can be beneficial in delivering 'optimum outcomes' in social behaviour, it would appear that a 'rush' through the earlier stages of entrainment and intersubjectivity is best avoided if the underlying trauma in autism/ASD is also to be resolved. In the next chapter, I examine in more detail how the recovering individual emerges.

CHAPTER 8

THE RECOVERING PERSONALITY IN AUTISM

Personal biographical recovery narratives frequently describe the individual's emergent (to adopt Temple's expression) personality during the recovery process. For example, Liam's mother writes:

> "Today, he (Liam) has developed into such an enthusiastic communicator. He exhibits an imagination that often leaves us and strangers awed….Professionals visiting the school with the intention of examining Liam were unable to find the 'autistic child' and asked for assistance!"
>
> (ATCA, *Website*, 2018)

Similarly, Tyler's mother describes how:

> "He (Tyler) was having numerous seizures, becoming aggressive at school and very unhappy. Fourteen months later…Tyler is so happy. His conversational skills have developed incredibly; his seizures have been reduced from every 5 days to as long as 6 weeks apart! He gives spontaneous hugs, talks about his feelings, has developed a great imagination and is more comfortable in groups and new situations."
>
> (ATCA, *Website*, 2018)

Donna (Chapter 4, Narrative 8) also developed into a creative and highly gifted musician, artist and writer with a considerable business sense. However, she still felt the need to protect her sensitivity from too much intrusion. Raun Kaufman's parents devoted three years to recovering him and subsequently developed the Son-Rise programme. As an adult, he writes:

"I was a very social kid and I had a wide circle of friends. Academically things went quite well. I went to my local public school growing up, but I spent my last three years of high school at an academically rigorous prep school. Throughout this period of my life, I really didn't think that much about my history of autism....During my time at college and after graduating, I spent four summers working at, and then helping to manage, a summer program for teens. Later on I worked at an educational centre in Southern California....I found the experience of working with kids to be so meaningful that it overwhelmed my interest in the business world, at least for a while. I get asked by many parents about my love life (and, yes, it can feel a bit strange to be asked for romantic details by someone you just met). Though I don't think it's appropriate to go into details about former girlfriends, I will say that I feel very lucky in this regard. I have had the good fortune to be with some truly wonderful and caring women in my life. Although I am not yet married, I have found a very meaningful sense of intimacy and fulfilment in these relationships."

He adds:

"I don't have any remnants of autism. I don't secretly crave a plate spin, and I don't find social situations in any way difficult. I'm just a regular guy, living my life. Ironically, it is the interpersonal areas that come most easily to me; I'm not so hot at the areas I should be good at, given my history – organisation, routine, technical subjects..."

(Kaufman, 2014. pp11-12)

Max's mother (Chapter 4, Narrative 5) describes the recovering Max one year after his treatment began:

"Max is a sociable fellow with many friends, and an excellent student working at his age and grade level. He takes piano and tennis lessons....He is resilient within his peer group, always able to defend himself with a kind of entertaining humour and charm. He is also a gentle soul, loved by teachers....I would still classify him as a bit more on the spacey side or forgetful side – especially in comparison to my older son, who is much more Type A. Max can tune out conversation easily if he wants to, gets a bit lost in thoughts, and sometimes does miss social cues. But, by and large, he is a more resilient teenager than his brother. He is loving school, has many new friends there, is doing well with his studies…likes the artistic counter-culture image, and is most interested these days in girls (he already has a girl friend or two), music, and his passion: computer animation."

(Lansky, 2003, p200)

Mark too (Chapter 4, Narrative 7) displays a sensitive, 'counter-culture' nature and was most at home in New Orleans:

"He truly loved New Orleans…it's laid back, non-conformist, and without snow.…He was making excellent money, getting involved in political causes, going to Mardi Gras and Jazz Fest and best of all, friends began to appear…offbeat characters with names like John the Tamale Man and Velvet the hot New Orleans mama with a brood of children and her part-time husband the cop."

(Stehli, 2004, p17)

I have suggested throughout that recovery in autism/ASD appears to correlate with and depend upon alleviation of the underlying limbic (allostatic) load and trauma. The subsequent shift in biochemistry away from fear-based functioning allows the innate exploration, curiosity and learning, that underpin social development, to establish. But how does this shift leads to the changes in 'personality' observed above? In the following sections, I summarise the current research base on this subject. (A more detailed analysis is provided in *An ecological theory of autism*, Poole, 2017).

WHAT IS PERSONALITY?

If we refer again to Figure 8 from Chapter One (shown below) illustrating the components of genetic identity (GI) it can be seen how personality is an expression of both inherited temperament and the functioning of the physical body, expressed within an individual's environmental context:

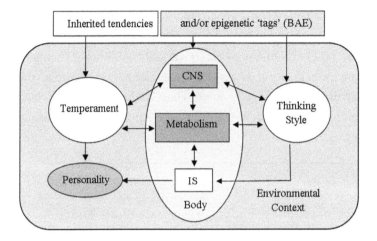

Personality as a Component of Genetic Identify

Temperament is the tendency to react to certain influences in a certain way. As Cloninger suggests:

> "...temperament describes what grabs our attention and how intensely we respond."
>
> (Cloninger, 2004, p42)

As shown, temperament is influenced by body-type and states (such as central nervous system/metabolism) and their related brain-wiring (thinking style).

CLONINGER'S FOUR TEMPERAMENT DIMENSIONS

From his research in this area, Cloninger (1996) has proposed four basic temperament dimensions; three of which are mediated through the major neurotransmitters: dopamine, serotonin and noradrenaline, as follows: 1) *Novelty seeking* (exploratory activity) relates to dopamine; 2) *Harm avoidance* (avoiding punishment, non-rewarding situations or novelty) relates to serotonin and, 3) *Reward dependence* (such as in obsessive or addictive behaviour) relates to noradrenaline. *Novelty seeking* and *Harm avoidance* are therefore opposite tendencies. As we all share these three major neurotransmitters it seems likely that we all express these three traits, but with some of us displaying dominance in certain dimensions. Cloninger

also found *Persistence* to be a consistent fourth temperament trait. As shown
in Table 14 below, each temperament represents a dimension with two poles
of (High to Low) extreme personality variants. Although we inherit a trait
dimension its expression is context-dependent. For example, the *Harm
avoidance* dimension may become High under certain environmental
influences, but Low – even to the point of 'optimism' and/or 'daring'- when
these alter.

Temperament Dimension	Extreme personality variants	
	High	Low
Harm Avoidance	Pessimistic Fearful Shy Fatigable	Optimistic Daring Outgoing Vigorous
Novelty Seeking	Exploratory Impulsive Extravagant Irritable	Reserved Rigid Frugal Stoic
Reward Dependence	Sentimental Sociable Warm Sympathetic	Critical Aloof Detached Independent
Persistence	Eager Determined Ambitious Perfectionist	Apathetic Spoiled Underachieving Pragmatic

Table 14 Four Temperament Dimensions and their Extreme Personality
Variants: After Cloninger (2004, p41)

Temperament appears particularly relevant to an individual's emotional life
(Mischel, 1993, p201). Work in the 1980s by Buss and Plomin described three
'dispositions' (inherited temperaments) in three main areas: 1) *emotionality/
reactivity*, 2) *sociability* and 3) *activity*. *Emotionality* or reactivity indicates
the tendency for easy physiological arousal and activation of the autonomic
nervous system (ANS) and towards demonstrating emotions such as anger,

fear and distress (Buss & Plomin, 1984). *Emotionality* therefore indicates a genetic pre-disposition to how easily an individual's nervous system and correlated emotions may be triggered. *Sociability* refers to the degree to which a person seeks interaction with others, and *activity* to the strength or intensity of their responses, ranging from hyperactivity to inactivity. Interestingly, in relation to sociability, Aron, 1996/2002) has suggested a 'highly sensitive person' (HSP) trait, which she defines as 'the tendency to turn inwards'. This clearly equates to a *harm avoidance* temperament. Aron estimates that 20% of the population may possess an HSP trait, although, in these individuals this may also represent a coping-strategy for dealing with sensory overwhelm. She notes that:

> "...studies of baby monkeys traumatised by separation from their mothers have found that these monkeys in adulthood behave much like monkeys born innately sensitive."
>
> (Aron, 1996, p13)

This suggests trauma may 'masquerade' as an HSP trait in those children whose dominant temperament is harm avoidance. As with much that was formerly considered fixed, we are now beginning to understand that genetic factors, including temperament traits, interact with environmental factors in their expression, thus personality is largely *epigenetic*. That is: our DNA inheritance is shaped by our 'real world' experiences, exposures and influences, through our internal biochemistry. Understanding the potential for this is important when we come to consider how personality appears to 'emerge' or alter during recovery.

HARM AVOIDANCE IN AUTISM/ASD

Differences in personality expression have been found to correlate with variations in brain structure. In relation to this, Herrington and colleagues state:

> "...numerous studies have posited that frontal lateralization associated with emotion reflects approach and avoidance motivation...left activity more associated with approach motivation and right activity reflecting avoidance motivation."
>
> (In: Canli, 2006, p135)

Melillo too, in his *functional disconnection syndrome model*, describes how:

> "The right brain is governed by what is known as avoidance behaviour,
> so it is the cautious brain.....Before the curious left brain can approach
> something, the right brain has to give its consent that it is safe."
>
> (Melillo, 2010, p64)

Aron (1996) has also referred to 'the brain's two systems' of approach and withdrawal. Citing work by Bates and Wachs (1994) she notes that 'behavioural activation' and 'behavioural inhibition' can be perceived as a 'pause to check' security system which ensures that it is safe before embarking forward. While the approach arm takes in sensory information and stimulates physical movement towards things, the withdrawal system does the opposite. The withdrawal arm will activate when there is a 'mismatch' and it is not clear if moving toward the object is safe. Aron (1996) considers this 'pause' activity to be 'a significant part of being intelligent' (p30). The tendency to withdraw may also correlate with low serotonin (GABA/ DHEA/serotonin pathway) and/or retained primary reflexes (derailed development). Most individuals with autism/ASD show a preponderance of right-hemisphere functioning, suggesting a chronic state of harm avoidance on Cloninger's proposed traits. In autism, this represents a survival (limbic) response following trauma. However, no simple genetic mapping has ever been found for personality traits. Rather, they are an expression of inherited temperament trait dimensions and genetic identity, expressed within our environmental context.

TEMPERAMENT/PERSONALITY RESEARCH IN AUTISM/ASD

There has been some interesting research into connections between autism/ ASD temperament and personality traits. For example, a twin study in Sweden by Kerekes et al. (2013) found children with ASD correlated positively with harm avoidance (were potentially high in pessimism, fearfulness, shyness and fatigue) and negatively with reward dependence (i.e.: were more inclined to be reserved, rigid, frugal and stoic). A further study by Picardi and colleagues assessed a cohort of twins (30% males) aged 18 and over (mean age 40) drawn from the Italian register. This sample was chosen because:

"...no twin study of autistic traits took account of the possible influence of state variables such as emotional distress, which has been found to be correlated with scores on autistic trait measurement."

(Picardi, et al., 2015, p5)

They are referring here to research by Kurita and Koyama (2006) who noted that 'distress' in their autistic sample had registered as part of their personality on the Japanese version of the *Autistic Spectrum Quotient* (ASQ). As before, Picardi and colleagues found the main associations between the autistic measures used and temperament were positive for harm avoidance and negative for novelty seeking and reward dependence. Genetic factors accounted for 44% of individual difference between the twins on the ASQ measure, with 20%-49% on Cloninger's *Temperament and Character Inventory* (TCI). That is: 56% of the ASQ individual difference between the ASD twins and 51-80% on the TCI – the majority in both cases – was non-genetic (i.e.: environmentally attributable). So that, although traits may be inherited (genetic), their expression, including as personality, is influenced by environmental factors.

PERSONALITY EXPRESSION AND HEALTH

We can understand Kurita and Koyama's (2006) finding that 'distress' might masquerade as 'personality' by recognising the importance of physical/psychological health on temperament traits – largely as a reflection of immune system involvement. For example, differences in personality expression can be observed in the varying behaviour of a person when sick with when well. Davies (2004) cites Eysenck's view that limbic system arousal (allostasis) is the key biological intermediary between a DNA trait and its expression. Thus, the state of the limbic system (and any accumulated allostatic load) will directly affect trait expression and, therefore, personality. As previously described, this 'load' will include inherited genetic mutations, and parental exposures and experiences (the BAE). Inherited temperament traits and subsequent personality expression will therefore be modified to reflect past or current health/illness, as illustrated in Figure 24, below. This connection has been noted in studies of schizophrenia (which used at one time to be confused with infantile autism). For example, a 'landmark' study by Wilson in 2016 found 108 regions of human DNA in which certain variants can raise the risk of schizophrenia. These were on a part of the genome that encodes proteins involved in immune function.

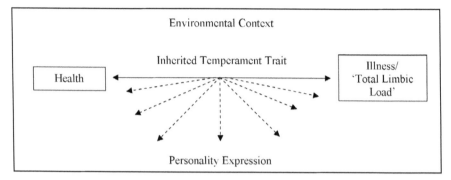

Figure 24 Personality Variations in Health and Illness

Wilson describes this as 'a puzzling find for a brain disorder' (Wilson, 2016, p12). However, it is understandable when we recognise that mental health is intrinsically related to physical health. Indeed, Wilson's immune system link supports this. If we transpose his finding to that of Cloninger's temperament 'extremes' we can now see how an individual in chronic trauma, toxicity and/or less than optimum health (mentally and/or physically), could express the harm avoidance Low 'extreme' (for example). But that, once health had been restored, they may then express the full trait dimension – even to the High variants of optimism and daring. For this reason, until full health has been restored (limbic load reduced) it could be difficult to know the full 'personality potential' of any ASD individual.

In Chapter 6 we explored the structure of recovery in relation to three domains, including of physical trauma/ill-health and toxicity (Domain 1). It was suggested that for full recovery to occur, this domain be addressed before progressing further. If personality expression is dependent on limbic health it follows that it is important to clear from the physical body anything toxic which may contribute to an allostatic (limbic) load. This includes chronic inflammation, allergic states and anything that impedes or lowers immune function generally. The benefit of this approach can be seen in the narratives. For example, Donna's path to recovery began after she consulted a naturopath who corrected her diet and addressed her hypoglycaemia and allergies (Domain 1). Further improvements in cognition (Domain 3) occurred on using Irlen Lenses for sensory integration difficulties (Domain 2). It is also likely that the external environment must adapt and respond to the changing needs of the child/individual as they recover, as with Max (Chapter 4, Narrative 5) whose home care and educational context was altered, as required.

STRESS AND TRAUMA EFFECTS ON PERSONALITY

Clearly, it is not just physiological aspects that can impact on health. Roberts and Jackson (2008) suggest that long-term mental states can also affect personality expression. Indeed, it is well known in the area of psychoimmunology that chronic stress can lead to illness and disease (Evans et al., 2000). In autism/ASD a high level of anxiety is considered to be the result of the autistic state. However, an ecological perspective suggests that this is at least equally due to the initiating trauma and motivational conflict, which result in chronic activation of the limbic system in fight/flight (HPA/cortisol pathway). As Mark Stehli's mother Pat writes:

> "Mostly, I recall overhearing him say that after AIT (audio-integration therapy) he felt a lessening of the constant feeling that he was being chased by a tiger. That was the first time I had any idea he had the 'fight or flight' response constantly colouring every experience."
>
> (Stehli, 2004, p19)

Temple also suffered high anxiety levels which were exaggerated under certain circumstances. However, as they reduced (from medication) she was able to express her true nature far more easily and make gains in her social abilities:

> "Gone are the frenzied searches for the basic meaning of life. I no longer fixate on one thing since I am no longer driven...with the passion subdued, my career and livestock equipment design business is going well. Since I am more relaxed, I get along better with people and stress-related health problem, such as colitis, are gone."
>
> (Grandin & Scariano, 1987, p138)

Temple also recognises that:

> "Autistic and dyslexic traits are probably normal traits that become excessive in certain individuals."
>
>> (Grandin & Scariano, 1987, p138)

Interestingly, Alexander's mother (Florica) describes the stressed Alex as returning to his 'autistic' self, after the distress of being bullied at school. And Donna Williams observes:

> "Under various degrees of stress or overload people can slip out of gear – from the significant back to the literal or further back to the sensory."
>
>> (Williams, 1998, p21)

These examples show that, under stress, the person is sent 'backwards' to an earlier stage of development and, in the case of an autistic person, sensory confusion. In dyslexia this stress effect has been described as a return to the 'favoured processing style' (Dennison, 1981) and/or to brain stem 'survival' functioning (Hannaford, 1995). Any prolonged mental stress/trauma may therefore create long-term (chronic) changes in the expression of personality (Roberts and Jackson, 2008). In autism this may include lack of brain hemisphere and sensory integration, leading to weak central cohesion (seeing parts but not the whole). It can also result in the dominant right-hemisphere function and high *Harm avoidance*, with low *Novelty seeking* and *Reward dependence*, described earlier. But once this 'extreme' need (for harm avoidance) is reduced the inner neurochemistry can alter and personality expression adjust to a less constrained and more expansive form.

LIMITED INTERESTS/DESIRE FOR SAMENESS/ STEREOTYPICAL BEHAVIOURS

As we have seen, in autism/ASD the individual is constrained by motivational conflict into a coping state, with limited opportunity for expression of their full personality potential. This is reflected in the behaviours of the 'triad of impairment' used in an ASD diagnosis (shown in Chapter 1) and again below:

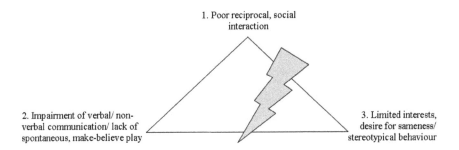

1. Poor reciprocal, social
interaction

2. Impairment of verbal/ non-
verbal communication/ lack of
spontaneous, make-believe play

3. Limited interests,
desire for sameness/
stereotypical behaviour

If we view the 'triad' in relation to personality expression we can see that corners 1) and 2) are the direct result of derailed development, while those of corner 3): limited interests, desire for sameness and stereotypical behaviours, reflect extreme expression of the personality of the individual while within the state of autism/ASD. This is supported by research from Bath University, UK, where researchers found that: 'some of the symptoms of Aspergers could be linked to levels of the stress hormone cortisol' (BU, 2009) which is triggered by the fight/flight mechanism. And also by Lord's study (Lord et al., 2013) which found that these stereotypical behaviours decreased sharply in Fein's 'optimum outcome' (OO) group (Fein et al., 2013) who were no longer diagnosable with autism/ASD. We can understand this finding better from an ecological perspective in which autism is the outcome of a state of chronic fight/flight constraining the individual to 'safe' behaviours. Staying with what is known (extreme *Harm avoidance*/right brain-hemisphere-dominant) occurs where a perceived threat to security is present. Alternatively, a premature 'leap' to left brain-hemisphere-dominant functioning (before the typical age of around 18-24 months) in order to control such insecurity, can result in rigid and/or obsessive activities. As we saw earlier, such behaviours can 'masquerade' as genetic in origin (Previc, 2007). However, if/when the inner neurochemistry is altered to one representative of security and relaxation, this will alter and expansion, exploration and learning become possible. The child is able to respond more fully to external environmental stimuli (individuals and events) and derailed/disrupted development may then 'catch-up'.

SEQUENCE OF RECOVERY

Development is a fully interactive process, with each step growing on previous attainments. Consequently, the recovery process may sometimes follow a specific path. For example, children in a DIR/Floortime programme appeared to improve in a particular sequence:

> "Within the first 3-4 months we would usually see greater joy and positive affect [emotion], along with more consistent relatedness (e.g. seeking out parents and caregivers). Even children who had been extremely avoidant and self-absorbed...83% of the children, which included children who proceeded very slowly, initially showed improvement in the range and depth of their engagement and pleasure."
>
> (Greenspan &Wieder, 1997)

These same children then:

> "...moved from simple to complex emotional motor gestures [in which] long sequences of reciprocal affective interaction...led to... the emergence of functional symbolic capacities. Creative and imaginative symbolic elaboration and the functional use of language always followed pre-symbolic affect, caring and communication."
>
> (Greenspan &Wieder, 1997)

Over time 58% of the children were able to use these emerging symbolic skills both creatively and logically:

> "Eventually, with a great deal of interaction and affect-[emotion] driven dialogues, the ability to abstract and comprehend the ideas of others emerged. Children did not get to this level unless their parents and therapists focussed on rapid, two-way symbolic communications. For example, it wasn't sufficient to listen to a verbal child and repeat what he said. Caregivers had to challenge the child to process incoming ideas...e.g. using affective tone, visual cues, multiple choices, and statements that inspired complex verbal responses to help children deal with more abstract dialogues."
>
> (Greenspan &Wieder, 1997)

This explanation describes the gradually more complex, emotionally-based and persistent, intimate interactions that are required between child and adult in order to develop 'higher order' reasoning and identification with others, and for which the 'magic square' of intersubjective relations forms the foundation (described in Chapter 7). This again shows how the full personality potential of the recovering child/individual can emerge once the underlying neurochemistry of fight/flight is reduced.

IS THERE AN 'AUTISTIC PERSONALITY'?

Some writers (e.g. Baron-Cohen, 2003) have proposed an essential, genetic difference between autism/ASD and typical individuals. But, when we understand that personality is a reflection of health, and subject to interactions between temperament and environmental factors, this hypothesis appears unlikely. Rather, although temperament and other aspects of genetic identity (GI) are inherited, their expression is not fixed. Due to their natural (healthy) susceptibility to specific environmental factors interacting with their innate temperaments, these susceptibilities may also be passed through the families of similar GIs (i.e. inherited). However, some GIs may be more likely to express autistic behaviours than others. Nevertheless the behaviours and characteristics of autism are not themselves genetically driven. As we have seen, they are the result of extreme personality expression, reflecting an underling allostatic/limbic trauma.

CONFLATING PERSONALITY WITH IDENTITY

In studying this area of autism/ASD 'personality' has frequently become conflated with 'identity'. For example, it is very common to read comments from parents concerning their children with autism/ASD suggesting that autism is 'part of who they are' and/or that the individual 'would not be who they are if they were not autistic'. This is usually stated as a defence against the idea of recovery or (more often) 'cure'. Indeed, for many autistic individuals themselves, 'cure' is conceived to be an insult and a denial of their 'real' nature. This is a very sensitive area to address. It takes place within the context of several decades of constructing autism as 'brain impairment', 'pathology in the brain' (Wing, 2003, p80), 'flawed genes' and/or of repeated statements that: 'autism is a lifelong condition and there is no cure' (Frith, 1993, p92). As a result, many young people and adults with autism have grown up to find themselves stigmatised and possessed of a permanent problem they can not themselves alter, even if they wished to. This situation has caused immense distress and hurt to many: one young girl in a *National Autistic Society* school was seen beating her head against a wall and blaming her brain for being 'autistic' after staff members had given her the "faulty brain" explanation. Other problems associated with this position include those of non-acceptance of difference, the needs of individuals going unmet, and fatalistic or low expectations of future improvement. In many of the writings, especially of women, there is evidence of failed attempts to prove that the ASD individual is somehow able to fit into the 'typical' world. For example:

> "…I am slowly leaning how to not spend my entire waking existence pretending I am just like you. I am not just like you. My brain is not like yours. I do not see the world the way you do. I like that. I don't care if you think this is awful and a waste of talent and time. I couldn't give a flying squirrel….I am autistic and I am proud of it. I see such beauty because of it. But I also see such agonising sorrow. So yes, I have depression. Is it any surprise?"
>
> (Kidney, 2014)

Angry (and unaware that 'typical' people also feel like this sometimes) writing such as this is a completely understandable and unfortunate result of decades of ignorance about the feelings and needs of autistic individuals. Nevertheless, I suggest that it is not 'autism' that we should celebrate (be 'proud' of) but the human spirit of the individual involved. The argument of this chapter is that this would (and does) remain, regardless of whether the individual has developed autism or not and/or recovered. And, indeed, some have argued against adoption of autism/ASD as an 'identity'. For example, Starr's response to Timimi (co-author of: *The myth of autism*) highlights a central difficulty:

> "There's much I disagree with in the book (not to mention some unfortunate errors of fact), and I am not as eager as the book's authors to do away with the entire concept of autism at the present time. But the book does make some important points, and I think

there is legitimate scope for a thoroughgoing critique of this sort...
if autism is anything, in the context of medicine, then it is a disorder.
This raises the question of whether it is possible to talk about
autism outside the context of medicine. In an ideal world, it might
be possible to talk about an 'autistic trait' one shares with a family
member...in the same way as one talks about a shared facial tic or
figure of speech...without the need for medicine or pathology to be
implicated in the discussion at all. But we don't live in an ideal world.
While autism is the subject of much informal discussion outside
a medical context, the medical meaning of autism is nonetheless
invoked at these discussions."

And concluding:

"...I think we already do think about autism as an identity, but I also
think that this may not be a good thing."

                                                              (Starr, 2014)

One does not need to live in an 'ideal world', however, to abandon the word
'disorder' or constructions of autism as 'brain flaw'. For example, in the
ecological theory described in this study, autism/ASD is a developmental
'derailment' (as coined by Rimland in 1964) rather than genetically-
determined pathology. The characteristics of autism (whether defined as
personality or identity) are the result of the individual's innate susceptibility
to environmental factors and their impact: physically and psychologically. To
recover from this derailment, differing degrees of health and repair will be
needed by different individuals. In some this 'recovery' will be 100 % possible,
while in others not anything like as much. In all cases, it is not the *personality*
of the individual, their *identity*, or their value as a human being that is in
question, but their happiness and life potential. It is clearly important that
we are all able to accept ourselves as we really are. But, the hypothesis of this
study is that it is only by recognising that autism results from factors which
are 'not us' that their limiting effects can be fully addressed in recovery.
Where autism is considered 'genetic' and/or 'fixed' these effects will become
compounded with the 'identity' of the individual. For example, Ari Ne'eman,
President of the *Autistic Self Advocacy Network,* writes:

"…it is important to remember that the particular qualities of autistic people, which may seem strange to the rest of the world, are actually valuable and part of their identity.…We don't think it is possible to fundamentally rewire our brains to change the way we think and interact with the world – but even if such a thing were possible, we don't think it would be ethical."

(In: Padawer, 2014).

Similarly, Greenberg states that autism:

"…is intrinsic to who we are…it's the hardware, not the software."

(In: Carpenter, 2015)

These passages present the clearest idea of the misunderstanding currently held that autism is: 'the way people are' rather than the result of their environmental experiences *interacting with* 'the way people are', and that this 'way' offers a flexible not fixed state of being for us all. Parallel with this is the further misunderstanding of the motivation and nature of recovery which, in the ecological theory of autism described here, is not to change the innate nature of a person but, rather, to liberate them to be 'who they really are' to the fullest, and free of the constraints created by the underlying trauma that brought the autism about. In fact, it is always possible to 'rewire' one's brain (should one wish it) without changing one's identity. This is called 'learning', 'adaption' or 'compensation' depending upon the context. We now know that the human brain is plastic in nature and responds to environmental stimuli. This means that life-long learning can occur. For example, research at Columbia University, US, found older people grow as many new brain cells as younger people and continue to develop neurons. This is in contrast to out-dated models of the brain, including those underpinning most autism research, as Baynes writes:

"For decades it was thought that adult brains were hard-wired and unable to form new cells."

(Baynes, 2018)

In short, where the brain is considered a fixed entity then clearly no change (or recovery) is possible. However, if it is understood to be a living organism and not 'computer hardware' recovery potential becomes logical. This is a vital point in understanding how recovery from autism/ASD can come about. And, although learning and adaption is much easier and quicker in the young (hence the preference for early intervention in autism/ASD) benefits can occur right through life, and at any age. So, in recovery, it is not the essential GI of the individual that is addressed, but the limitations due to the environmental factors and their effects which may limit full health and self-development.

NEURO-DIVERSITY: THE NEW ASD IDENTITY?

The previously labelled as 'impaired' have now grown up and written of their experiences and rightly rejected the labels stuck on them by 'experts' of the past. In response the UK, NAS has now officially abandoned Wing's concept of 'the triad of impairments' (although still using it for diagnoses). From this has grown a new perception of autism as a 'neuro-diverse' (ND) state based on brain difference (not 'flaw') with a 'neurotypical' (NT) label ascribed to the non-autistic 'typical' brain. In other words, autism/ASD is just a different, non-typical form of brain-wiring and sensory system. The 'ND' explanation therefore removes the stigma previously attached. In its support, those who are seeking to define (or re-define) themselves other than 'impaired' point to the lack of any biological evidence or 'gene for autism/ASD' (for example, Timimi, et al., 2011). And, it is the case that there is no such gene. However, this does not explain evidence of trauma in the writing of neuro-diverse individuals. For example:

> "In the past, skin contact was uncomfortable for me and I avoided it at all costs. Then, as time went by, I appeared to form strong attachments to certain individuals. I needed to be very close to them and was always needing them to hold or hug me. The stimulus of physical contact told me that I was okay and whenever one of these individuals could not be available to me, I moved into fear. Rocking myself and crying was my usual response, sometimes I would plead to be held and became very demanding."
>
> (Lawson, 2011)

This description by Wendy Lawson is a perfect example of what a distressed baby would feel and do. It is not in my view an example of 'neuro-diversity' (that is: different brain-wiring) but a reflection of trauma and delayed/derailed development. In addition, physical damage can (in theory) heal and the effects of trauma be recovered from, as Chapter 4 shows. In contrast, one would expect neuro-diversity to remain a fixed preference and/or sensory state. However, when one contrasts the unrecovered individual with their recovered/recovering state in the narratives, this does not appear to be the case. Rather, sensory overwhelm is often reduced to a manageable level – or even completely – and (generally) the individual becomes more comfortable socially. Logically, within the ND construct, this would not be possible (or even desirable). It is entirely understandable that individuals will be insulted by labels such as 'impaired' and 'faulty' and seek in their place equality and recognition of personal individuality and equity. The (only) problem with this new casting of ASD as neuro-diversity, as I perceive it, is that it inadvertently serves as an implicit acceptance of any developmental damage and harm which may underlie it. For example, Temple was able to access brain imaging services which showed she had experienced a physical trauma between the ages of 1-2 years of age. Damage clearly had occurred at this time in her development, although Temple does not interest herself with the possible reason/s for this. This harm – or compensation for it – may well lead to enhanced perceptual skills, as in Temple's case, by creating a diverse neurology (ND). But there is a difference between accepting a person as a unique human being in all their diversity and ignoring the fact that this may be harm-related; especially when at the same time we have increasing numbers of children who are being diagnosed as ASD and ADHD. So, while accepting diversity, we also need to ask why or how any underlying harm might have come about. It is of course more comfortable to ignore the idea that harm or damage in ASD may have unwittingly been done through environmental factors (with all that that implies) than 'it just happened due to genes we can't change'. Perhaps this is why recovery is not a subject most experts wish to explore? Nevertheless, masking trauma under the guise of 'neuro-diversity' allows the continuance of any such harm, including to others in the future.

DIFFERENCE BETWEEN GENETIC IDENTITY AND NEURO-DIVERSITY

It might now be necessary to ask: is genetic identity not the same thing as neuro-diversity? The answer is No. The difference between genetic identity

(GI) and neuro-diversity (ND) is important. GI is a term used to describe the fact that we all naturally vary in our 'brain-wiring' (thinking style), temperament and subsequent sensory systems, and modes of perception. This diversity is an evolutionary necessity allowing the maximum survival chance to a given community. In contrast the term ND may indicate brain differences but also incorporates those which are the result of trauma-states and harm, such as with Temple's neurologically-diverse perceptual skills. She recovered well from this harm 'in tune' with her genetic identity (GI): that is along the lines of her healthy, genetically endowed 'preferred' brain layout and thinking style. However, the trauma-driven behaviours of the ND individual in autism/ASD may sometimes be constrained to such an extent that the individual becomes developmentally 'stuck' in security-based functioning (extreme harm avoidance) and reduced social interaction. Baron-Cohen tangles with these facts whilst attempting to reconcile them with a traditional, genetic-determinist perception of autism/ASD:

> "What I have been interested in understanding…is how genes for autism survive in the first place. After all, autism limits one's abilities to read other's emotions and to form relationships, which in turn may reduce one's chances of having children and passing on one's genes."
>
> (Baron-Cohen, 2012)

The illogical nature of this situation leads one to conclude that autism/ASD is not necessarily neuro-diversity (ND) in action, but may also represent a state of damage. Yes, people are of differing GIs which, from an evolutionary perspective, *increase* our ability to survive. In contrast, ND states in autism/ASD may have the opposite effect.

THE DISTRESS OF AUTISM

There is currently a tendency to romanticise the autistic state (such as through films and TV detective dramatisations) while forgetting the physical distress. In fact, in ASD there appears to be a high degree of identifiable damage and physiological disorder, with considerable discomfort; extreme perceptual processing and overwhelm, in the presence of poor mind/brain integration, and severe health issues for many (see Chapter 4). As well as physical illness and damage there is also often very high anxiety, sufficient in one study for 84% of participants to be diagnosed with a discrete anxiety disorder (Lathe, 2006, p119). Clearly, such states represent more than just a 'different kind of thinking', although there may be that as well. Rather, these qualities reflect the type of physical damage/derailment experienced. Examples of disrupted development, such as that described by Mark Haddon in his autobiographical novel: *The curious incident of the dog in the night-time* are suggestive of the type of sensory overwhelm and poorly integrated sensory system individuals with autism/ASD typically suffer. Further examples are given by Alan Gardner, a garden designer, married for over 26 years and father of three. Considered 'quirky' at school, Alan says he: 'can't catch a ball' as autistic/ASD individuals: 'can't balance'. He explains:

> "I walk in straight lines, even in London, because that's where I want to go. We tend not to be very flexible in anything. We know what we want, how we want it, and we set about doing it."
>
> (Gardner, 2015)

Alan explains that he would rather evade emotions as they upset him: 'being ever so slightly shut off'. When invited to a barbecue one weekend he claimed to have had a 'complete meltdown', although:

> "Constant scheming and plotting really appeal to me. Just having constant goals stops me drowning in my own brainwaves."
>
> (Gardner, 2015)

Gardiner states that he 'loves bright colours and patterns' and 'doesn't care what people think'. He also re-iterates the ND hypothesis that:

> "Autism isn't a condition it is just a different way of seeing the world."
>
> (Gardner, 2015)

Alan considers that his physical difficulties are 'governed by the unique ASD mind'. With his particular perceptual ability of being able to see all the details at once in nature and replicating them in his garden designs, he gives autism as: 'an explanation, not a diagnosis or a condition'. With respect to Gardner, this is an 'explanation' that requires explaining. There is no logical connection between special perceptual abilities and poor balance (poor sensory integration) and physical difficulties resulting in a feeling of 'shut-off', which is more suggestive of the right hemisphere 'withdrawal/ harm avoidance' described earlier. Rather, as with Temple, there appears to be a combination of individual thinking style/GI, natural ability and severe sensory disruption and overwhelm, constraining personality to an extreme expression in certain situations. So, while it is obviously essential to improve the self-image and esteem of all autistic/ASD individuals, especially of those who have grown up with outdated and stigmatising attitudes from the past, I consider it equally important that the reason for any physical damage that may have occurred be fully understood. This includes states such as that described by Robyn Stewart, also on the high functioning end of autism/ ASD. She writes:

> "It feels as if my thoughts are in a series of cogs moving around in my brain...like someone has been eating toffee..."
>
>   (Steward, 2012)

Again, this does not appear to be simply a 'different way of thinking' (ND). Rather, it suggests a processing problem probably resulting from poor sensory integration and, as such, would have a physical/environmental aetiology, which it is important to identify. Consequently, whilst it is clear that we must (and do) accept and support diversity between individuals, this does not mean we have to accept the ND explanation without ensuring it does not stem from harm. This is especially so if we consider the 'life-long' impact of ASD. Further, where recovery from harm has taken place, such as described in the personal narratives of Chapter 4, we can seen that this has in no way altered the essential nature of these individuals but allowed each to shine more fully. And, a life without the stresses, worries and strains that the difficulties implicit in autism/ASD impose on the child/individual and their families is surely to be preferred where possible.

DIFFERENCE BETWEEN 'DAMAGE' AND 'IMPAIRMENT'

It could be argued that the term 'damage' used here is as insulting as 'impairment' in describing autism/ASD. For this reason it is helpful to examine the difference more closely. The meaning of impairment is: 'the state of being diminished, weakened, or damaged, especially mentally or physically'. This definition is therefore technically correct in ASD and (interestingly) inclusive of 'damage'. However, the historical association of the term 'impairment' with brain/gene 'flaw' and 'fault' and its implicit sense of being 'less than' (diminished) has become stigmatising of the individual. In addition, there is no reason given for the 'damage' other than an internal 'flaw' or 'fault' of the affected individual. In contrast, the use of the term 'damage' in the context of the ecological theory of autism/ASD proposed here is suggestive of the original (causative) trauma and harm and *not* the identity or personality of the individual. There is no stigma to this. If anything the theory implies a sense of 'other culpability' as yet unidentified (but see Poole, 2017, Chapter 8 for a review). In addition, this perception offers a potential 'way out' of some of the distress described earlier, for those who may want it, by proposing that 'repair'/recovery is a theoretical possibility.

THE PROBLEM OF LABELS

Sometimes a diagnosis or 'label' is helpful and necessary in order to access resources for the individual. For example, Amy, mother of a son (Alex) who 'lost' his autism diagnosis, states that her:

> "…ongoing struggle with the school is making sure he doesn't fall through the cracks, and that becomes harder without an autism diagnosis."
>
> (In: Carpenter, 2015)

This is partly because Alex retains special needs despite no longer given a diagnosis of autism. And:

> "…Amy says she is not confident that Alex has completely left autism behind. He still struggles in school, especially in reading comprehension and other areas that strain his still-immature language-processing skills. But he has learned coping and compensatory strategies that, at least for now, can convince teachers that he is understanding and processing information as any fifth grade student should."
>
> (Carpenter, 2015)

It is clear from this that diagnostic labels present a dilemma. Placing on one side the possible need for a change to a more developmentally congruent educational context for Alex, a diagnosis can act to provide necessary resources and support. However, losing the diagnosis does not in itself always equate to recovery (a difference explored in Chapter 6) which may require 'updates' in treatment programmes throughout the process. So, while it may be initially helpful to gain a diagnosis, and a better understanding of autism/ ASD from the 'inside', labels can be restrictive if they become our whole identity. Following her recovery, Judith Bluestone, at one time diagnosed with autism, states:

> "Am I autistic now? I don't think so. Even though my preferred modalities are solitude and written expression, and uncontrollable silliness and deep input rather than light touch, and my scripts and photos and rituals are still essential parts of me? No I am not autistic. How do I know for sure? Because the label is not who I am. I am who I have always known I was. I am Just Me. And, finally very proud of that, with all of the quirks that are part of me. I am Just Me."
>
> (Bluestone, 2005)

Interestingly, this contrasts with Florica Stone, mother of Alexander (Chapter 4, Narrative 1) who found that perceiving 'autism' as a permanent state, helped her accept and understand how to help her son. And also that of Louise Kidney, described earlier, whose decision to 'cut myself some slack' followed a state of burnout while working for the *US Government Digital Service*' and trying to look like everyone else' (Kidney, 2014). Of course, none of us can live trying to be like someone else, and the aim of recovery from autism is not to create homogenous, socially functioning individuals indistinguishable from others. It is to liberate individuals to be free to express themselves fully. Louise has taken the first step in her recovery by accepting herself as she is. The reduction of stress from this alone will be immensely healing.

A 'COPING' PERSONA?

At this point, it is perhaps of help to address some of the objections or caveats raised by autism specialists in relation to the research findings of

Fein's 2013 study (described in Chapter 2) where an 'optimum outcome' (OO) individual became no longer diagnosable on a standardised autism measure. For example, Carol Greenburgh, a special education professional, and mother of an autistic son, considers that, in some cases, people do not in fact 'lose' their autism but learn a coping mechanism which allows them to 'simulate a non-autistic persona' – something termed 'passing'. She considers that 'passing' uses a considerable amount of energy, placing strain on the individual. She states:

> "I don't want either me or my son using that energy trying to look 'normal'. I want us to use it trying to accomplish goals that we have set for ourselves."
>
> (In: Carpenter, 2015)

Professor Catherine Lord, director of the *Center for Autism and the Developing Brain* in New York, has also questioned how meaningful 'losing the diagnosis' is:

> "Perhaps these individuals improve on basic aspects of social behaviour that are striking in formal assessments, such as facial expression recognition, intonation or eye contact. But in the long run, that may be less important than flexibility, friendships and reciprocal interactions with familiar people in everyday life. People who retain symptoms of autism may do well even if they don't technically have an optimal outcome."
>
> (Lord, 2013).

She raises the presence of the substantial minority (7 of 34 participants) of OO individuals who nevertheless showed difficulties such as depression, inhibition impulsivity and hostility: features which were not seen in the group who retained their diagnoses. Given our new understanding of both the 'cause/s' of autism (underlying trauma) and nature of recovery (Chapter 6) we can now address these points. In the case of a 'passing' coping mechanism, this can occur where the deeper aspects of the trauma remain unaddressed and the focus has been on the cognitive aspects (Domain 3) alone. It may also apply in 'normalisation' approaches requiring conformity, with little personal autonomy or volition. Greenburgh is right, therefore, that it is clearly preferable to pursue the individual goals of the person concerned than impose socially acceptable behaviours on anyone. However, recovery – as opposed to 'losing the diagnosis' – enables both developmental derailment to re-instate as well as the underlying trauma to be addressed, at least to the degree that this is possible. Hence, with the seven children in Fein's study who developed problems it is possible that a more developmentally contingent intervention is required (Domain 3): one that more closely follows the intersubjective relationship described in Chapter 7. This would preferably be preceded by Domain 2 programmes.

A 'SUCCESSFUL' PERSON

Catherine Lord also considers that the concept of offering recovery has 'done damage' by setting up parents to believe that if they only followed the 'right' therapy, their child would no longer be autistic. She states:

> "There is just no evidence of that."
>
> (In: Carpenter, 2015)

In fact, there is evidence. But this misses the point that Lord is keen to make which, I think, is that we must recognise the strengths, value, needs and realistic nature of the individual concerned, rather than place pressure on them to be different from 'who they are'. In relation to 'losing a diagnosis of autism', she points out that:

> "It is not clear whether this group [OO] is more successful than those who continue to carry diagnoses."
>
> (Lord, 2013)

This comment must be placed within the context of Western cultural values. Such values are so tied into worldy achievement, hierarchy and status that it is perhaps inevitable that the 'recovered' from autism/ASD would be measured by some as 'more successful' than those who 'failed to recover'. It is also the antithesis of the humanistic psychology movement (in which this study of recovery is constructed) which is concerned only with the unconditional acceptance of each individual and of fulfilling our individual potential. It is therefore unfortunate that assisting some individuals to 'recover' should be cast as somehow 'unfair' on those who can't perhaps be helped 'as much'. Instead, we could welcome the possibility of enabling each of us to reach our own 'personal best' without comparison with others. And, understanding how recovery varies between individuals could help even those who may not fully recover as, by better understanding the difference, the stresses placed on some group members (such as described by Louse Kidney and others) can be more easily avoided or addressed.

'AUTIE/ASPIE PRIDE'

Another argument put forward against the desirability of recovery and associated practices is that losing a diagnosis of autism/ASD:

> "...deprives people of the opportunity to be part of the autism community, and that adults in this situation will sense that they are somehow different, but can't make sense of the feeling. In other cases, children may reject their history: If your whole life your parents have looked at autism as something that was this scary thing that, thank goodness, was no longer associated with you: that's a hard thing."
>
> (Ne'eman, cited in Carpenter, 2017)

This view depends entirely upon ones belief in autism as intrinsic to the individual (i.e. part of a genetically fixed ND identity). It makes the assumption that denying one's autistic past equates with denying ones 'real self', casting the no longer diagnosable person as a 'mis-fit'. However, Karen Exkorn, a physician whose son Jake made a full recovery, is convinced that this is not how he feels:

> "He (Jake) embraces his past and can talk about it."
>
> (In: Carpenter, 2015)

For Jake and his mother autism is part of their shared family history. However, Karen understands why it would seem hard for others to accept a better outcome:

"I'm not sure if I would have believed that full recovery was possible…if we didn't have a son who fully recovered."

(Cited in Carpenter, 2017)

Overall it appears that 'autie pride' and similar tags depend upon identification with a group or tribe in the same way as 'black pride' or 'gay pride'. These identities were/are felt necessary to the individuals concerned as a banner of self-acceptance in the face of stigmatism, ignorance and prejudice. But, ultimately, these labels still define an individual as a group member, rather than 'who they themselves are' as a unique person. This need for group (tribal) identity is part of human nature at present, and we can see it at its most harsh in the unhelpful comparisons felt by Mark (Chapter 4, Narrative 7) with his non-autistic Yale co-graduates. It is my hope that we will one day leave the need for such group membership behind, allowing our individual and unique human nature, in all its natural diversity, to be fully expressed and equally valued.

WHY RECOVERY?

Recovery from autism and its companion volume: *An ecological theory of autism* represent my personal journey through autism/ASD and the experiences and meanings of recovery for those affected. Now that the analysis is complete it is perhaps important to summarise why I consider recovery to be a feasible and desirable aim. Clearly, if the individual is happy, healthy and fulfilled the concept of 'recovery' will not appeal, or be relevant, to them. However, individuals with autism/ASD are frequently anxious, unhappy, unwell and difficult to care for. For example, Mikle South, associate professor of psychology and neuroscience at *The Autism Research Group*, McKay School, US, cites a voice message of a distraught 10-year old boy with autism/ASD asking:

> "How will things ever get better?...There's just something wrong with me Mom. I'm just broken."
>
> (BYU, 2016)

And a survey published in 2013 by the UK *National Autistic Society* indicated that 65% of diagnosed individuals said they: 'would like more friends' while 22% said they had: 'no friends at all'. It reported parents as saying that the transition to adulthood was like, 'falling of a cliff edge' (NAS, 2013). It is our role as carers and researchers to help free children from limitations and enable them to reach their individual potential. As Terisa Gabrielsen, a lead researcher at the McKay School, states:

> "...we have one goal...we want to make the lives of families better."
>
> (BYU, 2016)

Addressing the possibility of recovery, as described in this book, is one way of helping achieve this.

STATISTICS

There is also a more pragmatic reason for examining the possibility of recovery. In the UK there are more than 600,000 individuals diagnosed with autism/ASD, of whom a quarter do not speak and 85% do not work full-time. This poses a considerable financial burden. In 2014, a study by the *London School of Economics* (LSE) estimated the cost of autism in the UK at £32 billion per annum. This figure was more than heart disease, cancer and stroke combined: with £12 billion for cancer, £8 billion for heart disease and £5 billion for stroke. It is made up of residential accommodation, medical care and productivity loses. In the US, the cost was $175 billion per annum (LSE, 2014). Professor Knapp, who co-authored the study, explains:

> "Autism is more common than perhaps people realise...it's more than 1% of the population. Also the impact is across the lifespan, particularly for people with autism and learning difficulties, also known as low-functioning autism. Those individuals would need quite a lot of care and support from a pretty early age. You're talking about 60 or 70 years of support for people with this level of need."
>
> (In: Siddique, 2014)

Based on the assumption of autism/ASD as a 'lifelong' condition, even for those without additional learning difficulties, considerable support is required. The conclusion of the LSC is that further research is needed into early interventions with, presumably, yet more funding. In addition, some current interventions are less than satisfactory. For example, a landmark study by NHS England found more than 30,000 people with autism and learning disabilities are being wrongly prescribed anti-depressant and anti-psychotic drugs – often for years – without proper checks on their suitability and sometimes over the recommended safe limit. Worryingly, in the majority of cases there appeared to be 'no justification' for the prescription. These drugs act as a 'chemical cosh' (Donnelly, 2015). Carol Povey, director of the *National Autistic Society* states:

> "The high number of people on the autism spectrum being prescribed psychotropic drugs like anti-depressants and anti-psychotics is concerning and must be addressed urgently. Figures from one of

the reports reveal that autistic adults are prescribed antipsychotic medication at roughly 10 times the rate of the general population."

(In: Donnelly, 2015)

Much personal hardship, and a considerable amount of money, could therefore be saved simply by adopting the view that autism need not be 'lifelong' and recovery in some form, and to some extent, is both possible and desirable.

THE WAY FORWARD

The companion volume to this one, *An ecological theory of autism,* concluded that autism is about 95% environmentally driven and that its expression depends on our individual susceptibility, and type and timing of exposure, to a variety of environmental factors. Chapter 4 of this book showed that it is possible for many ASD individuals to recover from the negative effects of these interactions to a degree not previously considered possible; while Chapter 5 described the wide range of programmes that currently exist outside of conventional provision, but which have been found helpful by those writing of their recovery progress. I suggest it is now time for us, as parents, carers, therapists, educators and researchers, to embrace their 'real world' experiences and together find a better way forward.

REFERENCES

Achenbach, T. (1991). *Manual for the Child Behavior Checklist/4–18 and 1991 Profile.* Burlington, VT: University of Vermont Department of Psychiatry.

Achenbach, T. (1992). *Manual for the Child Behavior Checklist/2-3 and 1992 Profile.* Burlington, VT: University of Vermont Department of Psychiatry.

Achenbach, T. M. (1997) *Manual for the Young Adult Self-Report and Young Adult Behavior Checklist.* Burlington, VT : University of Vermont Department of Psychiatry.

Airey, T. (2014). A*dmiring autism: Busting 'autism myths' with a camera.* BBC News. Accessed at: http://www.bbc.co.uk/news/uk-england-27142806. September, 2017.

Amminger, G.P., Berger G.E, Schäfer, M.R, Klier, C., Friedrich, M.H, & M. Feucht. (2007). Omega-3 fatty acids supplementation in children with autism. (2007). A double-blind, randomised, placebo-controlled pilot study. *Biol Psychiatry.* Feb 15; 61(4): pp551-3.

Anderson, D., Liang, J., and C. Lord. (2014). Predicting young adult outcome among more and less cognitively able individuals with autism spectrum disorders. *J Child Psychol Psychiatry*; 55 (5): pp485-94.

Aron, E. (1996). *The highly sensitive person.* Secaucus, N.J. Carol Publishing.

Aron, E. (2002). *The highly sensitive child.* New York: Broadway Books.

ATC. (2011). Accessed at: www.autismtreatmentcenter.org/contents/about_son-rise/faq.php 2011). March 2016.

ATC. (2018). Accessed at: http://autismtreatmentcenter.org/contents/programs_and_services/high-functioning.php. March, 2018.

Autism Research Institute. (2010). Accessed at: http://www.autism.com/. June 2010.

Autism Research Institute (2015). Accessed at: http://autism.com/.Sept. 2015.

Autism Treatment Center (2017). *How the Son-Rise Program helped parents with autistic children.* Accessed at: http://autismtreatmentcenter.org/autism-education, March, 2017.

Baron-Cohen. S. (2003). *The essential difference.* London: Allen Lane.

Baron-Cohen, S. (2012). Are geeky couples more likely to have kids with autism? Scientific American. November 9th. Accessed at: http://www.

scientificamerican.com/article/are-geeky-couples-more-likely-to-have-kids-with-autism/. August, 2015.

Baron-Cohen, S., Allen, J. and C. Gillberg, (1992). Can autism be detected at 18 months? The needle, the haystack, and the CHAT. *British Journal of Psychiatry*, 161: pp839-843.

Barvalia, P., Oza, P., Daftary, A., and V. Patil. (2014). Effectiveness of homoeopathic therapeutics in the management of childhood autism disorder. Indian Journal of Research in Homoeopathy. Vol. 8 (3) July-Sept.: p147-159.

Bates, C. (2006). How fish oil unlocked my autistic son. Daily Mail, June 12th. Accessed at: http://www.dailymail.co.uk/health/article-373833/How-fish-oil-unlocked-autistic-son.html.

Bates, K., and T. Wachs. (Eds). (1994). *Temperament: Individual differences.* Washington, DC: American Psychological Association.

Baynes, C. (2018). Elderly people grow as many new brain cells as young, study finds. *Independent Online*. April 6th. Accessed at: https://www.independent.co.uk/news/science/brain-cells-ageing-old-people-grow-new-elderly-young-research-a8291056.html. April, 2018.

BBC. (2005). Quack autism cures must end. BBC, News. Accessed at: http://news.bbc.co.uk/1/hi/ health/3840629.stm. May, 2009.

Bell, J.G. (2004). Essential fatty acids and phospholipase A2 in autistic spectrum disorders. *Prostoglandins Levicot. Essent. Fatty Acids.* 71 (4): pp201-204

Berthoz, S., and E.L. Hill. (2005). The validity of using self reports to assess emotion regulation abilities in adults with autism spectrum disorder. *European Psychiatry* (20): pp291-298.

Beversdorf, D., Manning, S., Hillier, A., and R. Anderson. (2005). Timing of Prenatal Stressors and Autism. *Journal of Autism and Developmental Disorders.* Vol. 35, Issue 4: pp 471–478.

Bilder, D., Zimmermann, J., Miller, J., and W. MacMahon. (2009). Autism May Be Linked To Being Firstborn, Breech Births Or Moms 35 Or Older. Accessed at: http://www.sciencedaily. com/releases/2009/04/090427091115.htm. March, 2011.

Biller, J.A., Katz,A.J., Flores, A.F. Buie,T.M. & S.L. Gorback. (1995). Treatment of recurrent Clostridium difficile colitis with Lactobacillus GG. *J.Pediatr Gastroenterol Nutr.* Aug, 21(2): pp224-6.

B.I.R.D. (2017). Accessed at: http://www.birdcharity.org.uk/work/neurological-reflexes/. April, 2017.

Bluestone, J. (2005). *The fabric of autism.* Seattle, WA. Saphire Enterprises.

Blythe, S. (2006). Dissecting known factors in autistic spectrum disorders. *Medical Veritas*, 3: pp786-795.

Bock, K., and C. Staugh. (2007). *Healing the new childhood epidemics: Autism, ADHD, asthma and allergies.* New York: Ballantine.

Bolte, E.R. (2000). Short-term benefit from oral vancomycin treatment of regressive onset autism, *Journal of Child Neurology*, 15: p430.

BPS. (2007). Making progress on autism. *The Psychologist*, 20 (7) p410.

BPS, (2016). Neuro Harlow – The effect of a mother's touch on her child's developing brain. *The Psychologist*, Vol. 29 (10): p752

BPS. (2017). Desperately seeking validation. Conference Report. *The Psychologist*, July: p25.

Brazelton, T. and S. Greenspan. (2000). *The irreducible needs of children.* Cambridge, MA: Da Capo Press.

Brosnan, M., Turner-Cobb,J., Munro-Naan, Z., and D. Jessop. (2009). The absence of a normal Cortisol Awakening Response (CAR) in adolescent males with Asperger Syndrome (AS). *Psychoneuroendochrinology*, 34 (7): pp1095-1100.

BU. (2009). Autism linked to stress hormone levels. *University news,* University of Bath. April 2nd. Accessed at: www.bath.ac/uk/news/2009/04/autism-cortisol-link/. July 2010.

Buss, A., and, R, Plomin. (1984). *Temperament: Early developing traits.* Hillsdale, N.J.: Erlbaum.

BYU. (2016). Autism Research Group, Mckay School of Education. Accessed at: https://education.byu.edu/magazine/summer2016/autisms-answers. February, 2017.

Campbell, J. (2015). Mother helps cure son's misdiagnosed illness through internet research. *Independent online.* Accessed at: http://www.independent.co.uk/news/science/mothers-helps-cure-sons-misdiagnosed-illness-through-internet-research-10093866.html

Campbell-McBride, N. (2004). *Gut and psychology syndrome.* Cambridge, UK: Medinform.

Canli, T. (Ed.) (2006). *Biology and personality and individual differences.* New York: Guilford Press.

Carpenter, S. (2015). The children who leave autism behind. *Spectrum News.* Accessed at: https://spectrumnews.org/features/deep-dive/children-who-leave-autism-behind/. February, 2017.

Caron, C. (2011). *Nurse gives patient paralytic instead of antacid.* Accessed at: http://abcnews.go.com/Health/nurse-patient-paralytic-antacid/ story?id=14997244. January, 2018.

Centers, S. (2011). Accessed at: http://www.osteopathiccenter.org/autism. html March, 2012

Cloninger, S. (1996). *Personality.* New York: W.H. Freeman and Co.

Cloninger, R. (2004). *Feeling good: The science of wellbeing.* Oxford: OUP

Cohen, I. and V. Sudhalter. (2005). *PDD Behaviour Inventory (PDDBI).* Oxford: Hogrefe.

Cohen, Howard, Amerine-Dickens, Mila, Smith, Tristram. (2006). Early intensive behavioural treatment: Replication of the UCLA model in a community setting. *Journal of Developmental & Behavioral Pediatrics,* 27 (2): pp145-155.

Collins, N. (2014). *Grandmother dies after receiving wrong prescription.* Accessed at: http://www.telegraph.co.uk/news/health/news/11174710/ Grandmother-dies-after-receiving-wrong-prescription.html. January, 2018.

Cooper, J., Heron, T.E. & Heward, W.L. (2007). *Applied behavior analysis (2nd edition).* Upper Saddle River; N.J: Prentice Hall.

Cooper, R. (2017). Neurodiversityand dyslexia: Challenging the social construction. Accessed at: http://outsidersoftware.co.uk/wp-content/ uploads/2017/03/Neurodiversity-and-Dyslexia-Challenging-the-social-construction-of-specific-learning-differences.pdf. August, 2017.

Copeland, J. and J. Hodges. (1973). *For the love of Ann.* London: Arrow.

Conlan, L. (2016). Neurotribes: The legacy of autism and how to think smarter. *The British Journal of Psychiatry.* October. Vol. 209 (4): p353.

Cullen, L.A., & J. H. Barlow (2001). Parent's experiences of using touch therapy with children with autistic tendencies. In: *Proceedings.* Leicester: British Psychological Society.

Davies, M. (2004). Personality: Two ways of thinking about it. *The Psychologist.* Vol. 17 (11): pp 638-641.

Dawson, G. (2001). Mother is just another face in the crowd to autistic children. *Science Daily.* Accessed at: *https://www.sciencedaily.com/ releases/2001/04/010418072256.htm. May, 2017.*

DeCasper, A., and W. Fifer. (1980). Of human bonding: Newborns prefer their mothers' voices. *Science,* 208: pp1174-6.

Dennison, P. (1981). *'Switching on': The whole brain answer to dyslexia'.* Ventura, CA: Edu-Kinesthetics Inc.

Deweerdt, S. (2014). Repetitive behaviours disappear when autism does. Accessed at: https://spectrumnews.org/opinion/repetitive-behaviors-disappear-when-autism-does/ January, 2018.

Diamond, M., and J. Hopson. (1999). *Magic trees of the mind.* Plume: London, UK.

D.M, (2010). *Four-month old baby dies of overdose after mother given wrong prescription.* Access at: http://www.dailymail.co.uk/news/article-1246986/Four-month-old-baby-dies-receiving-fatal-dose-medicine-mother-given-wrong-prescription-chemist.html. January, 2018.

Donnelly, L. (2015). More than 30,000 people with autism and learning disabilities 'under the chemical cosh'. *Daily Telegraph.* July 14th.

DSM-V. (2013). *Diagnostic and statistical manual of mental disorders.* Washington DC: American Psychiatric Association.

DT. (2010). *Third of adults 'still take teddy bear to bed'.* Accessed at http://www.telegraph.co.uk/news/newstopics/howaboutthat/7947502/Third-of-adults-still-take-teddy-bear-to-bed.html. May, 2017.

DT. (2017). Is it ok for men to still own cuddly toys? Accessed at: http://www.telegraph.co.uk/men/11863886/Is-it-OK-for-grown-men-to-still-own-cuddly-toys.html

Edelson, S. (1996). *Interview*, June 9th. www.autism.com.

Edelson, S. and B. Rimland. (2006). *Recovering autistic children.* San Diego: Autism Research Institute.

EEPRU, (2018). *Prevalence and economic burden of medication errors in the NHS in England.* Policy Research Unit in Economics Evaluation of Health Care Interventions, Sheffield. UK.

Escalante-Mead, P., Minshew, J., and Sweeney, J. (2003).Abnormal brain lateralisation in high functioning autism. *Journal of autism and developmental disorders,* Vol 33 (5): pp539-543.

Escalona, A., Field, T. M., Singer-Strunck, R., Cullen, C., and K. Hartshorn. (2001). Autism symptoms decrease following massage therapy. *Journal of Autism and Developmental Disabilities.* Springer.

Evans, P., Hucklebridge, F. And A. Clow. (2000). *Mind, Immunity and health: The science of psychoneuroimmunology.* New York: Free Association.

Fantasia, V., Fasulo, A., Costall, A., and B. Lopez. (2014). Changing the game: Exploring infants' participation in early play routines. *Frontiers in Psychology.* Accessed at: http://journal.frontiersin.org/article/10.3389/fpsyg.2014.00522/full. June, 2017.

Fein, D., Barton, Eigsti, I-M., and E. Kelley. (2013). Optimal outcome in individuals with a history of autism. *Journal of Child Psychology and Psychiatry.* Vol 54(2): pp195-205.

Field, T. (2003). *Touch.* Cambridge, Mass: Bradford/MIT.

Field, T., Lasko, D., Mundy, P., Henteleff, T., Talpins, S. & M.Dowling. (1996). Autistic children's attentiveness and responsiveness improved after touch therapy. *Journal of Autism and Developmental Disorders,* 27 (3): pp333-338.

Fisher. M. 1988. Autism and holding: *Communication* 22(3): p75.

Fisher, P. (2010). Does homeopathy have anything to contribute to hormesis? *Human and experimental toxicology,* 29 (7): pp555-560.

Fisher, P. (2018). The Evidence. *Faculty of Homeopathy* website, Accessed at: https://facultyofhomeopathy.org/homeopathy-the-evidence/. May, 2018.

Fitzpatrick, M. (2009). *Defeating autism: A dangerous delusion.* London: Routledge.

Fraga, M., Ballestar, E., Paz, M., and Ropero, S. (2005). *Epigenetic differences arise during the lifetime of monozygotic twins.* Accessed at: http://twinsuk.ac.uk/wpcontent/uploads/2012/03/Fraga.PNAS_ 2005. pdf. February 2015.

Frith, C. (2009). Making up the mind. *The Psychologist,* Vol. 22 (10): pp842-845.

Frith, U. (1993). *Mysteries of the mind: Autism.* June: pp92-98.

Frith, U. (1989/2003). *Autism: Explaining the enigma.* Oxford: Blackwell.

Frymann, V. (1998). *The collected papers of Viola. M. Frymann: Legacy of osteopathy to children.* The Academy.

FS.Circle (2014). The cause of stimming. *Friendship Circle.* Accessed at http://www.friendshipcircle.org/blog/ 2012/03/22/the-cause-of-stimming-whats-your-stim/. November, 2014.

Gallagher, J. (2016). 'Super-parenting' improves children's autism. BBC, News. Accessed at: http://www.bbc.co.uk/news/health-37729095. May, 2017.

Gallagher, C., and M. Goodman. (2009). Hepatitis B vaccination of male neonates and autism diagnosis, NHIS 1997-2002. *J. Toxicol. Environ. Health A.* 73 (24): pp1665-77.

Gardner, A. (2015). 'Autism isn't a condition, it's just a different way of seeing the world'. Accessed at: http://www.telegraph.co.uk/men/thinking-man/11752863/Autism-isnt-a-condition-its-just-a-different-way-of-seeing-the-world.html. August, 2015.

Gates, D. (2018)Accessed at: www.bodyecology.com/autism.php. January, 2018.

Geller, S. (2004). *The big five personality traits.* Accessed at: https://www. safetyperformance.com/TheBigFive PersonalityTraits-GeneticandInherit edDeterminantsofBehavior.pdf. August, 2015.

Gerhardt, S. (2004). *Why love matters.* Hove, UK: Brunner-Routledge.

Glasson, E., Bower, C., Petterson, B., and N, Klerk, et. al. (2004).Perinatal Factors and the Development of Autism: A Population Study *Arch Gen Psychiatry,* 61: pp618-627.

Goldberg, M. (2011). *The myth of autism.* New York: Skyhorse.

Goldshmied, E., and D. Selleck. (1996). *Communication between babies in their first year.* London: National Children's Bureau.

Goodman, B. (2012). Why some children may 'grow out' of autism. Special Needs Digest. Accessed at: http://www.specialneedsdigest.com/2014/01/ why-some-children-may-grow-out-of-autism.html. February, 2017.

Grandin, T. (2014). *The autistic brain.* London: Ebury Publishing.

Grandin, T. and M. Scariano. (1987/96). *Emergence: Labelled autistic.* New York: Time Warner.

Gray, B. (2000). *Homeopathy: Science or myth.* Berkley, CA: North Atlantic.

Greenspan, S. (2004). *Greenspan Social-Emotional Growth Chart.* Oxford: Perason/PsychCorp.

Greenspan, S., and S. Wieder. (1997). Developmental patterns and outcomes in infants and children with disorders in relating and communicating: A chart review of 200 cases of children with autistic spectrum diagnoses. *Journal of Developmental and Learning Disorders.* (1): pp87-141.

Greenspan, S., and S. Wieder. (2006). *Engaging Autism.* Cambridge, MA: De Capo.

Griswold, A. (2016). Autism's brain signature lingers even after loss of diagnosis. *Spectrum.* Accessed at: https://spectrumnews.org/news/autisms-brain-signature-lingers-even-after-loss-of-diagnosis/. March, 2017.

Griswold, A. (2017). Compulsions, anxiety replace autism in some children. *Spectrum.* Accessed at:https://spectrumnews.org/news/ compulsions-anxiety-replace-autism-children/. February, 2017.

Gupta, M., Gupta, A., Schork, N., and G. Watteel. (1995). Perceived touch deprivation and body image: some observations among eating disordered and non-clinical subjects. *Journal of Psychosomatic Research.* Vol. 39, (4): pp459-464

Gutstein, S. (2011). Accessed at: www. autism.about.com/od treatmentoptions/a/RDI.htm. (September, 2011).

Gutstein, S. (2000). *Autism/Aspergers: Solving the relationship puzzle.* Arlington TX: Future Horizons

Gutstein S., and R. Sheely (2002). *Relationship development intervention with children, adolescents and adults.* London: Jessica Kingsley.

Hamilton, L. (2000). *Facing autism.* Colorado: Waterbrook.

Handle Institute (2009). Accessed at: http://www.handle.org/.

Hannaford, C. (1995). *Smart Moves: Why learning is not all in your head.* Arlington, Virginia: Great Ocean Publishing.

Happe, F. (1996). Studying weak central coherence at low levels: Children with autism do not succumb to visual illusions. *Journal of Child Psychology and Psychiatry,* 37: pp873-7.

Harrell, E. (2005). Fatty acids may be key to unlock autism. The Scotsman (Online). Accessed at: http://news.scotsman.com/?id=598582005. On: June 6th 2005.

Harris B., and R. Lewis. (1994). Physiological effects of massage. *International Journal of Alternative and Complementary Medicine.* February, p16.

Harris, J. (2016). *Journal of the American Academy of Child & Adolescent Psychiatry.* 'Book Review'. Vol. 55 (8): pp729-735.

Hayden, E. (1999). *Osteopathy for children.* Churchdown, Gloucester, UK: Hayden.

Hayden, E. (2000). Healing Touch. *Natural Parent,* July/August, p34-36.

Hecht, P., Hudson, M., Connors, S., and M. Tilley. (2016). Maternal serotonin transporter genotype affects risk for ASD with exposure to prenatal stress. *Autism Research,* Vol. 9 (11): pp1151-1160.

Higashida, N. (2013). *The reason I jump.* London: Hodder and Stoughton.

Hirstein, W., Iverson, P., and V.S. Ramachandran. (2001). *Autonomic responses of autistic children to people and objects.* Accessed at: http://www.ncbi.nlm. nih.gov/pmc/articles/PMC1088823/pdf/PB011883.pdf. June, 2014.

Hobson, P. (2002). *The cradle of thought.* London, Macmillan.

Houghton, K., Schuchard, J., Lewis, C., and C. Thompson.(2013). Promoting child-initiated social-communication in children with autism: Son-rise Progam intervention effects. *Journal of Communication Disorders.* Accessed at: http://comm.soc.northwestern.edu/aphasia/ files/2012/11/Houghton-Schuchard-Lewis-Thompson_J-of-Comm-Disorders_2013.pdf. April, 2017.

II Institute, Website (2017). Intensive Interaction Institute. Accessed at: http://www.intensiveinteraction.org/find-out-more/about-intensive-interaction/. July, 2017.

InfoRefuge, (2006-2013). Accessed at: http://www.inforefuge.com/science-of-smell-mother-infant-bonding. May, 2013.

Irlen East (2011). Accessed at:www.irleneast.com/research_into_irlen.htm. Feb. 2011

Isolauri, E., Juntunen, M., Rautanen, T. Sillanaukee, P. & T. Koivula. (1991). A human Lactobacillus strain (Lactobacillus casei sp strain GG) promotes recovery from acute diarrhea in children. *Pediatrics*. Jul, 88 (1): pp90-7.

James, G. (2012). Children can 'grow out of' autism, suggests study. Huffington Post. Accessed at: http://www.huffingtonpost.co.uk/2012/01/24/children-grow-out-of-autism_n_1226532.html. January, 2017.

Jarusiewicz, B. (2002) Efficacy of neurofeedback for children in the autism spectrum: A pilot study. *Journal of Neurotherapy*, Vol. 6 (4): pp39-49.

Jepson, B.and J. Johnson. (2007). *Changing the course of autism*. Boulder, CO. Sentient.

J.Hopkins, 2015. *Paternal sperm may hold clues to autism*. Accessed at: news/media/releases/paternal_sperm_may_hold_clues_to_autism. June, 2015.

Jones, G., Meldrum, E. and E. Newson (1994). *A descriptive and comparative study of interventions for children with autism*. Nottingham: University of Nottingham Publications.

Jones, J., and M. Johnson.. (2016). A revolution for the at-risk. *The Psychologist*, Vol. 29 (12): pp912-916.

Joosten, A., Bundy, A., and S. Einfeld. (2012). Context influences the motivation stereotypic and repetitive behaviour in children diagnosed with intellectual disability with and without autism. *J. Appl Res Intellect Disabil*. May, 25 (3): pp262-70.

Kagan, J. (1994). *Galen's prophecy*. New York: Basic Books.

Kaufman, B.N. and R. Kaufman. (1995). *Son-Rise: The miracle continues*. Tiburon, CA: H. J. Kramer.

Kaufman, R. (2014). *Autism breakthrough*. London: Vermillion.

Keenan, M. (2004). The tragedy and the shame. *The Psychologist*, 17 (2):pp72-75.

Kerekes, N., Brandstrom, S., Lundstrom, S., and M. Rastam. (2013). ADHD, autism spectrum disorder, temperament and character: phenotypical associations and etiology in a Swedish childhood twin study. *Comprehensive psychiatry,* Nov. 54(8): pp1140-7.

Kidney, L. (2014). After what I've been through, don't tell me I'm not autistic. *The Guardian Online.* Accessed at: https://www.theguardian.com/profile/louise-kidney

Kinney, D., Miller, A., Crowley,D., and E. Huang. (2008). Autism prevalence following prenatal exposure to hurricanes and tropical storms in Louisiana. Journal of *Autism and Developmental Disorders.* 38: pp481-488.

Klaveness, J. and J. Bigam. (2010). Accessed at: http://www.gfcfdiet.com/dietsurveysept2.htm#The GFCF Kids Survey.

Kobasa, S. C. (1979). Stressful life events, personality, and health: Inquiry into hardiness. Journal of Personality and Social Psychology 37 (1): pp1–11.

Kraemer, S. (2000). The fragile male. *British Medical Journal.* Vol. 321, 23-30 December: pp1609-1612.

Krug, D., Arick, J. and P. Almond. (1980). *Autism Screening Instrument for Educational Planning (ASIEP).* Portland, OR: ASIEP.

Kurita, H., and T. Koyama. (2006). Autism-Spectrum quotient Japanese version measures mental health problems other than autism traits. *Psychiatry and Clinical Neurosciences,* 60: pp373-378.

Lansky, A. L. (2003). Impossible cure: The promise of homeopathy. Portola Valley, CA: R.L.Ranch Press.

Larsson, H., Easton, W., Madsen, K., and Vestergaard, M. et.al. (2005). *Risk Factors for Autism: Perinatal Factors, Parental Psychiatric History and Socioeconomic Status.* Accessed at: htwww.sciencedaily.com/releases/2005/05/050521155202.htm. March, 2011

Lathe, R. (2006). *Autism, brain and environment.* London: Jessica Kingsley.

McEwan, B., and E. Norton Lasley. (2001). *The end of stress as we know it.* Washington. DC: Joseph Henry.

Laurence, J. (2013). Children can 'grow out of' autism, psychologists say, challenging the established view that it is a permanent, incurable condition. *Independent.* January 15th.

Lawson, W. (2000). *Life behind glass.* London: Jessica Kingsley.

Lawson, W. (2011). *The passionate mind.* London: Jessica Kingsley.

Lemer, P. (1996). From attention deficit disorder to autism: A continuum. *Journal of Behavioural Optometry,* 7(6): pp143-49.

Lewis, D., Bluestone, J., Savina, M, & W. Zoller. (2006). Imaging Cerebral Activity in Recovery from Chronic Traumatic Brain Injury: A Preliminary Report. *Journal of Neuroimaging,* Vol.16 (3): pp272-277.

Lonsdale, D., Shamberger, R. and T. Audhya. (2002). Treatment of autism spectrum children with thiamine tetrahydrofurfuryl disulfide: A pilot study. *Neuroendocrinology Letters,* Vol. 23 (4): pp303-308.

Lord, C. (2013). Optimum Outcome. *Spectrum News:* Opinion. February 15th. Accessed at: https://spectrumnews.org/opinion/viewpoint/guest-blog-optimal-outcome/. February, 2018.

Lord, C., Risi, S., Lambrecht, L., and E. H. Cook. et al. (2000). The Autism Diagnostic Observation Schedule-Generic: a standard measure of social and communication deficits associated with the spectrum of autism. *Journal of Autism and Developmental Disorders.* Vol. 30 (3): pp205-23.

Lovaas,O. (1987). Behavioral treatment and normal educational and intellectual functioning in young autistic children. *Journal of consulting and clinical psychology,* 55: pp3-9.

Lovell, A. (1978). *Simple Simon.* Tring: Lion.

LSE. (2014). Autism is the most costly medical condition in the UK. *The Guardian Online:* Accessed at: https://www.theguardian.com/society/2014/jun/09/autism-costs-more-cancer-strokes-heart-disease. May, 2017.

Marcus, O. (2017). *Masculine emotional intelligence.* Accessed at: http://owenmarcus.com/uncategorized/guess-what-turns-out-men-are-more-sensitive-than-women-part-1/. November, 2017.

McCandless, J. (2009). *Children with starving brains.* 4th Edition. Bramble Books.

McEachin, J., Smith, J., & O. I. Lovaaas (1993). Long-term outocmes for childen with autism who received early intensive behavioral treatment. *Americal Journal on Mental Retardation,* 97 (4): pp359-372.

McMillan, A. (2005). The use of Video Interactive Guidance (VIG) toincrease the attunement between children on the autisticspectrum and their mothers. Leicester: *British Psychological Society, Proceedings,* p5.

Mehler, M. and D. Purpura. (2009). Autism, fever, epigenetics and the locus ceruleus. *Brain Research Reviews,* 59 (2): pp388.

Melillo, R. (2010). *Disconnected kids.* New York: Perigee.

Melillo, R., and G. Leisman. (2009).*Neurobehavioral disorders of childhood: An evolutionary perspective.* New York: Springer.

Mill, J., Dempster, E., Caspi, A., and B. Williams. (2005). Evidence for monozygotic twin (MZ) discordance in methylation level at two CpG sites in the promoter region of the catechol-O-methyltransferase (COMT) gene. *American Journal of Medical Genetics part B: Neuropsychiatric Genetics,* 141: pp421-425.

Mills, H. (2002). MMR: The story so far. *Private Eye:* London.

Mischel, W. (1993). *Introduction to personality. 5th Edition.* Fort Worth: Harcourt Brace.

Montagnier, L., Aissa, J., Ferris, S. & J. L.Montagnier. (2009). Electromagnetic signals are produced by aqueous nanostructures derived from bacterial DNA sequences. *Interdiscip. Sci. Comput. Life Sci.* (1): pp81-90.

Moore, D. (2001). *The dependent gene.* New York: A.W.H. Freeman.

Morgan, C., and T. Bale. (2011). Early prenatal stress epigenetically programs dys-masculinization in second–generation offspring via the paternal lineage. Accessedat: http://www.jneurosci.org/content/31/33/11748.abstract. October, 2014.

NAS. (2010). *National Autistic Society* website, accessed: June 11th 2010. http://www.autism.org.uk/en-gb/living-with-autism/approaches-therapies-and-interventions/relationship-based-interventions/the-son-rise-program-a-parents-view.aspx.

NAS. (2013) Myths and Facts. *National Autistic Society* website. Accessed at: http://www.autism.org.uk/ about/what-is/myths-facts-stats.aspx. March, 2015.

Newton, R. (2008). *The Attachment Connection.* Oakland, CA, New Harbinger.

Nishitani S, Miyamura T, Tagawa M, Sumi M, Takase R, Doi H, Moriuchi H, and Shinohara K. (2009). The calming effect of a maternal breast milk odor on the human newborn infant. *Neurosci Res.* 63(1): pp66-71.

Norton, E. (2014). Parenting rewires male brain. Accessed at: http://www.sciencemag.org/news/2014/05/parenting-rewires-male-brain

Older, J. (1982). *Touch is Healing.* New York: Stein and Day.

Ornstein, A., Helt. M., Troyb. E., and K. Tyson. (2014). Intervention for optimal outcome in children and adolescents with a history of autism. *J Dev Behav Pediatr.* 35 (4): pp247-56.

Owers and Thorworth (1985). (Cited in Grandin, T. The Children's Centre of Neurological Development Research Section *Communication* Vol. 12 (3): December 1989.

Padawer, R. (2014). The kids who beat autism. *New York Times Magazine,* July 31st. Accessed at: https://www.nytimes.com/2014/08/03/magazine/the-kids-who-beat-autism.html. January, 2018.

Pardo, D.A., Vargas, D.L., & A.W.Zimmerman. (2005). Immunity, neuroglia and neuroinflammation in autism. *Int. Rev. Psychiatry.* Dec; 17 (6): pp485-95

Parracho, H.M., Bingham M. O., Gibson G.R., and A.L.McCartney. (2005). Differences between the gut microflora of children with autistic spectrum disorders and that of healthy children. *J.Med Microbiol.* Oct. 54 (Pt 10): pp987-91.

Partanen, E., Kujala, K., Tervaniemi, T., and Huotilainen, M. (2013). Prenatal Music Exposure Induces Long-Term Neural Effects. Accessed at: http://journals.plos.org/plosone/article?id=10.1371/journal.pone.0078946. July, 2017.

Peek, L. (2002).Thomas on the right track. *The Times.* March 5th, p11.

Picardi, A., Fagnani, C., Medda, E., and V. Toccaceli. (2015). Genetic and environmental influences underlying the relationship between autistic traits and temperament and character dimensions in adulthood. *Comprehensive Psychiatry,* April, 58: pp178-88.

Pickles, A., Le Couteur, A., Leadbitter, K., and, E. Salomone. (2016). Parent-mediated social communication therapy for young children with autism (PACT): Long term follow up of a randomised controlled trial. *The Lancet.* Accessed at: http://www.thelancet.com/journals/lancet/article/PIIS0140-6736%2816%2931229-6/full text

Poole, J. (2017). *An ecological theory of autism.* Leicester: Matador.

Potter, B., Orfali,S., and G. Scott. (1993). *Brain boosters: Foods and drugs that make you smarter.* Berkeley, Calif: bRonin.

Perry, B., Pollard, R., Blakley, T., and W. Baker, et al. (1995). Childhood trauma, the neurobiology of adaption, and 'use dependent' development of the brain: How 'states' become 'traits'. *Infant Mental Health Journal,* 16 (4): pp271-291.

Pfeiffer, B. & M. Kinnealey (2008). Autistic mannerisms reduced by sensory treatment. *Science Daily,* Apr. 27 Accessed at: http://www.sciencedaily.com/releases/2008/04/080425102403.htm. Feb 9th 2011.

Previc, F. (2007). Prenatal influences on brain dopamine and their relevance to the rising incidence of autism. *Medical Hypotheses.* Accessed online at: http://www.medical-hypotheses.com/article/S0306-9877(06)00497-X/abstract. May, 2013.

Reichenberg-Ullman, J., Ullman, R., and I. Luepker (2005). *A Drug-Free Approach to Asperger Syndrome and Autism.* Edmonds, WA: Picnic Point

Rimland, B. (1964). Infantile Autism: The syndrome and its implications for a neuronal theory of behaviour. London: Methuen.

Roberts, B., and J. Jackson. (2008). Sociogenomic personality psychology.

Journal of Personality. Dec. 76 (6): pp1523-1544.

Robinson, 2015. 'Stop Googling symptoms' Girl died from rare liver cancer after doctors refused to listen. Accessed at: http://www.dailymail.co.uk/news/article-3126052/Teenage-girl-told-stop-Googling-rare-cancer-killed-left-heartbreaking-messages-begging-doctors-seriously.html

Ronald, A., Happe, F., and, R. Plomin. (2005). The genetic relationship between individual differences in social and non-social behaviours characteristic of autism. *Developmental Science.* 8: pp444-58.

Rose, B. (2016). Jamie and his Lion: the adults who take their soft toys to work. *BBC News.* Accessed at: http://www.bbc.co.uk/news/disability-37560841. May, 2017.

Ross, C. (2009). *Human Energy Fields.* Richardson, TX: Manitou Communications Inc.

Rossi, E.L. (2002). *The psychobiology of gene expression.* New York: Norton & Co.

Roth, I. (2010). *The autism spectrum in the 21st century: Exploring psychology, biology and practice.* Milton Keynes: Open University.

Rothschild, B. (2000). *The body remembers.* London: W.W. Norton.

Rutter, M., LeCouteur, A., and C. Lord. (2003). Autism diagnostic interview-revised (ADI-R). Oxford: Pearson/PsychCorp.

Sallows, Glen O. & Graupner, Tamlynn D. (2005). Intensive Behavioral Treatment for Children with Autism: Four-Year Outcome and Predictors. *American Journal on Mental Retardation,* 110 (6): 417-438.

Salzen, 2016). Importance of maternal contact. Letter in: *The Psychologist,* Vol. 29 (11): p813.

Sanger, S., and J. Kelly. (1986). *The magic square.* Ealing, UK: Bantam.

Sawyer, M. (2016). 'Book Review' *Australasian Psychiatry.* Vol. 24 (6): p621.

ScienceDaily. (2010). Mother is just another face in the crowd to autistic children. Accessed at: https://www.sciencedaily.com/releases/2001/04/010418072256.htm. November, 2017.

Schopler, E., van Bourgondien, M., Wellman, G., and S. Love. (2010). *The Childhood Autism Rating Scale (CARS).* Oxford: Pearson/PsychCorp.

Schore, A. (1994). *Affect regulation and the origin of the self.* Hillsdale, N.J: Lawrence Erlbaum.

Schultz, R.T. (2005). Developmental deficits in social perception in autism: the role of the amygdala and fusiform face area. *Int. J. Devl. Neuroscience.* 23: pp125-141.

Seroussi, K. (2002). *Unravelling the mystery of autism and pervasive developmental disorder.* New York: Broadway.

Shattock, P. (2008). Peer-reviewed research on GF/CR diets. Accessed at: www.espa-research.org.uk//linked/publications.pdf. January 2011.

Shulman L., D'Agostino, E, and M. Valicenti-McDermott. (2015) When an Early Diagnosis of Autism Spectrum Disorder Resolves, What Remains? *American Academy of Pediatrics.* Accessed at: http://www.autismweb. com/forum/viewtopic.php?t=29107&start=20. March, 2017.

Siddique, H. (2014). Autism costs UK £32bn a year,analysis shows. *Guardian,* June 10th.

Silberman, S. (2015). *Neurotribes.* London: Allen & Unwin.

Silverstein, O., and B. Rashbaum. (1994). *The courage to raise good men.* London: Michael Joseph

Smith, T., Groen, A.D., and J.W. Wynn. (2000). Randomised trial of intensive early intervention for children with pervasive developmental disorder. *Am. J. Ment. Retard,* 105: pp269-285.

Solomon, R. (2007). Making progress on autism. *The Psychologist,* Vol. 20 (7): p410.

Son-Rise Programme (2010). Accessed at: *Autism Treatment Centre of America:* http://www.autismtreatmentcenter.org/. February, 2017.

Sorce, J., Emde, R., M., Campos, J. and Klinnert, M. (1985). Maternal emotional sig-nailing: Its effect on the visual cliff behavior of one-year-olds. *Developmental Psychology,* 21: pp195-200.

Starr, S. (2014). Is autism just another identity? *Spiked.* Accessed at: http:// www.spiked-online.com/newsite/article/12369. February 2016.

Steele, H., and M. Steele. (2001). Expectant fathers' (not mothers). Adult attachment interviews predict their children's mental health aged 11. Presentation at a conference of the Society for Research in Child Development. Minneapolis. Cited in *The Psychologist:* 2002, Vol. 15 (10): pp518-522.

Stehli, A. (2004). *Sound of Falling Snow.* New York: Beaufort.

Stern, D. (2002). *The first relationship (2nd Ed).* Cambridge, MA: Harvard University Press.

Stevenson, H. (2008). Private study links vaccinations to neurological disorders. *Natural News.* Accessed at: http://www.naturalnews. com/022642.html. Jan. 2012.

Steward, R. (2012). Living with Aspergers syndrome. Accessed at: http:// blogs.independent.co.uk/2012/10/19/living-with-asperger%E2%80%99s-syndrome-my-daily-experience-is-often-just-an-extreme-version-of-life/. July, 2015.

Stock, C. (2005). *The Out of Sync Child.* New York: Berkley Publishing

Stone, F. (2004). *Autism: The eighth colour.* London: Jessica Kingsley.

Stordy, J., and M. Nicholl. (2000). *The LCP solution.* London: Macmillan.

Sutton, C., Utting, D. and Farrington, D. (2006). 'Nipping criminality in the bud', *The Psychologist: Special Issue.* Vol. 19 (8): pp470-475.

TA. (2017). *Treating Autism* website. Accessed at: http://treatingautism.org.uk/our-approach/parents-stories/. February, 2017.

Teitelbaum, P., Teitelbaum, O., Nye, J., Fryman, J. et.al. (1998). Movement analysis in infancy may be useful for early diagnosis of autism. *Proceedings of the National Academy of Sciences,* USA, 95: pp13982-13987.

Timimi, S., Gardner, N., and B. McCabe. (2011). *The myth of autism: Medicalising Men's and Boys' Social and Emotional Competence.* Palgrave McMillan: Basingstoke.

Tinbergen, N., and E. Tinbergen. (1983/93). *'Autistic' children: New hope for a cure.* Oxford: Tinbergen Trust.

Trevarthen, C., Aitken, K., Papoudi D, and J. Robarts. (1998). *Children with autism: Diagnosis and interventions to meet their needs.* (2nd Edition). London: Jessica Kingsley.

Trevarthan, C., Barr, C., Dunlop, A-W., and N. Gjersoe. (Undated). *Supporting a young child's needs for care and affection, shared meaning and a social place.* Accessed at: https://www. scribd.com/ document/299843903/Supporting-a-Young-Child-s-Needs. November, 2017

Turnbull, A. (1996). Parents launch a plea for help for autistic Sam. *Salisbury Journal,* June: p1.

University of Washington (2001). *Press Release.* Mother is just another face in the crowd to autistic children. Accessed at: https://www.eurekalert.org/pub_releases/2001-04/UoW-Mija-1604101.php. May, 2016.

Upledger, J. (2011). Accessed at: http://onibasu.com/archives/am/55427.html. February, 2011.

Waal, N. (1955). A special technique of psychotherapy with an autistic child. In: Caplan,G. (ed). *Emotional Problems of Early Childhood.* New York: Basic Books.

Walder, D., Laplante, D.,Sousa-Pires, A., and F. Veru. (2014). Prenatal maternal stress predicts autism traits in 6½ year-old children: Project Ice Storm. *Psychiatry Research.* 219: pp353-360.

Wanveer, T. (2007). Autism Spectrum Disorder: How CranialSacral Therapy can help. *Massage Today,* July (7) Issue 7.

Weaver, I, Cervoni, N., Champagne, F. and A. D'Alessio. (2004). Epigenetic programming by maternal behaviour. *Nature neuroscience.* 7: pp847-854.

Weber, M. (1918). *Science as a Vocation.* Lecture given at Munich University. Published as: Wissenschaft als Beruf, 1922.

Williams, D. (1992). *Nobody nowhere.* London: Corgi.

Williams, D. (1994). *Somebody somewhere.* London: Corgi.

Williams, D. (1998). *Autism and sensing: an unlost instinct.* London: Jessica Kinglsey.

Williams, D. (1999). *Like colour to the blind.* London: Jessica Kinglsey.

Williams, D. (2004). *Everyday Heaven: Journeys beyond the stereotypes of autism.* London: Jessica Kinglsey.

Wilson, C. (2016). Teen gene link in schizophrenia? *New Scientist,* January 30th, p12.

Wing, L. (1986). *A question of Judgement.* London: National Autistic Society.

Wing, L. (1996/2003). *The Autistic Spectrum.* London: Robinson.

Wing, L. (2010). Clara Claiborne Park: Obituary. *The Guardian.* 4th August, 2010. Accessed at: http://www.theguardian.com/lifeandstyle/2010/aug/04/clara-claiborne-park-obituary.

Wing. L., and J. Gould. (1979). Severe impairments of social interaction and associated abnormalities in children: epidemiology and classification. *Journal of Autism and Developmental Disorders.* 9: pp11-29.

Yasko, A. (2014). *Feel good nutrigenomics.* Milton Keynes: Lightening Sources.

Yasko, A. (2017a). Accessed at: http://www.dramyyasko.com/our-unique-approach/ . March, 2017.

Yasko, A. (2017b) http://www.dramyyasko.com/stories-of-hope/. March, 2017.

Yehuda, R *et al* (2005). Transgenerational Effects of Posttraumatic Stress Disorder in Babies of Mothers Exposed to the World Trade Center Attacks during Pregnancy. *Journal of Clinical Endocrinology & Metabolism,* DOI: 10.1210/jc.2005-0550

Yerys, B., Nissley-Tsiopinis, J., de Marchena, A., and M. Watkins. (2016). Evaluation of the ADHD Rating Scale in Youth with Autism. *Journal of Autism and Developmental Disorders.* Vol. 47 (1): pp 90–100.

Zappella, M., Chiarucci, P., Pinassi, D. and P. Fidanzi et al. (1991). Parental bonding in the treatment of autistic children. *Ethology and Sociobiology,* Volume 12, (1) January: pp1-11

APPENDIX I THE ATEC QUESTIONNAIRE

ARI/Form
ATEC-1/11-99

Autism Treatment Evaluation Checklist (ATEC)
Bernard Rimland, Ph.D. and Stephen M. Edelson, Ph.D.
Autism Research Institute
4182 Adams Avenue, San Diego, CA 92116
fax: (619) 563-6840; www.autism.com/ari

Project/Purpose:

Scores: I	II	III	IV	Total

This form is intended to measure the effects of treatment. Free scoring of this
form is available on the Internet at: www.autism.com/atec

Name of Child _____ _____   ☐ Male   Age _____
    Last   First   ☐ Female   Date of Birth _____
Form completed by: _____   Relationship: _____   Today's Date _____

Please circle the letters to indicate how true each phrase is:

I. Speech/Language/Communication: [N] Not true   [S] Somewhat true   [V] Very true

N S V 1. Knows own name
N S V 2. Responds to 'No' or 'Stop'
N S V 3. Can follow some commands
N S V 4. Can use one word at a time (No!, Eat, Water, etc.)
N S V 5. Can use 2 words at a time (Don't want, Go home)
N S V 6. Can use 3 words at a time (Want more milk)
N S V 7. Knows 10 or more words
N S V 8. Can use sentences with 4 or more words
N S V 9. Explains what he/she wants
N S V 10. Asks meaningful questions
N S V 11. Speech tends to be meaningful/relevant
N S V 12. Often uses several successive sentences
N S V 13. Carries on fairly good conversation
N S V 14. Has normal ability to communicate for his/her age

II. Sociability: [N] Not descriptive   [S] Somewhat descriptive   [V] Very descriptive

N S V 1. Seems to be in a shell – you cannot reach him/her
N S V 2. Ignores other people
N S V 3. Pays little or no attention when addressed
N S V 4. Uncooperative and resistant
N S V 5. No eye contact
N S V 6. Prefers to be left alone
N S V 7. Shows no affection
N S V 8. Fails to greet parents
N S V 9. Avoids contact with others
N S V 10. Does not imitate
N S V 11. Dislikes being held/cuddled
N S V 12. Does not share or show
N S V 13. Does not wave 'bye bye'
N S V 14. Disagreeable/not compliant
N S V 15. Temper tantrums
N S V 16. Lacks friends/companions
N S V 17. Rarely smiles
N S V 18. Insensitive to other's feelings
N S V 19. Indifferent to being liked
N S V 20. Indifferent if parent(s) leave

III. Sensory/Cognitive Awareness: [N] Not descriptive   [S] Somewhat descriptive   [V] Very descriptive

N S V 1. Responds to own name
N S V 2. Responds to praise
N S V 3. Looks at people and animals
N S V 4. Looks at pictures (and T.V.)
N S V 5. Does drawing, coloring, art
N S V 6. Plays with toys appropriately
N S V 7. Appropriate facial expression
N S V 8. Understands stories on T.V.
N S V 9. Understands explanations
N S V 10. Aware of environment
N S V 11. Aware of danger
N S V 12. Shows imagination
N S V 13. Initiates activities
N S V 14. Dresses self
N S V 15. Curious, interested
N S V 16. Venturesome - explores
N S V 17. "Tuned in" — Not spacey
N S V 18. Looks where others are looking

IV. Health/Physical/Behavior: *Use this code:* [N] Not a Problem   [MI] Minor Problem   [MO] Moderate Problem   [S] Serious Problem

N MI MO S 1. Bed-wetting
N MI MO S 2. Wets pants/diapers
N MI MO S 3. Soils pants/diapers
N MI MO S 4. Diarrhea
N MI MO S 5. Constipation
N MI MO S 6. Sleep problems
N MI MO S 7. Eats too much/too little
N MI MO S 8. Extremely limited diet
N MI MO S 9. Hyperactive
N MI MO S 10. Lethargic
N MI MO S 11. Hits or injures self
N MI MO S 12. Hits or injures others
N MI MO S 13. Destructive
N MI MO S 14. Sound-sensitive
N MI MO S 15. Anxious/fearful
N MI MO S 16. Unhappy/crying
N MI MO S 17. Seizures
N MI MO S 18. Obsessive speech
N MI MO S 19. Rigid routines
N MI MO S 20. Shouts or screams
N MI MO S 21. Demands sameness
N MI MO S 22. Often agitated
N MI MO S 23. Not sensitive to pain
N MI MO S 24. "Hooked" or fixated on certain objects/topics
N MI MO S 25. Repetitive movements (stimming, rocking, etc.)

APPENDIX II BIBLIOGRAPHY OF PERSONAL RECOVERY NARRATIVES

The following titles formed the basis on which the original study was based. Since that time many more examples, largely internet-based have been published. Titles indicated with * represent examples in which the child or individual could no longer be classified as autistic on any standard measure following recovery. Titles indicated with ** represent anthologies of mixed recovered and recovering individuals.

*Autism: The Eighth Colour of the Rainbow. Florica Stone (2004). Jessica Kingsley: London

*A Real Boy. Christina Adams (2005). Berkeley Books: New York

*Climbing Out of Autism One Bite at a Time. Michelle Cheney (2001). Writers Club Press: San Jose

*Emergence Labelled Autistic: A True Story. Temple Grandin (1986/2005). Grand Central Publishing: Boston

*Facing Autism. Lynn. M. Hamilton (2000). WaterBrook Press: Colorado

*For the Love of Ann. James Copeland and Jack Hodges (1973). Arrow: London

*Let Me Hear Your Voice: A Family's Triumph Over Autism. Catherine Maurice(1993/1998). Robert Hale: London

*Louder Than Words. Jenny McCarthy (2007). Dutton: London

*Nobody Nowhere (1992), Somebody Somewhere (1994) Corgi: London (first two volumes of Donna William's autobiography); Like Colour to the Blind (1999). Everyday Heaven (2004) second two volumes: Jessica Kingsley: London

**Recovering Autistic Children. Edited by Stephen Edelson and Bernard Rimland (2003). Autism Research Institute: San Diego

**Son-Rise – A Miracle to Believe In. Barry Kaufman (1991). Doubleday: London (Contains six narratives of recovered and the recovering children)

*Son-Rise – The Miracle Continues. Barry and Raun Kaufman (1994). H.J. Kramer: Novato, California.

*Sound of a Miracle. Annabel Stehli (1991). Coubleday: London

**Sound of Falling Snow. Annabel Stehli (Ed). (2004) Beaufort Books: New York

*Unravelling the Mystery of Autism and Pervasive Developmental Disorder. Karyn Seroussi(2002). Broadway Books: New York

APPENDIX III IRP BLANK FORM

The form below can be photocopied if required.

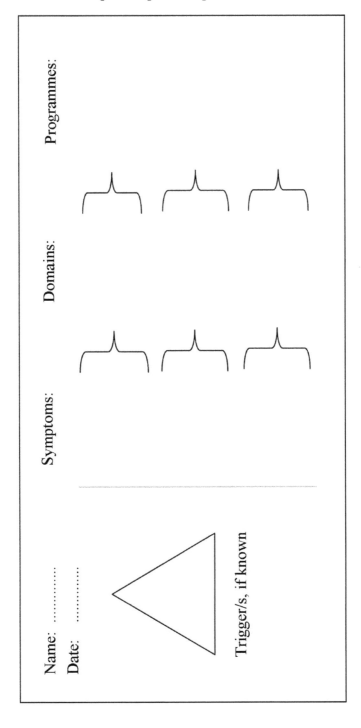

Lightning Source UK Ltd.
Milton Keynes UK
UKHW020633251120
374072UK00007B/667